Industrial Relations
in Australia and Japan

Industrial Relations in Australia and Japan

edited by

Jim Hagan and Andrew Wells

ALLEN & UNWIN

First published in 1994

Allen & Unwin Pty Ltd
9 Atchison Street, St Leonards, NSW 2065 Australia

National Library of Australia
Cataloguing-in-Publication entry:

Industrial relations in Australia and Japan.

  Bibliography.
  Includes index.
  ISBN 1 86373 740 5.

  1. Industrial relations—Japan—History—Congresses.
  2. Industrial relations—Australia—History—Congresses.
  I. Hagan, Jim, 1929– . II. Wells, Andrew.

331.0952

Set in 9.5/11.4 New Century Schoolbook by Robert Hood, Department of
Economics, University of Wollongong
Printed by SRM Production Services Sdn Bhd, Malaysia

10 9 8 7 6 5 4 3 2 1

Contents

Tables

Preface

This book began at one of the sessions of the Tripartite Mission to Japan in 1992. The Minister for Industrial Relations, Senator Peter Cook, the President of the ACTU, Martin Ferguson, and the Secretary of the ACCI, Brian Noakes, each outlined recent changes in Australian industrial relations to a large audience of Japanese business executives. My part was to sum up discussion.

We reviewed the proceedings later that evening. The program had probably achieved about as much as it could have, but it was obvious that a clearer understanding of the industrial relations of the two countries would require more than official presentations every few years, even if they were made by people as distinguished as members of the Tripartite Mission of 1992.

The Minister agreed that some continuing effort by scholars in both countries might create a better understanding of Australian and Japanese industrial relations, especially if their scholarship described not simply what it saw, but attempted to explain it in historical perspective. Accordingly, he authorised a grant to enable the Labour History and Industrial Relations Research Group at the University of Wollongong to bring together scholars and practitioners of industrial relations in both countries for a conference whose purpose would be to trace changes in the relations between employers and employees over the period of industrialisation in both Australia and Japan.

The conference was held in Wollongong in July 1993. This is the book of the conference, and it follows the pattern of the conference's organisation. On the first day, three Japanese scholars presented papers on the development of industrial relations in Japan from about the time of the Meiji Restoration (1869) until the present. The first paper covered the period from the Restoration until Japan's entry into the First World War; the second, the period between the World Wars; and the third, the period from 1945 until now. These papers were paralleled by three papers on the development of Australian industrial relations which covered the same periods. Discussion followed each pair of papers, and there was a plenary session at the end of the day. The second day followed the format of the first, except that the presentation was thematic, not chronological. Thus, the first two papers were about the role of the state in Japan and Australia respectively; the second pair, about the role of management; and the third, about the role of trade unions.

The papers themselves did not attempt comparisons between developments in Australia and Japan. The conference, and the book, mark a starting point for the labour historians of both countries. The discussion the papers provoked, however, made it clear that the mere juxtaposition of papers provided enough insight to suggest comparisons which would not only clarify the changing nature of industrial relations in both countries, but contribute to a better understanding of the process of industrialisation and its impact on both employers and employed.

It is with those expectations that the editors have written the first chapter. Just as this book is the first to set such a collection of essays between two covers, so the first chapter is, so far as we know, the first essay in the comparative labour history of Australia and Japan. It suffers, perhaps more than usual, from the faults of a first attempt, but it provides a beginning for future research.

The conference, and the book, mark an important development in the study of industrial relations and labour history in Australia. The editors and contributors wish to thank Senator Peter Cook for making it all possible; those officers of his Department who helped; the University of Wollongong for supplementing the original grant, and its Vice Chancellor, Professor Ken McKinnon, for summing up proceedings on the second day of the conference; Kathy Banks for making all the mundane arrangements of the conference actually work; Marie Ferri and Leonie Fromhold for deciphering manuscripts and answering innumerable enquiries; Senator Nick Sherry for his speech at dinner; Gai Warner and Michael Organ for their work on the bibliography; and Robert Hood, for patient and imaginative editing.

Jim Hagan
Professor of History
University of Wollongong

About the Contributors

Mr Michael Easson, until early 1994 Secretary, Labor Council of New South Wales. Michael Easson gained an honours degree in political science from the University of New South Wales and has completed postgraduate study at Harvard University on trade unions. He joined the Labor Council of New South Wales in 1978 and holds many appointments including member of the Australian Trade Union Training Council and the Australia–Japan Foundation . Recent publications which he co-edited and contributed to include *Transforming Industrial Relations* (Pluto, 1990), *Australian Industry—What Policy?* (Pluto, 1991) and *What Should Unions Do?* (Pluto, 1992). He is currently the chairperson of the Labor–Management Studies Foundation, Macquarie University, New South Wales.

Dr Andrew Frazer, Faculty of Law, University of Wollongong, Wollongong, New South Wales, Australia. Andrew Frazer is a lecturer in Law at the University of Wollongong, where he teaches Employment and Labour Relations Law. He holds degrees in Law and History from the University of Sydney. From 1987 to 1990 he was employed as a legal research consultant to the New South Wales Law Reform Commission. He has conducted research principally on the history of Australian labour law, and in 1991 he was awarded a PhD from the Research School of Social Sciences at the Australian National University for a thesis titled "Law and Industrial Arbitration in New South Wales, 1890–1912". He is currently continuing research on the history of the NSW industrial arbitration system for book publication.

Professor Jim Hagan is Dean of the Faculty of Arts and Professor of History at the University of Wollongong, where he teaches Australian History, and chairs the Labour History and Industrial Relations Research Group. He has published a large number of articles on various aspects of industrial relations and acted as a consultant on industrial affairs and education. The best known of his books are *A Short History of the Australian Council of Trade Unions* (Reed, 1977), *The History of the ACTU* (Longmans 1981), and (with Ken Turner) *A History of the Labor Party in New South Wales* (Longmans 1991).

Professor Ryuji Komatsu, Keio University, Tokyo, Japan. Ryuji Komatsu received his PhD from Keio University and has been a professor in the Economics Faculty of that university since 1976. Some of his major publications include *Formation of Enterprise-wide Unionism in Japan* (Tokyo, 1971), *Theory of Social Policy* (Tokyo, 1973), *Labour in New Zealand* (Tokyo, 1988), *and Modern Social Policy* (Tokyo, 1993). His current research interests are labour history in Japan and social welfare in New Zealand.

Associate Professor Raymond Markey, Department of Economics, University of Wollongong, New South Wales, Australia. Ray Markey is Associate Professor in Industrial Relations at the University of Wollongong, Australia. He is author of *The Making of the Labor Party in New South Wales* (Kensington [NSW], 1988), *The Trade Union Response to Technological Change in Australia* (Kensington, 1983), and *In Case of Oppression. The Life and Times of the Labor council of New South Wales, 1871-1991* (Pluto, 1994). He has also published a number of articles in Australian and comparative labour history, technological change and industrial relations, and industrial democracy. He has been a consultant to the Australian Department of Industrial Relations, the ILO, and a number of individual firms and trade unions in Australia and overseas. He is co-chairman of the International Industrial Relations Association Study Group on Workers' Participation and Self-Management.

Professor Takao Matsumura, Department of Economics, Keio University, Tokyo, Japan. Takao Matsumura gained his PhD in Social History at Warwick University in Britain and is Professor of Labour History at Keio University. Publications include *The Labour Aristocracy Revisited--Victorian Flint Glass Makers* (Manchester University Press, 1988). His current labour research interests are the Taff Vale Judgement and British Railway workers, and the Miners' Strike of 1984–85.

Mr Hajime Matsuzaki, Industrial Relations Research Centre, University of New South Wales, Sydney, New South Wales, Australia. Hajime Matsuzaki is a civil engineer who completed his Master of Industrial Relations Degree at the University of Western Australia. He is a lecturer on Japanese economy and industrial relations for the Trade Union Training Authority. Publications include *Japanese*

Business Unionism: The Historical Development of a Unique Labour Movement (Kensington, 1992) and he edits the University of NSW Industrial Relations Research Centre newsletter *Japanese Unionism Information*. His most recent work is *Unionism of the Construction Industry in Japan* (Kensington, forthcoming).

Professor Kazuo Nimura, Director, Ohara Institute for Social Research, Hosei University, Tokyo, Japan. Kazuo Nimura studied at the University of Tokyo and Hosei University. He has written, edited and co-authored a number of books in both Japanese and English. Works in Japanese include *History and Problems of the Japanese Labour Movement* (1966), *A Reassessment of the Early Japanese Labour Movement* (1979), *A History of the Osaka Labour School* (1982) and *An Historical Analysis of the Ashio Riot —A Social History of Mine Workers* (1988). Professor Nimura has also been a contributor to the following English language publications: *The Formation of Labour Movements 1870–1914—An International Perspective* (1990), *The Internationalization of Japan* (1992) and *Towards a Social History of Mining in the 19th and 20th Centuries* (1992). His current research interest is labour–management relations after the Second World War in Japan.

Mr B.M. Noakes, Executive Director, Australian Chamber of Commerce and Industry (formerly Confederation of Australian Industry). Bryan Noakes has worked as an employment, personnel and industrial relations officer in a number of prominent engineering companies in Australia. He served as industrial relations advisor, and assistant director to the Australian Council of Employers' Federations before becoming a director of the CAI Industrial Council. He has been an executive director of the Australian Chamber of Commerce and Industry for ten years and also holds a number of appointments including member, National Labour Consultative Council and deputy member, ILO governing body.

Associate Professor Tom Sheridan, Department of Economics, University of Adelaide, Adelaide, South Australia, Australia. Tom Sheridan is Reader in Industrial Relations History at the University of Adelaide. He received his PhD from the Australian National University, Canberra. His publications include *Mindful Militants* (Cambridge University Press, 1975), and *Division of Labour: Industrial Relations in the Chifley Years, 1945–49* (Oxford University Press, 1989). His research interests have concentrated on twentieth century issues and he is currently researching industrial relations during the Menzies years, 1950–65.

Mr Ben Watanabe, Visiting Researcher, Wayne State University, (USA), Advisor to the Asian Pacific Workers Solidarity Links and the Transnational Information Exchange. Ben Watanabe is an economics graduate of Keio University, Japan. He has been a full time staff member of the National Union of General Workers for thirty years, and held the office of Secretary General, Vice President and President of the Tokyo South District. He has written widely on labour relations in both Japanese and English journals and earlier this year delivered a paper at the Harvard Trade Union Program (Boston) entitled 'An Insider's Critique of Japanese Industrial Relations'.

Dr Andrew Wells, Department of History and Politics, University of Wollongong, Wollongong, New South Wales, Australia. Andrew Wells received his PhD at the Australian National University in economic history. He is a senior lecturer in history at the University of Wollongong who has written widely on urban, economic and labour history. His publications include *Constructing Capitalism,* (Allen & Unwin, 1989), and he co-edited with J.S. Hagan *The Maritime Strike: A Centennial Retrospective* (Wollongong, 1992). He is currently researching the history of the Australian Communist Party, 1920–85.

1 Industrial relations in Australia and Japan

Jim Hagan and Andrew Wells

How does one begin to compare the history of industrial relations in Australia and Japan? We asked our contributors to concentrate on answering an overriding question: how do you explain the changing relationship between employers and employees in either country?

There are obvious objections to such an approach. Unless carefully re-interpreted, the question assumes a uniformity which does not allow for the multitude of possible variations by region, industry, or size of firm. But it is possible to qualify answers to take account of these differences, and it is necessary to begin somewhere.

The strength of the question lies in its ability to subsume so many others. Any serious answer to it has to examine the process of industrial transformation, and the sectoral contributions to that process; the relationship of the economy to the major world industrial powers and the extent of collaboration or competition; inherited cultural values and prevailing forms of administration and political organisation. It was for that reason that we asked our contributors on the second day to address specifically the roles of management, trade unions and the state.

Of course, the last of these possesses a power which may override that of the others. But in Japan, the state itself was subject to tremendous external forces which also put massive indirect pressures on relations between employers and employees. When Commodore Perry sailed into Tokyo Bay in 1853 and offered the Japanese the choice between opening ports to trade or being bombarded, he was acting on behalf of the government of the United States. But several major European powers had exactly the same interest as Perry's government.

1

They too aimed at opening up the Japanese market to the sale of goods produced in increasing surplus quantity by their own industrial revolutions in manufacture. A series of commercial treaties achieved the aims of all of them, and Japan was plunged into a revolution which led to the overthrow of its centuries-old government and the installation of a new one legitimised by the restoration of the Meiji emperor in 1869.

What was to be the future of the new Japan? In their zeal for finding markets for their industrial surplus, the European powers showed strong interest in controlling the governments of those territories in which they saw market opportunities. If Japan was not to go the way of the others, it would have to industrialise in self-defence.

This became the policy of the new Meiji government. The government itself established new industries and renovated old ones. In this phase, the Japanese economy borrowed capital and skilled technical help from the foreign powers. But it was government policy to end that dependence as soon as possible. By the 1880s, the foreign experts were going home and the new Japanese ventures in private industry were being financed by domestic capital.

This required that Japanese finance be diverted into the new ventures, which meant that they had to offer superior profits. Combined with the need to undercut the prices of imported goods, that meant Japanese workers in the new enterprises would work for wages and under conditions that were inferior to those of similar industries controlled by the foreign competitors, in their homelands and elsewhere.

No such consequences followed in the Australian colonies. They were colonies within the British Empire, and their economies had followed a pattern of settler capitalism. British capital, and very little other, flowed in to fund a rapidly-expanding pastoral industry which supplied mills to England and Scotland with first-grade raw materials. British investors financed the coal companies which filled the bunkers of the (mainly British) steamers carrying British manufactures to Australia and back-loading with Australian primary products. Australian governments borrowed from British investors to build roads, railways and wharves for distributing British manufactures and transporting Australian wool back home.

British investment in Australia rough-hewed the shape of the Australian economy and its workforce in the nineteenth century. Manufacturing remained small scale and few manufacturing establishments were much above workshop size. Employment in the pastoral and mineral industries was much greater than in manufacturing, and there was a service sector which grew as the wealth of Australian people increased. Until 1890, the demand for Australian wool was strong and prices were high; British capital was readily available for private and public ventures. Australians, about half of them still British-born, and with substantial powers of self-government, felt no need to industrialise rapidly to protect themselves from the oppression of a foreign power, or to induce local investment in manufacturing by oppressing its workforce.

The nature of that workforce contrasted strongly with its Japanese counterpart. A large part of it was rural, but in Australia there was no peasantry that could serve as a significant source of recruitment for urban manufacture. It was overwhelmingly male, and by the 1880s the Australian workforce as a whole was about half British born and about half born in the Australian colonies. A large part of the latter fraction was often only one generation removed from British origins.

Those born in Australia had been raised against the background of the gold rushes that had begun to transform the eastern colonies at mid-century. Life on the goldfields had bred some disrespect for authority and enhanced beliefs in egalitarianism. British workers who came to Australia were the products of an industrial revolution that had been in progress for the better part of a century by 1850. They brought with them a knowledge of standards and conventions that they believed should regulate relations between employers and employees: what constituted a fair day's work and a fair day's pay.

They also brought with them a knowledge of how to bargain for that purpose. Engineers had set up the Australian branch of their British union even before their ship reached port. As the British trade union movement matured, its experience enriched the practice of Australian trade unions which operated in the forty years up to 1890 in conditions of strong demand for labour. By that year, the Australian trade union movement probably had the highest membership, proportionate to the workforce, of any in the world. Some of the unions had combined to form national organisations.

The Japanese industrial workforce was not heir to any such a legacy of practice and tradition. It was overwhelmingly rural—which meant that within one generation ideas, standards and customs appropriate to feudally organised rice-growing were transported to technically complex factories and workshops. Females outnumbered males in Japanese manufacturing until 1914, and in cotton and silk spinning (the largest employers) they made up an overwhelming majority.

In Japanese engineering, and building and construction, males predominated. Competition for their skills was strong and gave them a certain bargaining advantage. But they had no traditions of trade unionism or anything comparable to European experience as a basis for it. There had been guilds of artisans and masters in pre-Meiji times but they had not developed the same degree of independence as their European counterparts.

The chances of the new Japanese industrial workforce developing craft or industrial unions were further reduced by the persistence of the *oyakata* system. When the foreign experts departed, they left behind them a gap in the supervisory system of the new enterprises. To bridge that gap, managers reverted to the system of contracting work to a gang-boss, who would supervise his workers. The gang members' first loyalty was to their *oyakata;* when the first unions began, they often included *oyakatas,* and the unions' success depended on their presence. The unions were unstable, small, usually limited to one enterprise, exclusive, and narrowly focused. Outside the handful of trade unionists, there was a secondary labour market, many times larger, that was unprotected by law or collective bargaining.

The *oyakata* system also produced problems for the employers. Loyalty to the *oyakata* meant that a manager might suddenly lose his workforce. With technological development, firms began to replace *oyakatas* with foremen they appointed. They also began to attract skilled workers' loyalty directly to the firm through training programs, promotions systems, bonus schemes and the prospect of lifetime employment.

There has been some controversy over whether this kind of paternalism resulted from the transposition of feudal obligations or from prudent managerial practice. Whichever is the case, it is certain that Japanese employers did not like the competition for the loyalty of their employees that the unions offered, and resented the slight amount of bargaining power that a very small number of unions had been able to gather by the late 1890s. They sought the help of the government, which obligingly legislated to repress trade unions and to outlaw strikes.

Cooperation of this kind between employers and the government was not surprising. Large-scale manufacturing and other businesses that had their origins in pre-Meiji times were represented directly in the Diet, whose members were elected on a franchise that precluded any working-class representation. The Meiji government had intervened heavily in the economy from the beginning and it sold off the enterprises it had established to private buyers, who were often old-established merchant firms. The Diet and the government had a keen interest in preventing industrial disturbance from injuring production and they applied traditional methods of quelling it.

The Lower Houses of the Australian colonial parliament were elected by manhood suffrage. Several of their members owed their election to the belief that they were 'friends of the working man', and after the parliaments decided to pay their members, Labor parties were able to exert their sometimes considerable influence on policy and administration. Those industrial employers who sat as members of parliament had often risen from the ranks of tradesmen and were proprietors of small businesses.

What emerged as policy from the Australian parliaments of the nineteenth century was a 'colonial liberalism'. Governments did not intervene in trading and manufacturing, but they did intervene, and heavily, in supplying economic infrastructure which would help the development of the economy through private enterprise. From the 1880s, governments also intervened in the economy by assuming responsibility for setting up systems of technical education which (since the instruction was not specific to any particular workplace) had the effect of establishing a potentially mobile skilled workforce.

The governments themselves were benign employers and, before 1890, they left industrial relations pretty much to individual employers and trade unions. Employers sometimes sought solutions to disputes in the common law and statute law inherited from England. Some of this was repressive, but before the Great Strikes of the early nineties, they did not make frequent use of it.

After the Great Strikes resulted in the defeat of the labour movement, the colonial governments established tribunals to set minimum wages and to arbitrate industrial disputes compulsorily. Three years after its establishment in 1901, the government of the Commonwealth of Australia did the same. The courts of compulsory arbitration dealt not with individuals but only with unions that registered with them. This requirement built unions into the system, assured their future, and multiplied their numbers and their membership.

From 1904, the demand for labour became increasingly strong. Unions were able to bargain with advantage. They were able to encompass the unskilled as well as the skilled within their membership, limit contracting in manufacture, spread conditions achieved by the stronger bargainers to the weaker, keep a check on wage differentials, and prevent the unregulated development of a secondary labour market.

2 Employers and employed in Meiji Japan

Hajime Matsuzaki

The Meiji Era in Japan began with the restoration of the Emperor in 1868. By that time, many Asian countries had been colonised by the Western Powers: British India, Burma and Malaya, French Indochina, the Netherlands East Indies, the Spanish Philippines, and Portuguese Macao. The Opium War had broken out in 1840 between Britain and China and ended with the British colonising Hong Kong. Avoiding colonisation by those powers became a Japanese obsession. Popular slogans in those years, such as *fukoku kyôhei* (rich country and strong army) and *wakon yôsai* (Japanese ethos and Western technology), reflected a main direction of the country and the desire to modernise effectively. The era was characterised by a rapid and enthusiastic westernisation and a great reliance upon a flood of western imports. In 1875, a prominent Japanese thinker, Yukichi Fukuzawa, likened the life in this era to 'living two lives'. This mixture of indigenous Japan and imported Western influences was a distinct and dynamic change and it formed a characteristic historical setting for the development not only of labour relations but of the country itself.

Japan before the Meiji Restoration

Japanese medieval times are generally reckoned to have begun in the late twelfth century. Then, and for seven centuries up to the beginning of the Meiji Era in the late nineteenth century, the Japanese economy was of the kind that European historians (with the history of their own countries in mind) have described as 'feudal'. The land of Japan was

6

owned by aristocrats, temple authorities, and a class of independent warriors known as *samurai*. Between landlords and the serfs who worked their lands and were bound to the soil, there was the obligation of loyalty and obedience on one side, and protection and care on the other.

But not all Japanese were bound in this way. As in medieval Europe, a market economy and market towns developed on the basis of surplus products, including crop and handiworks, and the gradual introduction of money as a means of exchange. In the towns lived free men: merchants and artisans and labourers who worked for them. By late medieval times, which ended in the late sixteenth century, some of these towns were developing national and even international markets. Merchants, masters and craftsmen within them had begun to establish organisations which were granted monopoly by a landlord and regulated production and marketing in much the same way as European guilds. When Christian missionaries came to Sakai, the largest of the towns, they found its trading activities familiar enough to think of it as a 'Japanese Venice'.

Initially, samurai landlords in revolt utilised the economic power of these towns to win battles in the Warlike Age, which lasted throughout the sixteenth century. When a few prominent samurais were completing national unification, they began to check the developing independence of these trading towns and finally forced obedience from them. In 1603, the Tokugawas emerged victorious from a succession of wars and succeeded in establishing a national government at Edo (Tokyo). This government claimed authority over all Japan and endured until the Meiji restoration of 1868. After the Tokugawas' victory, most Japanese towns were reformed into 'castle towns' which were politically designed for the maintenance of the feudal system. The Tokugawas enforced a strict caste system consisting of warriors, peasants, artisans and merchants.

The Tokugawas regarded the potential independence of the guilds within towns with suspicion, and they believed that the spreading of Christianity by missionaries was subversive. They dealt with both problems by banning Christianity in 1613 and, in 1641, declaring a policy of isolation which restricted free opportunities for foreign trade and removed one of the main sources of the growth of the guilds. As well, they permitted operation of only those guilds that were prepared to obey the government's policies of restriction and control. As a result, Japanese guilds did not develop the strength and independence of their European counterparts. Edo, the biggest castle town, grew to have a population of about a million by the end of the Tokugawa Era.

Despite these restrictions, Japan's commodity economy was growing as the Edo Era came to a close. In general, handiwork goods were produced by putting out domestic work. But a primitive factory system had appeared in manufacturing silk and cotton thread and cloth, making bean paste and brewing sake. By the time Commodore Perry arrived in 1853, merchants and financiers were able to offer that challenge to landed authority that the Tokugawas had first feared. Their overthrow was the result of both internal and external pressure.

Commodore Perry arrived with a fleet of four warships. In the name of the government of the United States, he demanded the opening of ports to allow the merchants and manufacturers of his nation access to Japan's population of thirty million; alternatively, he would 'open a battle immediately and find out who wins'. The Tokugawa government agreed to open the ports and concluded similar treaties with the Netherlands, Russia, Great Britain and France. This humiliating diplomatic defeat resulted in economic turmoil and a civil war which lasted until 1868. The defeat of the government ended a regime which had lasted almost three centuries and resulted in the restoration of the Meiji emperor as titular Head of State.

By the time of the Emperor's restoration, the Japanese economy had reached an early stage of capitalist development similar to that of Western countries one or two centuries before. It had developed a commodity market for the distribution of a wide range of goods; it had a money banking system; and there was some speculative investment. Moreover, some merchants had accumulated relatively large amounts of capital, and this was available for new ventures.

These developments helped cushion the impact of the large-scale western imports on the Japanese economy. Cultural differences also provided some protection. For example, English-manufactured cotton goods did not sell as well in Japan as British traders had anticipated. They were of thin texture only and did not meet all market demands, because Japanese buyers also sought products made of thick texture for winter and working wear.

Despite these qualifications, it remains true that the commercial treaties laid the economy of Japan open to the operation of economies much more developed than her own. The Meiji restoration signalled the end of feudalism. The new government abolished the feudal hierarchy and the system of landholding on which it was based. It inaugurated the Imperial parliament and acknowledged the right to freedom of economic activity. It also planned an industrial revolution which in the space of a few decades would take sectors of Japan's industrial system from small-scale workshop and domestic manufacturing through to large-scale factory production.

The Meiji industrial revolution

The Meiji industrial revolution mixed indigenous and imported elements in a process which aimed to catch up with the industrialisation of Western powers without being swallowed by them. This process was vulnerable to external pressure; in it, the state played the role of economic leader, and from it emerged a dualistic economic structure. To this process, the Japanese brought their traditional work ethic and a less individualistic mentality than their Western competitors.

The Tokugawas' consistent policy of incorporating guilds into the government power structure had resulted in delaying the evolving division of labour into clearly-defined functions and associations for employers on the one hand, and employees on the other. At the beginning of the Meiji era, feudal ties remained significant and this was the case between labourers and capitalists, whether the latter were well-established or involved in new ventures.

There was another important aspect of the feudal relationship. When the Meiji era opened, a number of large merchants were based on a quasi-family community, the House, in which succession and organisation were dominated by blood relationships. The persistence of this traditional bond guaranteed a close relationship between business and government and helped the Meiji government take the initiative in the industrialisation of Japan. The government decided that Japan's best defence against the encroachment of foreign powers lay in the rapid establishment of industries which could compete successfully with the products of Western countries. This required the most effective use of financial and human resources, so the government established enterprises in strategic industries, including coal mining, iron and steel, shipbuilding, armaments, and silk and cotton spinning.

With the exception of railways, arsenals, posts and telegraphs, the government had sold most of these enterprises by the end of the nineteenth century. This privatisation offered great business opportunities to the rising industrial capitalists, like Mitsui, Mitsubishi, Sumitomo and Yasuda. They and the state were closely connected in the process of the industrialisation and the militarisation of Japan.

The government showed little interest in the industrial sector outside that part dominated by the large companies. It took only a few minor measures, like banning the guilds, shortening apprenticeships, and prohibiting slave labour. Thus developed a dual industrial structure, in which modernisation was confined to the large companies. These imported western machinery, and hired Western engineers and technicians to install it, train staff in its use, and manage their work on the shop floor.

Cotton and silk spinning

Cotton and silk spinning had existed as domestic industries long before the Meiji restoration. Women and children had spun thread from materials supplied by a 'thread master' who collected the spun thread and sold it. Their earnings were a useful, even necessary, supplement to the earnings of peasant households.

The rapid increase of exports due to the opening of ports resulted in a rapid inflation. In particular, the price of silk thread soared and hit silk-weaving shops. The commercial treaties of the 1860s exposed these industries to competition from European factories and they virtually collapsed. In addition, the introduction of monetary taxing forced a large number of peasants to borrow money for paying their taxes. Their indebtedness plunged peasant agriculture into poverty; in the three years from 1884 to 1886, one third of the entire arable acreage of Japan was given over to mortgagors. The resulting misery produced a huge social problem for the government. It had also to consider the large sum that thread imports added to the trade deficit. Since the treaties made protection impossible, the government had to adopt policies which would enable Japanese industry to meet foreign competition on its own terms. Because the government wished to depend as little as possible on foreign capital, the restructured industry would have to raise its own capital domestically.

Following this policy, the government established model filatures in both the cotton and silk industries. They gave preference in employment to the daughters of dispossessed samurai, and working conditions were benign. An eight-hour day was common, following the imported European system, and managers encouraged workers to think of themselves as co-partners in a patriotic venture. There was a conscious sense of reciprocal obligation, in a carry-over from the *samurai*'s former feudal relationship. It was not surprising that such an operation was unprofitable.

This phase ended when the government began to sell its enterprises to private industry, and in the rapid expansion of the cotton and silk spinning that followed. Textile mills were the most important producers of consumer goods in this process; in 1882, they accounted for one-half of all private factories, and employed three-quarters of all factory workers in Japan. The process of expansion that followed drew heavily on female labour. In 1900, female workers numbered 62 per cent of the labour force in private factories, and in 1910 their proportion was 71 per cent.

In cotton and silk spinning, their proportion was even greater and it increased as the substitution of ring-spinning for mule-spinning allowed for the employment of more 'weak-muscled females'. They were typically the daughters of peasants impoverished by the ruin of their domestic handicraft industry. Frequently their fathers had agreed to indenture their labour for some years ahead in return for a loan predicated on their future earnings. They began work at age fourteen, recruited by agents who told of great and exciting prospects for factory girls in the big towns.

The reality was very different. Commonly, the girls lived in dormitories into which they were locked when they came off shift—for the sake of their morals, employers sometimes said, and the arrangement also had the advantages of making absconding difficult and ensuring that they were available for longer hours of work than if they had to travel. Conditions in the dormitories were often crowded and unsanitary, and were notorious enough to provoke a government inquiry near the turn of the century. The girls paid for their accommodation out of their wages.

Wages in the spinning factories were low compared with wages in the established crafts. When the largest of the cotton-spinning companies, the Osaka Cotton Spinning Company, began operations in 1882, it deliberately set its wage rates at about two-thirds of the going rates for skilled tradesmen. It was clear about its motives: the company had to meet foreign competition; it had to buy expensive foreign machines; and it had to attract investment capital away from more certain ventures. The way to do this was to promise ample profit.

Those few who did so were all males. Although in the Kansai mills the median wage for both female and male workers was within the range 21 to 30 yen, only one female in ten earned more, and males predominated in the higher wage grades. Throughout the cotton-spinning industry in Japan, average female wage rates were between about half and 60 per cent of male rates in the 1890s. This meant that some girls found themselves actually owing money to their employer once they had paid their fines and their board.

What wages they achieved were made only after long hours of work. Working hours were at first set according to daylight hours, so that working hours were long—fourteen hours and more—in summer time, but became much shorter in winter. With the introduction of gas, and then electric lighting, factory managers instituted a night shift, and shift hours settled down generally to twelve, with a total of one hour off for meals. Allowing time for cleaning-up on Saturday and starting-up on Monday, this was about a 70-hour week, which some factory managers thought reasonable on the grounds that people of low peasant grade had no right to better expectation. Indeed, official factory publications had as their principal theme the nobility of a joint enterprise in which employers and employees were able to serve Japan, and Christian missionaries occasionally visited the factories to remind the workers of their duty.

This did not prevent employees from occasionally indulging in wildcat strikes. There was no trade union organisation in cotton or silk spinning, but occasionally workers at a particular factory banded together and withdrew their labour in protest, generally against some variation in wages or hours. Despite the existence of a reserve army of peasant labour, market forces sometimes helped them. As new factories opened, so they competed with the more established ones for experienced and skilled labour, even to the point of attempting to kidnap or press-gang them.

To prevent this, employers made several attempts to combine into associations whose members would agree not to hire workers who did not have a clear certificate of discharge from their previous employer. These attempts were not very successful, but the government assisted. The Public Peace Police Act exposed strikers and organisers of labour to heavy penalties.

Heavy industry

Exploitation and repression of workers in an infant cotton-spinning industry has not occurred in Japan only. What was more distinctive in the history of Japanese industrial relations was the organisation of labour in heavy industry.

Here the gap between traditional methods of organising the workforce and that required by modern technology caused serious problems. Most of the skilled workers available to the government-owned and privatised factories were still organised according to traditional guild practices. An *oyakata*-master contracted to supply the services of tradesmen. Managers could not employ them directly and this posed several difficulties for the organisation of a technologically advanced factory. The tradesmen's first loyalty was to their *oyakata* master and the gang frequently switched its services to other employers in pursuit of greater skill and higher reward.

By the turn of the century, some companies were developing methods to cope with the high turnover of skilled workers. They introduced initiatives like wage ladders and yearly and bi-annual pay rises instead of day wages and piecework rates. Despite their efforts, the *oyakata*-masters still managed to retain a large, if diminishing, control over skilled workers until the end of the Meiji era.

Meanwhile, factories became larger, skills more complex, and the reorganisation of skilled workers more pressing. Japan fought two short wars in the ten years between 1895 and 1905 and these put great pressure on heavy industry. The inflation and temporary unemployment which followed the conclusion of each led to a series of strikes and resulted in the formation of a clearly identifiable trade union movement.

Faced with this additional challenge to management's authority, large companies aimed at more direct control of their workforce. They developed a paternalistic philosophy which sought to enclose their workers ideologically within a framework of company loyalty. They established education and training programs, provided welfare benefits and company housing, and began to reorganise the *oyakata*-masters as foremen. They began to offer longer terms of employment and promotion by seniority. By 1914, labour turnover had diminished significantly.

As a result of this internalisation of the skilled labour market, a dual labour market emerged. The large and modernising companies offered superior wages and conditions. According to a survey conducted by the Ministry of Agriculture and Commerce in 1914, the average wage of employees in firms with more than 1000 employees was 46 per cent greater than those in firms with five to nine employees in the machine and tool industries. In metal refining, the corresponding figure was 52 per cent.

Construction industry

The construction industry was affected by the introduction of western technology too, but to a much lesser extent. The development pattern of the industry was considerably different. Since the Tokugawa Era and even earlier, construction work had tended to be carried out in two sectors. One was mainly engaged in large-sized building work and civil engineering work such as the opening of irrigation canals and highways and embankments which were planned and executed by government. These works used a large number of manual labourers under the supervision of government officers. The other sector was mainly engaged in the building of castles, temples and houses and was carried out by traditional skilled artisans. This sector had comparatively well-developed craft guild associations.

The Meiji industrialisation required a great number of large buildings and civil engineering projects. This extensive demand brought plenty of opportunity to establish companies which undertook the execution of these works from the government and growing private companies. Since imported technology was quite limited within this area, the executor of these projects relied almost totally upon manual labour. So, in order to meet this demand, these contractors needed labour suppliers, who developed in time into subcontractors. Since there was an unlimited supply of labour, these labour suppliers were in an overwhelmingly favourable position, and often employed gang organisations who relied on violence to recruit by force and to ensure work discipline. Hence, the working conditions of such manual labourers were extremely poor and even slave labour was common. This situation was paralleled in the mining industry. With the growth of the construction industry, these contractors began to use sub-subcontractors. In this way, this sector multiplied its layers of subcontractors and gradually developed into a multi-layered subcontracting system. Modernisation in terms of improvement of working conditions was very slow.

The house building sector, on the other hand, relied upon a traditional skilled workforce and the relatively developed craft guilds. In 1872, the government banned guild organisation, and in 1885 its Trade Association Ordinance attempted to guide those that had survived away from the organisation of labour. But since the imported technology had only a negligible effect upon this sector, the traditional work practices were not destroyed decisively and the master–journeyman relationship remained. The guild-like practices of building craftsmen survived relatively well throughout this era and developed as proto trade associations despite government pressure.

Trade unions in the Meiji era

The guilds in the building industry also became the basis for organisations which had some of the characteristics of Western trade unions In the 1880s, sawyers in Tokyo had an organisation which covered the trade almost completely. There were two bodies for journeymen and masters which operated separately but had an agreement with the timber merchants to exclude from the trade workers who did not belong to these bodies. The journeymen's association negotiated with the masters' association about wages and the latter in turn negotiated with the timber merchants, based on the agreement with the former. There is also evidence that plasterers in Tokyo organised their association in 1881. It may be controversial as to whether these organisations are regarded as craft unions or guilds, but it is apparent that they were in the process of separating into masters' and journeymen's bodies.

The dominance of traditional work customs among Japanese workers also affected early trade unionism. In 1897, the first unequivocal attempt at western-style unionism appeared when *Rôdôkumiai Kiseikai* (Association for Organisation of Trade Unions) was formed. The leaders of this union had returned from San Francisco strongly influenced by the American Federation of Labor. For them, the American experience seemed transferable to Japan.

Under the leadership of the Association, Japanese craftsmen began to form western-type unions and organised themselves into craft-based unions in certain industries. The first was *Tekkô Kumiai* (Iron Workers' Union) formed in 1897 with 1180 members in ship yards, railway shops and arsenals. By the end of 1899, its membership had increased to 5400. In a major private railway company, Nippon Railway, the union, *Nippon Tetsudô Kyôseikai* (literally, Nippon Railway Corrective Association) was formed in 1898 with some 1000 members who were mainly engine drivers. In 1899, typographers organised the Typographers' Union with some 2000 members.

These unions were the first attempt at Japanese trade unionism. Their activities, however, did not go much beyond those of a friendly or mutual-aid society. Since most local unions were based on a company which provided them with skill-training, so these unions did not control the supply of skilled labour. They were short-lived because of their weakness, as evidenced by the high mobility of their members and an insufficient financial base to provide mutual aid.

In addition, they were oppressed under the Public Peace Police Act passed in 1900. The fierce anti-unionism of the Meiji government strongly bore the character of a preventive policy which it had decided on in advance, influenced by developments in western countries. Employers too had hostile attitudes towards unionism in general. In this environment, these unions' most important objective was upgrading the social position of their workers, to offset the influence of the still remaining feudal social hierarchy.

The pattern and number of industrial disputes clearly divide into two periods: before and after 1897, when the first trade union movement appeared. Before then, disputes took the form of spontaneous riots and disturbances, mostly in mining and the textile industries. But after 1897 and coinciding with the rapid development of the Japanese capitalist economy, disputes increased in modern factory industries and railways. This represented the beginnings of organised industrial action rather than spontaneous outbursts.

In the recession that followed the Russo–Japanese War (1904–05), accompanied by a social unrest due to tax rises and inflation, industrial disputes greatly increased. In 1907, the number of disputes reached the highest peak of the Meiji Era and subsequently remained at a quite high level.

In this environment, the first socialist movement appeared, although it was brutally crushed by the government within a few years. Meanwhile, the rapid growth of Japanese industry significantly increased the number of factory workers. In heavy industry they grew from 32 000 in 1897 to 180 000 in 1914, by which year factory workers overall numbered 950 000. The significant increase in the size of the workforce gave a firm foothold and a longer life to the union movement. In 1912, *Yûaikai*, the Friendly Society, was established. Its membership in 1917 was estimated at 20 000. This union was characterised by moderation at first, but it adopted a more militant line later. Finally winning nationwide coverage in 1921, it developed into *Sôdômei*, the Japan Federation of Trade Unions.

Conclusion

The industrial revolution that took place in the years of the Meiji Restoration saved Japan from military and political domination by western powers. Preservation of independence was one of the aims of the government's policy, and the government and the people succeeded in fulfilling it in fact. Why Japan could remain independent and industrialise so rapidly and why only Japan alone in Asia could successfully achieve both targets have long been key questions for Japanese and other historians.

As seen in the cotton and silk spinning industry, the extremely harsh exploitative working conditions seem to be one important reason. But it is difficult to conclude that such poor working conditions were exclusively a Japanese phenomenon. Even though they might not be exactly the same, there were similar cases in other Asian countries. So, whereas it may be correct that such work practices were an element in the achievement, it cannot explain why Japan alone remained independent. More specific reasons should be found.

This paper has focused upon the origin and background factors of the dual structure of the economy as well as the labour market. In particular, from the industrial relations point of view, such an approach has been accompanied by the question: how did the Japanese economy develop so successfully in such a short period without facing crises in its labour movement resulting from poor working conditions?

During the Tokugawa Era, the Japanese economy developed considerably and reached the early stage of capitalism. On the other hand, the feudal system still remained a very strong influence. The resulting economy met the full competitive force of western capitalism.

The nature of the Meiji Industrial Revolution was produced by a mixture of two different elements, the indigenous tradition and the imported modern structure, which together made the fundamental framework for the later period. The indigenous tradition was characteristically based on the feudal system in which the political and economic sectors were unseparated. From the industrial relations point of view, this unseparated nature was evidenced in industrial organisations, in particular in the guilds which did not have clear separation into companies and craft unions as in the West. In a sense, the Meiji Industrial Revolution meant that the unseparated stage of guild organisation met the separated stage of it as imported from the West. In other words, it meant in practice the intermingling of traditional work practices based on the master–journeyman relationship and the modern factory production system. Although it is difficult to simplify various outcomes from diverse industries into a single picture, the case of heavy industry illustrates a typical shift from a discordant mixture of elements to a unique and reasonably harmonious system. Its most important result was the emergence of internalisation of the labour market and the dualistic structure of the economy.

Thus the undifferentiated nature of economic and political power within Japanese capitalism also helped to create state-led industrialisation and the dualistic structure of economy, based on a close relationship between the state and the business world. In order to maximise the effect of industrialisation, the government invested financial and human resources in particular strategic industries and sectors. As a result, each industry tended to have two segmented groups. One was the large government-run or private corporations with modern production facilities and the other was small producers still largely influenced by the feudal tradition. This technological segmentation was another aspect of the dualistic economy.

Thus some uniquely Japanese features emerged in the development of the Meiji economy. The first was the amalgamation of traditional and modern, or indigenous and imported, which were generated by the gap in the development of capitalism. The second was the dual structure of the industrial economy and labour market. The third was the state-led economic development aimed at bridging the economic and military power gap between Japan and the Western Powers. Another important feature of this type of economic development was the tendency to oppress the labour movement, which government and business both regarded as an obstacle to their policies. The compound of these elements produced a Japanese uniqueness that expressed itself in a distinctive form of industrial relations as well as in economic development per se.

3 Australia, 1870–1914

Raymond Markey

Australia, along with New Zealand, had a unique system of labour relations by 1914. It was based upon compulsory state arbitration, which sought to eliminate industrial conflict, to moderate the impact of market forces upon wages, and to encourage responsible trade unionism. In this context, by 1914, the unionised proportion of the Australian workforce had reached 45 per cent, the highest union density in the world.

As late as 1890, it would have been difficult to predict these outcomes. The most industrialised and populous colonies of New South Wales and Victoria already enjoyed the highest union densities in the world, but the unions had sought gains through either unilateral regulation or collective bargaining, largely on a regional or occupational level. State arbitration of any kind was barely discussed. How and why such significant developments occurred requires a close examination of the major parties' industrial relations and the social and economic context between 1870 and 1914.

Social and economic context

From 1870 to 1890 the Australian colonies experienced an economic boom, with rapid population growth, extensive immigration, high export income from wool and minerals, extensive capital inflow, and an economically interventionist state. By 1890 the Australian colonies had amongst the highest levels of urbanisation, labour productivity, wages, working-class home ownership and union membership in the world. They were renowned for their prosperity, egalitarianism and social mobility. Sydney and Melbourne building workers were the first in the world to gain an eight-hour day in the 1850s. Metal workers followed in the 1870s. The colonies also enjoyed unusually democratic government, based upon a reasonably extensive male suffrage. This 'workingmen's paradise' provided a fertile environment for the establishment and growth of trade unions.

However, prosperity was always qualified. Many workers lived in city slums, a growing low-wage sector emerged in manufacturing, concentrated amongst women and juvenile workers, and underemployment was embedded in the cyclical nature of much industrial activity and the casual basis of many jobs. Outwork was a common feature in the clothing industry. Working conditions came under increased pressure from the mid-1880s. Employers adopted a tougher industrial relations stance, especially in major industries experiencing structural problems. The changing composition of the Australian labour force reflected the structural shift towards industrial growth, with the primary sector share falling from 40 to 30 per cent, secondary industry expanding from 25 to about 30 per cent, and the tertiary share of the labour force growing from about 12 to 23 per cent.

Australian manufacturing was characterised by low capital–labour ratios and small scale, even though the average size of industrial units doubled from 1881 to 1901, and in some industries, such as railways, brewing, and gas production, larger productive units were more common. In Sydney in 1900, the median size of establishments was between four and nine employees, while 88 per cent of all manufacturing establishments employed less than thirty hands. Unlike mining and the pastoral industry, where Australian technology led the world, manufacturing technology in Australia was largely British, which was already uncompetitive by the end of the century.

Australian workers were drawn either from Britain and Ireland or were born in the colonies, where capitalist relations of production were already dominant, even in rural industry. Whilst many Irish immigrants to the colonies came from a rural background, many from Britain originated from the cities. The attraction for so many of these immigrants to the colonies lay in the possibilities for independence from wage labour, in the goldfields or on the land which seemed so plentiful in Australia as compared to Europe. These dreams were more often than not shattered in the harsh reality of colonial life. Nevertheless, the ideal of independence bred a workforce imbued with a strong sense of its own worth, and a corresponding lack of deference in relations with employers. This was complemented by the importance in colonial industry of traditional craft workers with their expected advancement into the ranks of small masters; skill counted more than capital until the end of this period. Finally, these tradesmen brought with them from Britain a strong consciousness of the tradition and practice of independent craft unionism, which flourished in Australian circumstances.

Trade unions, 1870–1890

By the 1870s the union movement was well-established, particularly in New South Wales and Victoria. Most unions were based upon traditional crafts in building and metal trades, in the printing industry, and amongst coopers, bakers, cabinetmakers, coachmakers, shipwrights, bootmakers, and saddle and harness makers. These tradesmen represented a 'labour aristocracy', with high wages, a high degree of job control, and prospects for social advancement. Their unions were usually small and localised, with a significant degree of participatory democracy, although some formed loose colony-wide associations, and two were actually branches of British unions: the Amalgamated Society of Engineers (ASE) and the Amalgamated Society of Carpenters and Joiners. Most unions were concentrated in capital cities, which were the locus of most secondary industry, although they were also beginning to appear in the larger provincial towns, such as Newcastle.

Craft union strategies reflected, and reinforced, their members' relatively privileged position. They strongly supported apprenticeship systems, which restricted labour supply, making skilled labour scarce and its unions strategically well placed to maintain good wages and conditions through unilateral regulation. Consequently, modern collective bargaining was limited. Most craft unions also developed benefit policies which attracted and disciplined members, since disobedience to union rules could void such benefits. The high fees required to maintain benefit funds reinforced the exclusiveness of craft unionism. Some craft unions even functioned as 'uplift' organisations, providing their members with libraries, trade journals and debates for their 'improvement'.

However, colonial craft unions were not always as industrially docile as many commentators have suggested. Strike propensity was not an accurate indication of militancy, because different opportunities faced workers in different industrial environments. Craft unionists frequently gained their demands without striking because of their strategic bargaining power. This was the essence of classical unilateral regulation as defined by the Webbs. Facing many small to medium-sized employers usually, they were also able to pick them off one at a time, using the 'strike in detail'.

Unionism also gained some substantial inroads amongst semi-skilled and unskilled labour in the 1870s. New South Wales coalminers, wharf labourers, and seamen organised unions early in this decade. The Amalgamated Miners' Association (AMA) was formed in 1874 on the Victorian goldfields. At the same time, a closer community of interests began to emerge amongst unions. The most substantial indication was the formation of the Sydney Trades and Labour Council (TLC) in 1871. Its authority developed slowly, especially since it was dominated by craft unions, but its title and objects recognised common interests between tradesmen and labourers. Wharf and building labourers affiliated from the outset, and the TLC deliberately encouraged unskilled organisation. Slowly it assumed a role as a general representative of Sydney workers, and even those elsewhere in the colony. It adjudicated demarcation disputes between affiliates and intervened, when invited, in some industrial disputes with employers, especially when they involved co-ordination of affiliated unions or support for extensive strike action. Its most spectacular success was the 1874 iron trades dispute for the eight-hour day. Over the next decade or so, similar labour councils emerged in other capital cities and in regional centres such as Broken Hill.

Unionism expanded dramatically in the 1880s amongst previously unorganised semi-skilled and unskilled workers. New mass unions covered the shearers and rural workers, metal miners and southern and western coalminers in New South Wales, railway workers and navvies. Maritime workers organised more extensively (geographically) and intensively, including even marine engineers and ships' officers. In the cities, gas, brewery, road transport, and clothing and textile workers, including women, also unionised.

Two of the greatest organisational achievements were the spread of the AMA from its Victorian base into New South Wales metal mining, and the formation of the Amalgamated Shearers' Union (ASU) in 1886. The ASU was based predominantly in New South Wales, but had branches in Victoria and South Australia. The Queensland Shearers' Union originally organised separately. From 1890, the ASU organised shed hands in the General Labourers' Union, with which it amalgamated in 1894 to form the Australian Workers' Union (AWU). Following parallel developments, the Queensland Workers' Union amalgamated with the AWU in 1904. Later, organising throughout rural industry and amongst unskilled factory workers, this became a general union, and Australia's largest.

However, these unions were atypical for the time. The seamen organised the only other intercolonial union. With the exception of a general female union, all other unions organised on a craft or occupational basis, as indeed did the AWU initially. The AMA and ASU/AWU were also exceptionally large, even allowing for the ASU's exaggerated claims of 20 000 members in 1890. By 1889, the AMA had 7000 members at Broken Hill alone, and many more in Victoria. By 1911, even before its expansion outside the pastoral industry, the AWU claimed 47 000 members.

Most unions remained small in the 1880s, with a membership in the hundreds rather than thousands. Some were even smaller. This was especially the case amongst urban manufacturing and building unions, even the largest of which, the ASE, printers, butchers, and bootmakers, had less than 2000 members in 1890. The larger unions were those of navvies, road transport workers, shop assistants, coalminers, railway workers and maritime and wharf labourers.

Union penetration also varied between industries. Coalminers achieved virtually 100 per cent density, and locomotive engine-drivers and maritime unions 75 per cent or more. Many craft unions' density was as high, although technological change and productive reorganisation were increasing the number of non-union, semi-skilled workers in their workplaces. Some unskilled unions such as the Gas Stokers' also achieved high coverage. However, union density was particularly low in clothing and textiles, in food production, and amongst women generally. Piecework, high seasonality of employment and outwork hindered unionism in these cases. Even the ASU/AWU's membership was somewhat volatile because of the short, five-month, shearing season, the itinerant nature of the workforce, and the high proportion of small landholders and their sons amongst shearers.

Notwithstanding these qualifications, the unionised proportion of the workforce in New South Wales and Victoria, which had the bulk of union membership for Australia, was extraordinarily high by international standards. Although no reliable statistics exist for the period prior to 1901, it has been estimated that by 1890 total union membership in each of these two colonies reached about 65 000. This represented 21.5 and 20.3 per cent, respectively, of the workforce. Such an impressive organisational achievement involved fundamental changes in the nature of industrial relations.

Specific threats to established wages and conditions, real or perceived, provided the momentum for the organisation of many new unions in the 1880s. However, in order to build continuous associations, the new unions relied upon the 'habit of association' in working-class communities, with shared occupational experiences and cultural values. Coalminers and maritime workers provided the most powerful early examples. During the boom of the 1870s and 1880s, the direction of economic development, the expansion in the size of industrial units, the decline in opportunities for independence from wage labour in petty commodity production, and productive reorganisation spread the 'habit of association' across a broader range of workers. This was especially true where labour was concentrated in manufacturing, at Broken Hill mines, in the railways, and even amongst shearers.

Union membership growth was only one expression of a broader mobilisation of the working class in the 1880s. Labour councils were organised in most capital cities and some provincial cities from the early 1880s, and the prestige and authority of the older Sydney TLC increased notably, as it assumed the leadership of the working class rather than of a narrow group of unions. It grew from representing less than half of all New South Wales unions in 1885, with 9583 members, to representing 40 000, or two-thirds of all New South Wales unionists, in 1891. Seven Intercolonial Trades Union Congresses were organised between 1879 and 1891. They developed a political reform platform, and in 1891 adopted a scheme for unified industrial and political organisation in the Australasian Labour Federation (ALF). Although this scheme did not reach fruition, it nevertheless reflected a less tangible ferment.

Radical and socialist ideas flourished. The Australian Socialist League was formed in Sydney in 1887, and soon spread to Melbourne. In cities, socialist organisations appeared; despite low membership, their newspapers reached larger audiences, and some union officials became socialists. A mood of militant self-confidence and willingness to undertake joint action increasingly characterised the unions, the language of class intensified, and industrial relations were increasingly depicted in terms of 'capital versus labour'.

Employers, 1870–90

Employer organisation also expanded in the 1880s. In the 1870s the characteristic form of employer organisation was in local masters' associations in the trades, paralleling the craft unions, such as the Master Builders, Master Plumbers, and Master Printers. They were not exclusively, or even predominantly, industrial relations organisations. In many respects, they and the craft unions shared common interests, in maintaining high standards for the trade, and in opposing 'cheap' employers outside the masters' associations. Employers outside these associations pioneered productive reorganisation and engaged less skilled employees who were non-unionists. There were examples where these associations bargained with unions, notably over the dispute which led to the granting of the eight-hour day by the Iron Masters' Association in Sydney in 1874, and on occasions with the

Master Builders' Associations of the different colonies. However, these were exceptional cases, because the predominant craft union method of unilateral regulation at this time left limited scope for collective bargaining.

The nearest to an industry organisation of employers in the 1870s was the Northern Coal Sales Association, the 'Vend', representing the largest coalowners in the Newcastle region of New South Wales. It essentially functioned as a cartel, fixing the price of coal and dividing the market amongst producers. However, in doing so it gained the cooperation of the union in a unique collective bargaining framework. The rationale for a cartel was excess capacity. This also affected the union. By restricting production, the Vend sought to maximise the price for coal. Wages were paid by the piece, the 'hewing rate' per ton of coal won, and in the early 1870s the union agreed to tie the hewing rate to the price for coal, on a sliding scale. In this way, it attempted to share the benefits of higher prices. Consequently, it was tied to the cartel policy, since restrictions on production for individual firms had the added effect of sharing work, when the available workforce was excess to requirements in all except the busiest periods of production.

The Steamship Owners' Association of Australasia (SOA) was formed in 1878 by eighteen Australian companies involved in the coastal shipping trade, which was then a major means of transport and communications. There was a close association, and even overlapping membership, between the SOA and the Vend, since coal provided both fuel and a major cargo for shipping, and some coalowners invested in shipping interests. The SOA was not initially an industrial relations body, but mainly sought to restrain competition by price-cutting, as shipowners invested in larger capacity ships. Nevertheless, from 1884, when the SOA achieved substantial unity amongst its own constituents, it conducted annual collective bargaining on a national industry basis simultaneously with all of the maritime unions. This was the first instance of national, multi-union industry bargaining in Australia.

Pastoralists' Associations also emerged in the 1880s, initially in response to the formation of the ASU and QSU. Consequently, their primary function was industrial relations from the outset. By about mid-1890 there were colony-wide associations in all of the sheep grazing colonies of New South Wales, Queensland, Victoria and South Australia. At this point, the shearers' union leaders sought industry-wide agreements in each colony. They were attracted to this strategy in New South Wales and Victoria especially, because of the difficulty in disciplining the ASU's volatile itinerant membership, and because of the large numbers of small to medium-sized sheepowners, with whom they faced an endless round of industrial skirmishes in order to establish union wage rates and conditions. The ASU, therefore, supported closer employer organisation. However, the difficulties which the ASU faced in organising their members were shared by the Pastoralists' Associations. During negotiations with the New South Wales and Victorian associations in June to July 1890, the ASU was painfully aware that they did not represent a majority of sheepowners, or even those who owned the majority of sheep, in those colonies. In the ensuing months, as the membership of these organisations increased, as the Queensland regional associations federated into a colonial organisation, and as the colonial associations formed an intercolonial federal council, their motivation was opposition to the unions themselves, rather than establishment of a stable collective bargaining framework.

This was one reflection of employers' growing economic difficulties in key sectors of industry from the mid-1880s. Wool industry prices fell, with expansion into marginal land requiring greater capitalisation. Shipping suffered from over-competition, and coalmining from excess capacity. These industries not only produced large unions, but also the strongest and most organised employer resistance to union conditions and demands.

Peak councils of employers also emerged in the 1880s. Beginning in Sydney in 1826, colonial Chambers of Commerce were long established. However, whilst they were occasionally involved in organising employers to resist unions, their principal function was as trade organisations. Similarly, the colonial Chambers of Manufactures (formed in Melbourne in 1865, in Adelaide in 1869 and in New South Wales in 1885) were primarily trade organisations, which lobbied strongly for protective tariffs. Closer organisation of employers primarily for industrial relations occurred with the formation of colony-based employers' federations or unions, in 1885 in Victoria, 1887 in South Australia, and 1888 in New South Wales. The latter and the TLC in New South Wales sought a framework agreement for joint conciliation of disputes in 1889, but neither could gain the support of their constituents. Events had already passed beyond this possibility.

By the end of the 1880s, a number of key leaders in the new organisations of employers also spoke in terms of class warfare. As with the pastoralists' associations, the main momentum for the organisation of employers' federations was that unions must be resisted, rather than bargained with. These were extremely unstable circumstances for the further development of collective bargaining.

In 1890, the growing class consciousness and closer organisation of both unions and employers reached flashpoint in the great maritime strike, the largest ever experienced in the colonies. The complicated details leading to this conflict need not concern us here. However, the broad trends are revealing for the alignment of forces at the time. In August, seamen and wharf labourers struck in support of marine officers locked out for affiliating with the Melbourne Trades Hall Council. The conflict quickly spread to miners, road transport workers and shearers throughout the eastern and southern colonies. Shearers were dragged into the dispute because of their agreement for mutual support of the wharf labourers who would not handle non-union shorn wool. In some cases, notably the metal mines at Broken Hill, the employers rushed to lock out workers first.

The original issues were quickly subsumed in the employers' war cry of 'freedom of contract', by which they meant the right to hire non-union labour, and in the unions' reply of 'defence of unionism'. The strikers were led by an intercolonial union conference, and by Labour Defence Committees in Sydney and Melbourne, and the Employers' Federations coordinated anti-union activity. In October 1890, the strikers were forced to return to work on employers' terms because relatively high unemployment assisted the employers in organising strikebreakers, and because of the intervention of the state on their side. The form of this intervention was not new, but its scale was. Troops and artillery were dispatched to the coalfields and 3000 special constables were enrolled from amongst white-collar workers, small traders and professionals for crowd control. Hundreds of strikers were charged under Master and Servants Acts, or for assault and affray during picketing and demonstrations. Most importantly for the long term, the peak councils of unions and employers had become command centres for industrial warfare.

The role of the state

Australia was characterised by a democratic and economically interventionist state in this period. The six Australian colonies separately enjoyed democratic self-government under the distant British constitutional monarchy, each with its own state apparatus. Government capital outlays in Australia, mainly in the provision of transport and communications, amounted to between one-third and one-half of total capital outlays to 1900. The Australian colonies established significant public enterprises in the railways. Infrastructure development remained the major focus of colonial government in a vast, recently settled continent, and in most other areas the state was wedded to laissez-faire ideology.

Nevertheless, the colonial governments did intervene in one further area of significance, namely, technical training. By 1888, New South

Wales had established a state technical education system, and other colonies soon followed. It is significant that the TLC played a major role in lobbying for the creation of this system. By achieving this centralised system of labour market training, the unions maintained apprenticeship and an external labour market in which skills were portable between employers. Employers acquiesced because skilled labour was scarce and the state effectively subsidised their training costs.

Finally, the colonial Australian state never systematically repressed the unions. The colonial state neither encouraged unionism at this stage, nor seriously hindered it. Some unions had registered as friendly societies because it was the only means of gaining legal status prior to the 1880s in most colonies. South Australia passed the first Trade Union Act in 1876, followed by New South Wales in 1881 and Victoria in 1886. However, legal uncertainty until then was not a major impediment to union organisation, except perhaps that officials who absconded with union funds or members in arrears for fees could not be sued. Even under the Trade Union Acts, strict regulation of picketing remained, with penalties for 'intimidation', 'molestation', or 'watching and besetting'.

Master and Servants legislation regulated labour relations more generally, and more harshly than in Britain because of colonial labour shortages. It provided for up to three months' gaol and confiscation of wages for misconduct, including disobedience or breach of contract, after summary trial before local justices of the peace, who were frequently employers. Only in the 1880s did magistrates replace justices of the peace. Breach of contract commonly arose out of desertion of a job before discharge by the employer, and all servants were compelled to receive a certificate of discharge before leaving an employer's service. Servants could also sue an employer for non-payment of wages and compensation for ill-usage under the Act, but these were civil proceedings as opposed to criminal proceedings against servants, and do not appear to have been very successful. The Master and Servants Acts were commonly resorted to by employers during labour shortages, especially in rural industry. Their provisions were also frequently implemented against striking workers, on the grounds of disobedience. The militant coalminers were regularly subjected to prosecution in this way. However, this usage was not consistent enough to prevent strikes. Otherwise, the state did not usually intervene in industrial relations, with the exception of the militant coalminers, against whom they regularly sent troops during strikes.

The depression of the 1890s and the breakdown of industrial relations

From 1891 the colonies' financial and economic structures reeled from the combined impact of falling wool and metal prices and cessation of British capital inflow. State developmental works virtually ceased. A highly speculative land boom from the late 1880s burst when prices fell, causing the temporary failure of most financial institutions during 1892–94, and the loss of savings by many small depositors. Unemployment reached about 30 per cent. Thousands tramped the countryside, and many workers' homes were repossessed. Despite rearguard union actions, wages and conditions for those who remained employed declined significantly.

A series of major strikes occurred during the great depression of the 1890s, repeating the main themes of the maritime strike. Employers were emboldened by their 1890 success and the economic climate to impose wage reductions or 'freedom of contract' or both upon shearers in 1891, Broken Hill miners in 1892, seamen in 1893, shearers again in 1894, and coalminers in 1894–96. Most of these conflicts involved state intervention, in the form of troops, and conviction of strikers for desertion of duty, assault, riot or picketing. In the 1891 and 1892 strikes, the union leaders were gaoled for conspiracy. Many smaller disputes occurred amongst urban unions.

The unions disintegrated. Most of the new urban unskilled unions completely collapsed, as did the AMA at Broken Hill, and the wharf labourers. Those which survived, such as the AWU, most craft unions, the Victorian AMA, and railway unions, were severely weakened, as were the labour councils.

The Labor Party and state arbitration

The labour councils' response to the industrial carnage of the 1890s was to form Labor Parties. The first major successes were achieved in New South Wales and Queensland, where the new party gained a substantial parliamentary presence as early as 1891 and 1893 respectively. As envisaged by their founders, these parties were to be working class in composition and objectives. Their original platforms were similar to those of the European social democratic parties of the late nineteenth century, concentrating upon political reforms necessary for working-class political intervention, and industrial legislation such as factory regulation and the eight-hour day. In these ways, the Labor Party offered the potential to neutralise the state apparatus which had intervened so decisively against unions in the 1890s strikes, and to gain broad union objectives for improving working conditions, when the limits of industrial action in this direction had been so clearly shown at that time.

Initially, there was also a significant socialist influence in these platforms, with its high point evident in the plank for 'nationalisation of the land and the whole means of production, distribution and exchange', in 1891 in Queensland and in 1897 in New South Wales. In both cases, however, these planks were short-lived, and the parties came under the control of moderates committed to republican nationalism, the extension of state employment, some welfare measures (notably the old age pension), and gradual industrial reform. By the end of the 1890s, the dominant ideology of the labour movement had become Laborism, which sought the civilisation of capitalism by a strong trade union movement associated with the Labor Party.

Compulsory state arbitration did not initially appear in the Labor Party platforms. It had rarely been an issue prior to the 1890s, and certainly enjoyed no union support while industrial means seemed effective. It was first discussed in 1891 at a royal commission into strikes in New South Wales. That commission heard evidence from twenty-one union leaders and fifteen employers. Most agreed with the commission's report that the maritime strike could have been avoided if there had been a board of conciliation. However, most witnesses were unclear about the distinction between collective bargaining and conciliation, or between conciliation and arbitration, and all wished to appear at their best in public. Most favoured some system of conciliation and/or arbitration, but only a third of the unionists and one employer favoured a state system of arbitration.

In 1892, the New South Wales government passed the Trades Disputes Conciliation and Arbitration Act. Councils of Conciliation were established with two representatives each from unions and employers, and failing settlement at that level, a dispute could go before a Council of Arbitration, consisting of one representative each, with an impartial judicial chairman. However, the Act did not provide for compulsory reference of disputes to the Councils, nor enforcement of awards. As a result, it was irrelevant in the 1890s, because employers simply refused to submit disputes to the Councils.

Although some unions and the TLC had supported the legislation, the union response was unenthusiastic. From 1893, some Labor parliamentarians pressured the government for further legislation providing for compulsory reference of disputes to arbitration on the application of one party only, and enforcement of awards. These demands were fuelled by an 1894 New Zealand Act providing for compulsory arbitration and enforcement of awards, and by the establishment in Victoria from 1896 of wages boards with power to enforce minimum wage rates. These boards, however, lacked arbitral powers in disputes, and were composed of equal numbers of employees and employers with an impartial chairman. Nor did they offer unions a role. For these reasons, wages boards were not the preferred system of the unions. Indeed, the unions did not openly support compulsory arbitration until the end of 1898, when the TLC finally adopted this policy. Even the Labor Party did not adopt the policy on its platform until 1899, despite the earlier efforts of its parliamentary leadership.

Compulsory state arbitration became attractive to the unions as a strategy for guaranteeing their very existence. Nevertheless, the unions as a whole did not wholeheartedly embrace the policy; hence their late acceptance in the 1890s, after the worst of the depression was over, and when the TLC was only a shell of the widely representative body that it had been in 1890. The socialists on the left steadfastly opposed state arbitration, and they gained some wider support based on traditional working-class distrust of the state, especially after the experiences of the 1890s. Many craft unions also considered that they were strong enough to achieve their ends independently. Even when arbitration became the policy of both unions and the party, unions were unwilling to abdicate the right to strike, although the system was supposed to render industrial action superfluous.

The most enthusiastic supporters of the 'new province for law and order' were clearly the parliamentary leaders of the Labor Party. Its prominence in Labor policy at the end of the 1890s reflected the dominance of the moderate parliamentary leadership by that time, after a long internal struggle for control of the party. The moderates finally succeeded due to an alliance with the AWU, which delivered a high proportion of rural seats to the Labor Party. The AWU was particularly attached to arbitration because of its difficulties in organising itinerant rural workers and bargaining with large numbers of employers. Arbitration also epitomised the ideology of Laborism. Even so, it was liberal governments which introduced the state arbitration system in the early 1900s.

The national settlement of the 1900s

The early 1900s provided the circumstances for the application of Laborism, with recovery from the depression, the federation of the colonies into the Commonwealth of Australia, and the growing electoral success of the Labor Party. After the bitter class conflict of the 1890s, a high degree of national political consensus emerged. The national settlement between the classes of the early 1900s was built upon four main policies. 'New protection' was the cornerstone. It extended an earlier Victorian protectionist alliance between manufacturers and labour, with more explicit trade-offs between different class interests, and involved a significant extension of the role of the state. New protection committed the Commonwealth to a tariff on cheap overseas goods to protect domestic manufacturers. In return, workers received a White Australia policy to protect them from 'cheap labour competition' from Asia; a compulsory state arbitration system which was meant to nurture unionism and guarantee 'fair and reasonable wages'; and the beginnings of a welfare state with the old age pension.

The federation of the colonies in 1901 still denied Australia a unitary national political structure. The six colonies became States in the Commonwealth of Australia, the British Crown ceding defined powers to it, as prescribed in a constitution, whose normal arbiter was the High Court. The implications of this federal/State structure had far-reaching implications for the nature of the industrial relations which emerged.

The single most important impact of this structure was the creation of a dual federal/State system of arbitration. Section 51 (XXXV) of the constitution granted the Commonwealth government its industrial powers, specifically to legislate with respect to 'conciliation and arbitration for the prevention and settlement of industrial disputes extending beyond the limits of any one State'. This does not allow the federal government to legislate generally over employment conditions, but only to establish tribunals. These only had jurisdiction where an interstate industrial dispute existed. In all other areas, the States retained industrial powers and indeed, in most cases, established their own conciliation and arbitration tribunals. These constitutional complexities soon created a thriving new industry in labour law.

The first State to effectively introduce compulsory arbitration was New South Wales in 1901. Western Australia legislated similarly in 1900 and 1902, followed by South Australia and Queensland in 1912. Victoria and Tasmania maintained wages board systems instead. However, in 1904 the Commonwealth also legislated the Conciliation and Arbitration Act. Since Western Australia had a tiny population and unionised workforce at this stage, the major players in the new system to 1914 were New South Wales and the Commonwealth.

Essentially, the Acts established systems of tribunals (boards, courts, or a combination of the two). They also provided for the registration and regulation of associations of employees and employers (although unlike employees, employers need not register to be a party to proceedings). Collective bargaining remained possible outside the systems, or in addition to its awards which set minimum standards.

However, the systems were compulsory in that they could be invoked without the consent of both, or even either, parties; tribunal awards were binding on both parties; and the use of direct industrial action was prohibited during the implementation of tribunal procedures. Enforcement of awards and prohibition of industrial action were soon supported by penal clauses, which provided for fines or deregistration of the parties.

The new systems rapidly extended their impact upon industrial relations in Australia. By 1914, over 1000 tribunal awards, wages board determinations and legally registered industrial agreements existed throughout the country, covering about 80 per cent of all unionists, or over a third of all Australian employees. Given the lukewarm support for arbitration from unions as a whole in the 1890s, this indicated, to some extent at least, what Turner has described as 'the domestication of the trade unions to the arbitration process' (Turner 1965, pp. 34, 40). There were three important reasons for this.

First, the political and industrial circumstances of the time tended to lock the unions into support for compulsory state arbitration. In the 1890s the Labor Party had committed itself to the principle of arbitration in the absence of a mass union movement. When the unions re-emerged in the 1900s, they too were committed to the new system to the extent that they accepted the party as their political representative. Most did. Arbitration was part of a complex political formula of trade-offs between Labor and non-Labor, under the umbrella of new protection. Opposition to arbitration might have jeopardised these arrangements. The employers' organised opposition to arbitration pushed unions still further towards support for it. In a sense, the struggle over wages and conditions was conducted by proxy, through the political and legal struggle over the nature of arbitration machinery which ensued in the early 1900s.

Secondly, arbitration systems produced changes in the structure and nature of unionism itself. The unions which had been decimated in the 1890s depression were typically the small, localised bodies with a high degree of participatory democracy. Apart from the strategically-placed crafts, those that best survived the depression included some of the large new unions in transport, rural industry and mining. With the exception of the coalminers, they tended to be more bureaucratic and centralised. The AWU exemplified this organisational trend. Arbitration relieved such unions from the responsibilities of participatory styles of organisation, because courtroom methods of operation encouraged amongst officials specialised skills, which did not necessarily depend upon close interaction with rank-and-file members. Arbitration facilitated larger unions spread over a number of localities, which added a dimension of bureaucratisation to union structure. This trend affected even the traditionally participatory crafts. Furthermore, the Commonwealth arbitration system encouraged the federation of State-based organisations, as most unions had been, whilst maintaining strong State branches with access to the State tribunals. Paradoxically, however, arbitration also nurtured small, unskilled unions whose independent industrial viability would otherwise have been difficult to maintain.

Under these circumstances, the Commonwealth and State arbitration systems fostered three main client groups amongst the unions. The first was the AWU, which was the largest Australian union, and by far the most politically influential. Amendments by a federal ALP government to the Commonwealth Act in 1910, allowing unions to organise in more than one industry, enabled the AWU 'to swallow up smaller unions which thought they could get by on militancy alone'(Macintyre 1983, p. 363). The second group consisted of those weaker organisations representing unskilled labourers, which were able to secure recognition and delay absorption by other unions. The New South Wales Act specifically encouraged these unions by taking occupation or 'calling' as the basis for union recognition, and by accepting a low minimum membership (as low as twenty in the 1908 amendments) for the purpose of registration. The third group, craft unions, could thus benefit from widespread unionisation of the workforce in an entire industry, whilst maintaining their own separate organisations. Out of these three groups came the large general unions, the semi-skilled and unskilled occupational bodies, and the separate craft organisations which characterised Australian union structure for most of the remainder of the century.

The third reason commonly offered for union support of arbitration in the early 1900s was its assistance in the recovery of unionisation from the 1890s depression. Registration under the Acts gave unions corporate identity, qualified preference for union members in employment ('other things being equal'), a monopoly of organisation in designated industries, and obliged employer recognition which had been denied in the 1890s. These institutional benefits offered unions an alternative to industrial action. More generally, the institutional assistance given unions by arbitration partially compensated for the unevenness of economic recovery in the early 1900s. Employers retained the advantage in important sections of the labour market because of an excess of unskilled labour and the impact of technological change upon some trades; unemployment reached 10 per cent in 1901–04, and hovered around 6 per cent until 1910. Notwithstanding these limitations to economic recovery, Australian union membership grew from 97 000, representing 6 per cent of the workforce in 1901, to 523 000, representing 45 per cent of the workforce in 1914.

Nevertheless, the support which arbitration offered for the recovery of unionism in general has been exaggerated. Union growth in States with wages board systems, which did not support unions, was as vigorous as in New South Wales. Economic recovery was sufficient to allow substantial unionisation. Perhaps the belief that arbitration provided a shelter encouraged the formation of many unions. However, the advantages of arbitration in practice were limited. It is by no means clear that the granting of a qualified union preference in employment was important in facilitating trade union growth, especially in the Commonwealth sphere. Some detailed studies indicate that the manner in which arbitration operated could actually hinder the development of unionism amongst the unskilled. In New South Wales, many of the problems which unions encountered with the arbitration system resulted from legal obstacles imposed by the Supreme Court. It ruled the declaration of a common rule throughout an industry invalid. The declaration of an actual dispute was deemed necessary in order for the Arbitration Court to exercise jurisdiction, and a union could not act as an agent for employees until a dispute existed, thereby denying employees the protection of their union during initial negotiations for an award. Unions also discovered that arbitration was a costly process in terms of legal expenses.

These developments were largely the result of a concerted employers' campaign to restrict the operation of the arbitration system. Spurred on by what they saw as a mounting threat in that system and the Labor Party, employers developed more broadly representative organisations, especially around the State-based Employers' Federations. They organised for industrial and political purposes, raising political funds, lobbying government, running candidates in elections and supporting non-Labor parties, with which they had close links. Most importantly, they directed much of their energy towards frequently successful legal challenges to the jurisdiction and early decisions of the arbitration courts. Their actions clogged up and slowed down the New South Wales court's activities, so that legal costs escalated. Even if successful in gaining a favourable award, unions faced the prospect of it being overruled by a higher court. By 1907 the unions considered the New South Wales Act useless as a result.

As the situation in New South Wales deteriorated for unions, the Commonwealth Court appeared to offer them better prospects. This was largely due to the famous Harvester judgment delivered by Justice Higgins in 1907. He instituted the concept of an irreducible 'living' or 'basic' wage, theoretically regardless of market forces, as the reference point for federal wage determination. The level at which he set this represented an increase of 27 per cent for unskilled award rates. More importantly, the decision had a major impact on the long-term structure of Australian wages, particularly as the States also adopted their own basic wages, beginning with New South Wales in 1914. Henceforth, until 1967, most award wages consisted of two components: the basic wage, and margins for skill or other considerations. Furthermore, the needs of a family unit, consisting of a male wage-earner, plus wife and children, was adopted as the basis for calculating the cost of living to be covered by the basic wage. Given the community assumption that women's wages were supplementary to a male breadwinner's, this decision structured a low-wage regimen for women. From 1912 the female basic wage was set at 54 per cent of the male.

The Harvester judgment impacted slowly upon wage structures. Initially, few unions took much account of it, and those that did were most likely to be disappointed that the decision ran counter to their policy of claiming a fair share of profits. Even in conjunction with its later State equivalents, the basic wage did not cover a majority of the workforce until the 1920s. Nevertheless, from this time Higgins gave a number of judgments favourable to unions, among them the introduction of the 48-hour week in federal awards. These decisions offered a powerful incentive for the federation of State unions to gain access to the Commonwealth Court. By 1914, two-thirds of union members belonged to 79 interstate unions.

But now employers managed to clog up the Commonwealth Court with a series of appeals to the High Court, which effectively reduced the powers and jurisdiction of the federal tribunal. In 1906, State government employees were removed from federal jurisdiction. The establishment of common rules, covering all employers regardless of whether they were party to a dispute, was also disallowed. Consequently, when it came to power in 1910, the Labor Party sought constitutional amendments by referenda, but without success.

Frustration with the obstacles to arbitration and an upswing in the economy produced an upsurge of industrial action by unions from 1908. By then, the coalminers had already withdrawn their registration under the system in disgust. In 1909 they launched a major industrial campaign for improved conditions. In the same year, Broken Hill miners were locked out when they resisted a 12.5 per cent wage reduction, and a major tram strike occurred in Sydney. In 1912 a general strike also occurred in Brisbane over tramway employees' assertion of their right to union membership.

In each of these confrontations, the unions were defeated, ultimately by the intervention of the state. This was most blatant in the case of the New South Wales coalminers in 1909, when, after enacting special legislation providing for severe penalties for persons inciting or encouraging strikes, five of the miners' leaders were gaoled, and trial by jury was suspended. The State government also imprisoned the Broken Hill miners' leaders, after dispatching armed police and strikebreakers. As Turner emphasised, the process of domestication of the unions required that the state discipline those which acted outside the arbitration system (Turner 1965, pp. 36–44).

The circumstances of the early 1900s indicated, however, that the process of domestication was incomplete. By the end of the first decade of the twentieth century, socialists and syndicalists in the Industrial Workers of the World found fertile ground amongst miners, transport workers and other unionists disillusioned with the performance of the arbitration system and the Labor Party which had so strongly advocated it. For a time, they challenged moderate Laborism for the leadership of the labour movement. In this sense, arbitration remained the major political reference point that it had been since the late 1890s.

Conclusion

By 1914, the Australian system of labour relations was firmly established. The system built on entrenched workforce traditions and employer approaches to labour relations, in the context of labour shortages. Perhaps the single greatest feature of these was the propensity of the Australian workforce in the nineteenth century to form trade unions. Australian employers increasingly concentrated upon dealing with unions representing whole occupations, and never succeeded in establishing internal labour markets. The major distinguishing feature by 1914 lay with the role of the state. In Australia, it confirmed and extended external labour market strategies and employer preoccupations with unionism. The state did this through the compulsory arbitration system, which encouraged unions and awarded wages and conditions on an occupational basis. Henceforth, the political sphere of conflict between labour and capital became a major determinant of the structure and nature of industrial relations in Australia, particularly because of an established democratic tradition which allowed the unions to organise an effective Labor Party.

4 Labour relations in Japan between the wars

Takao Matsumura

It has often been argued that the origins of the Japanese employment system can be traced to the original practice of a small number of large commercial enterprises like Mitsui. Here, it is claimed, the traditional ethos of the Japanese family (called 'ie') was adapted to the organisation of a modern industrial enterprise, where relations between employers and employees were seen in terms of a 'family enterprise' and were directly comparable to those between the head and the children in the family. Chie Nakane describes this as 'a vertical society' (Nakane 1974), and in his pioneering study of the Japanese factory system, J.C. Abegglen argues that the system was based on the traditional willingness of both workers and managers to see the enterprise as a family-like community in which their own welfare was dependent on its prosperity. Such beliefs were reinforced by the traditional vertical structure of social dependence (Abegglen 1958). It is also possible that Confucianism played a major role in generating the system and the particular work ethos of Japanese people—for example, the acceptance of authority, loyalty and deference to superiors—clearly was and is of great importance.

But the origins of the specific characteristics of industrial relations in Japan—employment for life, seniority wages, mutual loyalty and 'enterprise unionism'—need to be considered more specifically in their historical context. If we look at the origin of the system in terms of economic circumstances, managerial strategies, state power, and the nature of the labour movement, then it will become clear that the system was the creature of the rational, profit-maximising behaviour of managers who were seeking to adapt their strategies to the specific characteristics of the Japanese labour market (Taira 1970; Crawcour

1978). In this chapter, I would like firstly to talk about the labour market, then managerial strategy and finally trade unionism between the Wars.

Labour market

During the First World War, capital became more concentrated and the Zaibatsu groups established their position as leaders of Japanese industry, commerce and finance. The war changed dramatically the structure of the working classes in Japan. The number of workers in heavy industry, light industry and construction increased rapidly from 211 000 in 1914 to 255 000 in 1920. The number of female textile workers also grew rapidly, though not as fast as male workers. Numbers in factories employing over five persons increased by 60 per cent in the same period to reach 46.8 per cent of the total work force in 1920.

After the summer of 1915, the growing demand for munitions from Russia stimulated the Japanese economy and caused labour shortages. Most of the additional workers were recruited from agriculture. Labour mobility between the factories increased—particularly in shipyards, machine factories and steel mills—and industrial managers became preoccupied by the problem of securing a stable supply of skilled and semi-skilled labour for their factories. They attempted to counter high mobility by wage increases and agreements to prevent poaching between themselves. This was not very effective however (Gordon 1985, p. 163).

The prosperity brought by the First World War continued for a short while after the Armistice, but in April 1920 the boom ended. Many banks failed and the market in silk, Japan's major export commodity, shrank. The golden era of wartime had ended and before recovery could begin, the 1922 Washington Conference on disarmament further damaged Japan's heavy industries, which relied heavily on military procurement.

Throughout the 1920s, the Japanese economy staggered from depression to depression until 1929, when it suffered even greater damage from the world depression. It was during the long-term depression of the decade that the characteristic Japanese pattern of industrial relations took shape. The increase in the number of factory workers during the decade was not very large (from 1 550 000 in 1920 to 1 800 000 in 1928) and the rate of increase per annum was only 1.5 per cent compared to 18 per cent between 1914 and 1919. During the war, labour mobility in heavy industry had been as high as 70–90 per cent per year, but in the late 1920s the rate of labour mobility fell to about 10 per cent. In contrast to the war-boom period, it now became a risky and difficult matter even for the skilled worker to move from factory to factory. Hence the desire to stay with a particular company grew very strong and more men than before hoped to remain with their first employer from initial employment to retirement.

The world depression in 1929–30 proved a disaster for Japanese heavy industry. 1931 was the severest year, when Japan's exports fell by 70 per cent compared with 1929 and at least 2 000 000 were unemployed. Even the university elites were affected and the title of a popular film—*I Went to University, But ...*—became a cliché of the era. In 1931 Japan came off the Gold Standard and Finance Minister Takahasi's deficit spending policy had some effect, so that Japan's recovery came earlier than recovery in the West.

In 1931, Japan began the invasion of China, and after military intervention in the northern part of China (Manchuria) in September 1931 (the 'Manchurian Incident') Japanese military expenditure also began to rise steeply. Heavy industrial enterprises were among the chief beneficiaries, but despite the recovery the labour market only gradually shifted from a situation of over-supply to one of labour shortage. Individual companies did not repeat the tactics they had followed in the First World War but behaved cautiously, continuing to employ most new recruits as temporary workers. This gave permanent workers added incentives for staying with their companies.

The labour market is a necessary but not sufficient condition to explain the establishment of life-time employment. So we should take managerial strategy into consideration.

Managerial strategy

Among the various managerial strategies, what I want to stress is 'in-company technology training'. During and after the First World War, some managers preferred to try to establish a stable and trained skilled workforce within their companies in order to meet the rapidly increasing demands of new technologies. A translation of Taylor's *The Principles of Scientific Management* appeared in 1913, only two years after its American publication. To introduce the Taylor system, the traditional master system had to be reorganised. For instance, Sumitomo abolished the master system around 1921 and instead adapted the permanent employee system. In the Mitsui Shipbuilding Company, the Kobe Iron and Steel Company and the Shibaura Machinery Company, technological training programmes were set up. The managers looked to employ inexperienced young boys with good educational qualifications after graduation each year in March or April. These became a favoured group expected to supply the future leaders. The companies did not teach manual skills to the newcomers but concentrated on those skills needed for high levels of technology, and in-company technology training schemes rather than reliance on courses provided by public technological schools became standard procedure in many large companies in the 1920s. It was natural that workers who received high levels of technological training from their companies should have developed a strong sense of loyalty, and this was how the tradition of life-time employment in industry developed from its beginnings in the Meiji era.

Seniority base wages were supplemented by other inducements, such as retirement funds and non-wage welfare benefits for workers who stayed with the company. Despite the decrease of ability after the age of forty, wages continued to increase until retirement, and family subsidy, housing, travelling and clothing costs relevant to productivity were supplied. These were introduced roughly in parallel with the seniority base wage system. Managers were generally opposed to state welfare schemes as well as to the proposed legislation on health insurance in 1920, because this would have meant that non-wage welfare in the company would have lost much of its effectiveness.

The problem to be answered is why Japanese managers were able to establish 'in-company technology training' rather easily without opposition of the workers. In Japan, there was a form of apprenticeship, but one that differed from its English counterpart. In England and in many other European countries, the apprenticeship system constituted the process through which artisans mastered the skill of their trade and became journeymen. In England in the mid-nineteenth century, such men had organised national craft unions which were able to regulate the entry of apprentices and ensure high wage-rates. In Japan, there were urban craft guilds during the Tokugawa period, and in Tokyo, for example, the masons and sawyers maintained their craft guilds until at least 1889, though machinists and others in modern industries did not reproduce these earlier journeymen's organisations. As a result, they were never able to regulate entry into the trade or set wages through negotiations with their masters, and when new technologies began to be imported from the industrialised countries in the West, it was too late for them to establish an apprenticeship system.

This meant that in Japanese industry there was no stratum of artisans in the English sense, and this was why both craft and industrial unions subsequently proved difficult to establish, even though *Yûaikai* did attempt to create such an organisation. But it was the workshop rather than particular occupations, crafts, or even individual industries that continued to be the basic unit of organisation.

A few industrial unions, such as the gun workers and the Tokyo Electric Machinery Iron Union, were established in 1920, but attempts to set up industry-side craft and industrial unions failed. Collective action never went beyond company-specific issues. Even the successor to the *Hyôgikai*, which had been the most active proponent of industrial organisation, decided in 1929 to devote its energy to workplace struggles.

Recently, historians have begun to question whether the training systems in the larger companies were as successful in the 1920s as the managers expected. In a comparative study of the employment conditions of white-collar staff (*Shokuin*) and workers (*Kôin*) in the Hitachi Company, Shinji Sugayama has shown that attempts to encourage long-term service by hiring graduates and offering seniority wages began systematically for white-collar staff in the late 1920s. It was also applied to other workers in part, bringing about a new stratification of the labour market in both large and small factories. However, management efforts to elicit long-term service from workers were limited in effect and inconsistent. Workers hired after graduation from high school comprised only 10 per cent of all the recruits between 1920 and 1939. Wages did not necessarily rise with seniority, and income differentials between junior staff and workers amounted to a factor of four in the late 1940s. When business was slow, older workers with seniority were the ones most often fired. To regard relations in the Japanese employment system in this period as 'a paradise' is therefore misleading. So the stereotyped understanding of the characteristics of industrial relations in Japan should be reviewed by case studies, as Sugayama has done (Sugayama 1989, p. 554).

Trade unionism

Thirdly, I would like to refer to trade unionism, because this was closely related to the formation of a unique industrial relations system. The economic boom caused by the First World War made the trade unions more confident and aggressive and after 1917, labour disputes increased rapidly. The Russian Revolution had a dramatic impact on Japan because it gave hope to those who had been insisting on the need for revolutionary changes in society. In 1918, large-scale 'rice-riots' took place and shook the government. Starting as protests by housewives in a remote village against the sharp increase of the price of rice, the riots quickly spread throughout the nation and involved several million people. Troops were mobilised to repress the rioters, and the repression of the riots was seen by many as the desperate act of a dying *ancien régime*. The number of disputes over claims for wage increase reached a peak in 1919. Factory workers began to organise rapidly and the number of unions grew: in 1918, there were 107 unions, in 1919, 187 unions, and in 1920, 273 unions. Steelworkers, shipbuilders and machinists were particularly militant and even the *Yûaikai,* which had originally been founded in 1912 by Suzuki Bunji, a Christian social reformer, as a tame and harmless institution, began to take a different form and attitude.

These changes meant the abandonment of the old principles of harmony between capital and labour and the adoption of something more akin to class-struggle. The *Yûaikai* changed its name to the 'Great Japan Trade Union Federation' in 1919 and took the decision to become the national co-ordinating centre for craft and industrial unions (Large 1972). In 1920 and 1921, strikes broke out in a number of large enterprises—for example, at the Kawasaki Dockyards in Kobe, where 35 000 men were involved.

Facing these militant movements, managers expelled independent trade unions from their enterprises and tried to establish welfare systems in their company. Also they set up what were called 'factory councils'. Since 1918, the government had officially encouraged the introduction of factory councils and forty-eight shipyards, arsenals, steelmakers, machine and metalworking factories introduced factory councils in the period from 1919 to 1928. The Yokosuka Naval Yard, with 17 500 employees, was the first to institute a factory council in 1919. The Kure Naval Yard, with nearly 19 500 employees, and Yahata Ironworks, with about 18 000 employees, followed in 1920, then the Mitsubishi Nagasaki Shipyard in 1921. The introduction of factory councils in these large-scale industries reached a peak in 1921, mainly in those industries controlled either by state capital or by the Zaibatsu groups (Nishinarita 1988, pp. 200–1; Totten 1967).

The real issue, however, is the aim and results of introduction of the councils. In contrast to the factory councils (or factory committees) in the West, which provided a means for conducting negotiations between managers and trade unionists, factory councils in Japan were designed to prevent independent trade unions from coming into the firm or, where any unions existed, to get rid of them. From the beginning, the councils were designed to function as substitutes for trade unions. Managers usually allowed workers to elect council members, but the candidates were generally limited to senior white-collar workers. Managers offered workers a chance to express views on wages or work conditions, but they always limited the council to an advisory role. In the early 1920s, there were some attempts to use the councils as spring boards for establishing unions, but such attempts proved illusory and by the end of the 1920s, managers had succeeded in banishing almost all strong unions from the major shipyards, machine factories and steel mills.

As a result, independent trade unions were eliminated from the large enterprises and only in medium and small scale firms were workers able to remain organised. The result, shown in Table 4.1, was that industrial disputes and collective action shifted from the larger enterprises to smaller factories. Although trade unions continued to exist in name in the arsenals and in some of the larger enterprises, their role was limited to electing labour representatives for the ILO, and they were no longer independent trade unions. The failure of the labour movement in the larger enterprises in the 1920s and the establishment of the factory councils were therefore two sides of the same coin, and constituted some of the essential conditions for the emergence of the modern Japanese pattern of industrial relations.

Table 4.1 Participants in labour disputes (%), Japan, 1921, 1926, 1930

	Number participating in labour disputes					
Year	1–14	15–99	100–299	300–399	>1000	No. of Disputes
1921	11.0	57.8	19.1	8.9	3.2	246
1926	27.0	51.9	15.9	3.6	1.6	495
1930	30.9	53.4	11.0	3.6	1.1	907

Labour Ministry, 'Labour Disputes in our Country shown by Statistics', cited in Nimura 1969, p. 63.

Industrial relations during wartime between 1931 and 1945

After the 'Manchurian Incident' in 1931, a highly nationalistic climate developed. In 1933, Japan withdrew from the League of Nations and in 1938, from the ILO. Japan's war industries were now enjoying spectacular gains. Unemployment virtually disappeared and wages were rising. As a result, the trade unions also gained strength through increased membership and in fact, union membership reached its highest peak for the pre-war period in 1936, with a total of 420 000 members, even though this was still less than 8 per cent of the total industrial work force. But the outlook of the trade unionists remained unchanged. In March 1933, for example, one of the leaders of the Japanese Seamen's Union wrote to his friend Edo Fimmen, general secretary of the International Transport Workers Federation, to describe his impressions of Japanese trade union after returning from several years service in London:

> From my experience with the trade union movement in Europe, I think that the functioning of Japanese trade unionism has in many respects not yet reached maturity. A reform is required not only in the organisation of trade unionism but to recreate a trade union spirit among the organised workers. For one month I did my best to attend various trade union meetings to tell them about trade union organisation and trade union spirit which the trade unionists in Europe have experienced in fighting for the establishment of trade unionism during the last hundred years (Letter from S. Mogi, 31 March 1933).

The number of disputes and the numbers participating in disputes decreased from the time of the 'Manchurian Incident' up to 1935, but a sharp rise in disputes in small factories in 1936 and 1937 brought the *Sanpô* movement to life.

War with China broke out in 1937, and what was called the 'China Incident' quickly became a full scale war as the Japanese invasion spread like a flood over China. This 14-year war was to be the longest that Japan had ever fought, and its eventual outcome was war with the United States in 1941. At the time of the invasion of China there were almost no trade unionists left who would oppose the invasion. On the contrary, the All Japan Labour Federation passed a resolution at its annual convention in October 1937 which declared: 'We give our most sincere thanks to the officers and men of the Imperial Army who ... with the Imperial Navy did so much to add to the nation's glory throughout China since the incident began ...' (Large 1981, p. 203). In March 1938, the National Mobilisation Law was passed, providing the government with emergency powers to control human and material sources in time of war. The first regulations were ordinances limiting labour mobility and controlling wages, which were put into effect in 1939. Signs began to appear in the shops: 'Waste not, want not, until we win'.

From then until the war ended in 1945, the government issued regulations in rapid succession. The National Registration System was introduced in 1939, requiring individuals with special skills to register with the government. This system was gradually expanded to require the registration of all workers regardless of special skills. At the same time, all males aged sixteen to twenty were required to register whether they were workers or not. In 1944, registration was extended to males aged from twelve to fifty-nine and unmarried women from twelve to thirty-nine, and in the final period of the war, high school pupils were mobilised into heavy industries. The National Workbook

Law of 1941 required all workers to carry workbooks registered with the local Employment Agency, in which were recorded their employment histories, current status and wages. The law covered six million workers, roughly three-quarters of the national industrial workforce. In 1942, a comprehensive anti-turnover ordinance was introduced to reduce the rising rate of labour turnover, making it almost impossible for workers in heavy industries to move legally from one factory to another. As labour shortages became more severe with the development of the war, increasing numbers of Koreans were forced to come to Japan to work in mining and munitions factories. The exact number is still not known, but it is estimated that about three million Koreans were working in Japan when the war ended. Their working conditions were extremely wretched and if they attempted to escape, they were killed. In Nagano prefecture, for example, many Korean workers were killed once construction of the munitions factories was completed because they knew the secret lay-out and structure of the factories.

After the China War started in 1937, industrial relations were drawn into the orbit of 'Sanpô', short for 'Industrial Service to the Nation'. The Sanpô movement had been founded in 1936, and was initiated by the far right wing of the labour movement, the Kyôchôkai, and the Home Ministry's Police Bureau. The reason for introducing Sanpô into all factories was to harmonise labour-management relations, to prevent disputes, to ensure industrial peace and thereby to facilitate war production. The factory councils of the 1920s were taken as a model and the policy was implemented through the Sanpô Federation, which was officially supported by the Home and Welfare Ministries in July 1938, before being superseded by the government-run Sanpô association. 'Enterprise as one family' was a typical slogan. All other unions were eventually dissolved, but the Sanpô was seen by many contemporary workers as a more sophisticated version of earlier enterprise unions and most previous trade union leaders cooperated with the Sanpô. All employees from the company president to the temporary workers were members of the organisation and the Sanpô leaders declared that the traditional distinctions between white- and blue-collar should be ended. A new spirit of 'industrial service to the nation' should replace the selfish spirit of personal interest and workplace confrontation.

The impact of the Sanpô movement on industrial relations was considerable and helped to diffuse in-factory training schemes in both large and small factories where such programs had previously been either weak or non-existent. Instead of seniority-based wages, Sanpô established the formula of 'family-supporting' wages, that is a minimum rate for each age bracket, and an extra allowance for each dependent.

Uniform annual pay increases to all workers, regardless of their length of service to the firm, became the general tendency after the onset of the Pacific War, but once this stage of the war began, the emphasis on harmony gave way to more practical concerns about attendance, efficiency and productivity. The slogan, 'Imperial Work Ethic' replaced 'Enterprise as One Family'. It was not long before life for working people became increasingly wretched and finally disastrous.

To conclude, then, it would clearly be quite wrong to see the typical features of contemporary Japanese industrial relations as an ideal which has made high rates of economic growth possible. Employment for life, seniority wages, mutual loyalty and enterprise unionism were developed in a fairly haphazard fashion during the 1920s and in a period of long-term depression. The changes occurred only in the larger enterprises and were possible only because they were combined with the simultaneous employment of temporary workers and women, and the development of a system of sub-contracting to smaller outside companies. Immigrant Korean workers also began to play an increasingly important part in the labour force. In return for the sacrifices they made, a certain section of the Japanese labour force was rewarded with a relatively secure system of industrial employment. But such a system, it must be remembered, was also premised on the exclusion of an independent trade union movement.

5 A failed 'passive revolution': Australian industrial relations, 1914–39

Andrew Wells

This chapter surveys Australian industrial relations from 1914 to 1939. For the purposes of this discussion, industrial relations are defined as the power relations between management and employees (or between capital and labour) as they occur in the workplace. These relations have a number of dimensions. Firstly, industrial relations have a workplace character; the specific pattern of this division of labour, the employment of technology and management strategy, set the scene for industrial relations at the point of production. Secondly, in the Australian context, worker and management interests in the formation of wage levels, defined hierarchies of skill and conditions of employment have been mediated through a formal state-sponsored system of arbitration. Industrial relations in this sense is a study of the system of representation, negotiation and legal enforcement of work relations. These relations are shaped by the State and federal systems of arbitration. Thirdly, insofar as industrial relations are an aspect of a wider ensemble of social power relationships (class relationships—posited on property rights conferred by private ownership and control of productive resources, and the related capacity to appropriate and deploy the social surplus), they should be placed within the wider field of social, political, intellectual and ideological relationships.

From a theoretical perspective, any attempt to fetishise and give higher priority to one group of these relations generates a tendency to miss the wider social pattern of the power relationships between workers and their employers. The entire ensemble of these relations is what Gramsci theorised as hegemony and E.P. Thompson termed 'the social formation'. The material discussed in this chapter is centred on

industrial relations in the narrower—workplace and institutional—
sense, but the *explanation* for specific patterns of industrial relations
in their wider sense and their transformation over time is sought in a
broader Gramscian framework. Thus, in searching for analytical and
explanatory categories, the discussion widens. Social class remains
determinant in shaping an entire social formation, including its
material and ideological character. So much for definition and theory.

Economic and political context

Between the beginning of the First and the Second World Wars, the
Australian economy underwent a complex process both hard to
comprehend and define. In broad terms, the high-wage, relatively
prosperous economy was a product of its long-run relationship with
Britain. From the 1830s, Australia was viewed as a settler capitalist
society, available for exploitation and integration within an imperial
division of labour. This role was characterised by the flows of free-
immigrants and investment funds from Britain, the development of a
relatively sophisticated and highly profitable pastoral, mining and
agricultural economy supported by a large publicly-owned
communications infrastructure, and an urbanised population engaged
in service, financial and manufacturing activity. These patterns were
a consequence of a largely open economy, dominated by Anglo-colonial
finance capital, a capitalist structure of ownership over extensive
national resources and an exploitative and racist attitude towards the
pre-European Aboriginal population and non-European immigrants—
free and indentured. Indeed, as N.G. Butlin has recently suggested, the
success of this colonial economy was posited on the coerced transfer of
knowledge, natural resources and embodied labour from Aboriginal
people to European 'settlers'.

In the 1890s and in the early 1900s, there was a significant reaction
by white settlers against the economic, financial, political and military
requirements of this previously dominant Anglo-Australian
relationship. Economic depression, industrial conflict and financial
chaos provided the context for this questioning. At an economic level,
this meant a reassessment of the dependence on the pastoral,
agricultural and mining industries in Australia. What has been called
'colonial liberalism' was a loose attempt by politicians and intellectuals
sympathetic to the manufacturing interests in Melbourne and elsewhere
to sketch out the essential features of this post-colonial political
economy. It was not until the 1920s, however, that the substance of this
new conception became, in part, reality. A necessary prerequisite was
a political transformation of the colonial state. A sober assessment of

the economic structure of settler capitalism suggested that the advantageous circumstances which gave European Australians a high living standard and considerable political freedoms in the late nineteenth century were unlikely to be replicated in the early twentieth century. Although the new federal structure would inhibit rapid economic transformation, colonial liberalism and ascendant Laborism shared a similar developmental conception. Central to this conception was a policy to industrialise the economy and enhance the skills and wages of the urban workforce.

What has been discussed in a previous chapter as 'new protectionism' and 'Laborism' captures the spirit and practical steps needed to create the basis of a new political economy. But it is important to recognise that the traditions and the economic interests created in the settler colonies were not about to disappear. The waves of pro-British patriotism evident at the beginning of the First World War and the power of Imperial sentiment to split the labour movement over the question of conscription for overseas military service under British direction, are clear examples of a colonial rather than a genuinely national outlook. Moreover, the significance of primary-export industries reliant on borrowed money from London, and the tight web of mercantile and financial links between Britain and Australia, was maintained, even strengthened. The war and the widespread post-war disillusionment, especially heartfelt by workers and ex-servicemen, suggested that Australian imperial subservience was losing its hold, notwithstanding Australian policies to encourage soldier settlement and welcome British immigration to Australia, to solve their overcrowding and to provide agricultural produce to meet insatiable Imperial needs. But the most accessible and productive lands in Australia had already been appropriated; expansion required costly public and private outlays in communications and land improvement, and the pattern of international trading relations turned against primary exporting industries. In the 1920s, the movement of export prices, indeed the worsening terms of trade as a whole, demonstrated the importance of trying to complete the reorientation of the economy begun in the previous decades.

The cumbersome and excessively complex federal political structure was a major barrier to direct economic reorganisation. It is easy to overlook the important consequences of the post-colonial state, as shaped by a *laissez-faire* ideology and well-developed market relations with a dominant imperial power, in weakening the capacity of that state to restructure the economy, the separation between the political sphere and the economic field, where private interests dominate, being central to the liberal state. The colonial and post-colonial state, though strongly involved in resource ownership and communication infrastructure investment, was acting to support private activity. It was not imbued with a strong ideological commitment to public ownership or regulation; these were expedient or temporary measures.

The only possible solution to the forging of a new political economy in this constitutional and institutional context was to deploy the powers of the Commonwealth government over tariffs and wage conditions (powers conferred on the central government) and coordinate these initiatives with State government enthusiasm for public works expenditure and industrial investment, technical education and growth in urban employment. This form of industrialisation was necessarily limited by the complexities of rivalries and distrust between governments, the limited size of the domestic market, the lack of a heavy armament industry and the absence of proximate and accessible export markets. The institutional, political and market barriers to sustained industrialisation were thus formidable. Nevertheless, the costs of the war had generated a large overseas debt, so the introduction of tariffs and a Commonwealth income tax in 1919–20 were required to avoid an impending fiscal crisis. This worked to assist industrial investment. Industrial production—generally based on import substitution—became a dynamic part of the economy for much of the 1920s. Indeed, the immediate post-war period, characterised by all the signs of deep-seated political and industrial discontent, was stabilised in part by the growing, if selective, use of state repression, but more importantly by the growing signs of an impending economic boom.

Despite a serious wave of strikes in the period 1916–21 in the coal, maritime and railway industries (and a general strike in New South Wales) and a challenge to the legitimacy of the Arbitration system by the radicalised left-wing of the labour movement, the basic tenets of Arbitration survived. Thus the key notions, increasingly the concern of the Federal Court of Conciliation and Arbitration, that the distribution of national income between capital and labour should be determined by a legal quasi-state instrumentality, and that the cost of living should be considered in framing a Basic Wage, was maintained. Between 1912 and 1930, the whole machinery of wage fixation was thus developed and extended in the context of the federal and State governments assuming enhanced responsibilities for training workers and supporting and fixing their wages and conditions. Industrial relations were thus strongly shaped by the state.

Within this framework of state-arbitrated wages and award conditions, the position of the skilled manufacturing artisan in the employment hierarchy was coming under attack. A distinction needs to be made here between the so-called traditional colonial manufacturing activities—food-products, soft and alcoholic beverages, clothing and footwear, milling and baking, to take some obvious examples—where technical sophistication was not essential and the new emerging industries like iron and steel, motor cars, electrical appliances and chemical products, where new technology and production methods were decisive. In the new industries the trend was to import British, European or American technology and production techniques. These had a substantial impact on devaluing and displacing important sections of the manufacturing workforce. It thus followed that the position of skilled tradesman, especially in the engineering trades, was being undermined (but not destroyed) and the determination of awards in the industrial courts both reflected and underwrote this significant change. Had this pattern of change been supported by a stable international production, trading and financial system, the Australian economy may have consolidated its industrial transformation and even developed an export capacity. But it was vulnerable to and institutionally incapable of rapidly responding to sudden changes in the imperial economic system (itself embedded in the international economy).

The pattern of apparent economic prosperity was broken by the onset of an international capitalist depression in the late 1920s. Once again the pattern of the 1840s and 1890s was repeated. In the late 1920s, raw material prices fell and overseas borrowing dried up. This time, in contrast to the 1890s, the foreign debt was essentially public; incurred in the borrowing for infrastructure by state governments anxious to encourage industrial development, transport improvements, electrical generation and transmission and agricultural intensification. A fall in export increase and a cut-back in public spending and employment had immediate consequences for the manufacturing and service sectors. Unemployment and a balance of payments crisis were the most tangible aspect of the Great Depression in Australia. While the leading historian of the depression places significant emphasis on economic distortions produced well before the Wall Street Crash (public and private miscalculation and mismanagement), this follows from his essentially neo-classical and general equilibrium cast of mind, not from a balanced judgement about the Australian political economy as a whole. Schedvin likes to argue that the public-supported manufacturing strategy was a mistaken and politically motivated departure from Australia's comparative advantage in land-based export industries and that a necessary economic correction was inevitable irrespective of international factors. This is not an entirely helpful judgement about the causes of the depression for historical and theoretical reasons. Be that as it may, by 1930 unemployment rose steeply, the balance of payments deficit was serious and the crisis in public finance was substantial. A federal Labor government led by Scullin, constrained by the constitutional and economic realities of the time and its own ideological conservatism, was no more able to avoid some unpleasant measures to remedy the crises than its conservative predecessors.

Eventually the government's response involved a major devaluation of the Australian currency (to bring the already substantial discounting of the Australian pound, supposedly on a par with sterling, to an official resolution), a vigorous attempt to reduce import costs by using embargoes, quotas and increased tariffs, and a contraction of public expenditure and employment. The formal agreement negotiated in May 1931, the so-called 'Premier's Plan', was an agreement mostly concerned with public employment, wage levels and overseas borrowing and repayments. The 'Premier's Plan' is largely a misnomer; the actual compromise agreement was in large part an abdication of political responsibility by elected parliamentarians in their attempts to solve a national economic emergency in the face of 'expert advice' from local and British bankers and financiers and the recently established economics profession. Needless to say, the mainstream labour movement, including the populist but largely rhetorical New South Wales Premier Jack Lang, had few alternative ideas and strategies to ameliorate the impact of the depression. A Labor government was completely ineffectual in a situation where about one-third of the workforce, a large slice of the labour movement's constituency, were unemployed. Balancing the budget and cutting expenditure were not radical or even humane solutions. A split in Labor ranks, reflecting its policy vacuum, meant that political initiative returned to the conservative United Australia Party and thus, in keeping with liberal and market ideology, economic recovery was to be the painful consequence of a long, drawn-out international recovery, itself partly a consequence of military spending.

One important aspect of the slow process of recovery was the relative neglect by Australian governments and entrepreneurs of the potential for regional trade with Asian raw-material purchasers. This would have been in opposition to the accepted policy of concentrating on supplying the British market. So even when market opportunities from Asia beckoned, traditional Empire loyalties were respected— such was the power of the past. The Ottawa agreement of 1932 and the 1936 Trade Diversion tactics had similar implications. Rather than develop the growing Japanese interest in Australian wool and wheat (by the early 1930s Japan was Australia's second largest buyer of these commodities) and encourage their desire to import minerals from Australia, these government measures gave Britain trade preferences, and by 1939 had resulted in an erratic and unwise return to a trading dependency on the United Kingdom. So as raw material price slowly recovered—wool considerably faster than wheat—and primary exports diversified, Australia was resuming its role as a supplier of raw materials and foodstuffs to Britain. From a British point of view, this seemed especially desirable as a possible future war with Germany would require strategic access to Australian and Empire raw materials. Meanwhile, as N.G. Butlin rather tersely noted in his survey of economic developments, the manufacturing sector that expanded to supply the local market, even in these depressed times, typically looked to British investors, technology and management practices in establishing new factories or modernising old ones, thereby avoiding what we would now call industrial best practice. So one conclusion we might draw is that Australia was badly served by its politicians, diplomats, financiers and industrialists in the mid-1920s to the late-1930s. Their policies, sentiments and actions strengthened an already well-entrenched economic and military alliance with a declining world economic and naval power and in so doing they failed to diversify Australia's trade, cultural and political relationships.

A curiously neglected characteristic of this inter-war period was the long-run economic stagnation. In 1938/39, the real domestic product per head was almost exactly what it had been in 1920/21. Even more curious was the employment and wages pattern that emerged in the 1930s. It appears that for the employed workforce, real wages were not significantly reduced in this period, despite the nominal 10 per cent reduction in wages that the Commonwealth government determined in 1931 and the consequent flow-ons to State tribunals. So, although unemployment peaked at around 30 per cent in 1930–2, and the ravages of unemployment deeply affected those it touched, the majority who remained in work were more insulated from the direct impact of unemployment, but not the widespread fear of joining the jobless, than one might have expected. To understand this apparent contradiction, we now turn to the institutionalised aspect of industrial relations—that is, the Arbitration system—before examining workplace industrial relations.

The institutional context of industrial relations

The system of arbitrated wages and conditions established in the Australia colonies and New Zealand had a central role in the shaping of industrial relations. Without a clear understanding of the system's operations, powers and impact, we cannot reconcile two statements made by well-respected Australian labour historians.

Fitzpatrick, writing in 1941, states without much elaboration:

> The trade union movement was able to improve its organisation
> beyond measure, in the quarter of a century between the wars. This
> vastly improved organisation was probably the principal factor in
> making possible a slight increase in real wages. (Fitzpatrick 1941,
> p. 340)

In his study of the same period, Macintyre concludes a lengthy
survey of the political and social impact of the depression thus: 'By
1931 the unions were powerless, the ALP was routed and a large
proportion of the population reduced to helpless indigence' (Macintyre
1986, p. 274).We will return to resolving this paradox subsequently.

The Australian arbitration structure had its origins in colonial
wage boards. The New South Wales Act of 1901 and the Commonwealth
Court of Conciliation and Arbitration established in 1904 were the
central innovations in establishing the modern structures. Fundamental
to these Acts and the institutions they called forth was the loss of trade
unions' power (especially the legal right to strike) in return for
legitimising the role of trade unions in securing for their members a
recognition of their members' skills and a minimum living (or basic)
wage plus margins for defined skill. The determination of this 'basic
wage' became the province of the Commonwealth Court, even though
only a minority of workers and their unions were directly subject to its
awards. The living wage (the cost of reproducing labour power), not
relative market power of individuals or groups of workers (or indeed
the market position of their employers), was the starting point for
industrial negotiation; furthermore, immigration restrictions, clear
designations of skill and protectionist policies buttressed this state-
mediated compact between capital and labour. The Labour Movement's
dependence on these principles is normally part of any definition of
mainstream labour ideology of the period (viz. Laborism).

The most significant consequence of this institutionalised
arrangement was that the system encouraged the organisation of
employers and employees. What the system delivered to both parties
was a legally enforced collective bargaining procedure which established
the Award as the binding set of rules throughout an industry. This
enhanced very considerably the capacity of unions to attract and
expand membership. Many unions were born with the state acting as
midwife. Thus, union membership grew quickly; 53 per cent of the
workforce was unionised by 1920. The depression saw membership
falling; they bottomed at 43 per cent in 1934. On a comparative basis,
even allowing for the decline, these percentages were much higher
than those in Great Britain, to make an obvious comparison. To take

the greatest advantage of the system, unions registered under both Commonwealth and State industrial systems. Over time the pattern of State awards generally followed those of the Commonwealth Court.

In theory, though not in practice, the involvement of unions and unionists in this system meant loss of the *de jure* right to strike in exchange for participation in an extended State *de facto* law-making instrumentality. The industrial relations system of Australia thus provided unions and unionists with simultaneous legal protection and industrial subordination. The Court recognised the law-making and enforcement primacy of the parliamentary and legal systems, as well as accepting the established property, ownership and management rights implicit in the concept of private property in a capitalist society. The Australian Court consequently accepted the right of private owners and managers to select, control, promote, demote and dismiss their workers. Freedom to sell one's working capacities to an employer was to coexist with essentially coercive relations with that very same employer within the workplace. While the Court occasionally ruled on questions of procedure or due process, it accepted what one academic authority called:

> ... the capitalistic order in the present shape, and assumes that any large change in the organisation of industry is a matter solely for the people or their representatives in Parliament (Foenander 1947, pp. 211–2).

The Arbitration Court not only provided a framework for regulating industrial relations, it also created an innovative means for determining the minimum wage level. In 1907, Mr Justice Higgins introduced a 'Basic Wage' by calculating a sum that might purchase an austere standard of living for a working-class family. The essence of this system remained in place until the early 1920s. In 1921, Justice Higgins, the principal architect of the Court and its wage-fixing philosophy, retired to be replaced by increasingly conservative personnel on the bench. In the period of employer consolidation, conservative government and then economic depression, attempts were made to change the Court's powers, in keeping with a bench increasingly concerned with the employer's ability to pay and remain profitable. When these attempts failed, a successful campaign was waged to modify the established principles of wage fixation and extend the role of the capacity-of-employers-to-pay concept.

During the mid 1920s, the increasingly reactionary Bruce–Page National government did in fact attempt a substantial change to the Commonwealth Arbitration system. This was an attempt to give employers greater freedom to vary wages and conditions. Firstly, penal provisions were introduced in 1926 and secondly, after proposing that the Commonwealth exercise a monopoly in industrial arbitration (to bring troublesome unions under control and remove the room to manoeuvre provided by State jurisdictions), it responded to very considerable labour movement opposition by going to the 1929 elections on a promise to transfer industrial power (except in the maritime industry) to the States. Bruce's campaign did not impress the electorate. His political ineptness during a systemic depression ended over twelve years of Nationalist Party ministries. A pledge to maintain Arbitration had much to do with the election of the Scullin Labor government in October 1929. Its victory at the polls gave it a clear House of Representatives majority, but not a Senate majority.

So the Arbitration system remained and its existence and operation may help explain the curious and contradictory features of the labour market during the 1930s noted earlier. The most systematic statistical and conceptual work in this area has been recently undertaken by Professor Bob Gregory and his colleagues at the Australian National University. Their research shows that the general characteristic of the unemployed during the depression (such as age, gender, skill, education) was not much different from the employed. But once unemployed, it was very difficult to return to work—so most unemployment was long-term with consequently little job rotation and minimal use of part-time workers. Moreover, they argue that despite the Federal Court's reduction of nominal wage levels by 10 per cent in February 1931— when the basic wage concept was undermined by a 'capacity of industry to pay' idea—and even allowing for the very high levels of unemployment, real wages were not reduced. And despite the fact that the Harvester basic wage notion was not restored until 1937, Gregory and his co-researchers assert: 'During the Depression real wages measured in terms of consumer prices were above their historical trend' (Gregory et al. 1985, p. 5).

For those in work, especially in unionised areas of the economy, there were obvious limits to the employers' offensive. Unions and the Arbitration system were sufficient to moderate a wholesale attack by employers on workers' conditions and wages. It follows that the apparent opportunity for employers to rapidly restructure the economy (as occurred during the 1890s depression in a situation of falling real wages and union disintegration) was never actually realised in the somewhat different circumstances of the 1930s. This helps explain an equally curious phenomenon. The role of the manufacturing sector in generating new employment in the mid- to late-1930s is widely accepted by economic and labour historians but the actual figures for capital outlays contradict the notion that this expansion was based on rapid technological change. Capital to labour ratios in manufacturing actually fell during the recovery phase. To be more explicit, there was a drastic decline in large factories and the growth of smaller ones. It was therefore the impact of the tariff and devaluation and the reorganisation of production that made manufacturing more profitable, not so much wage reductions *per se*.

These arguments are consistent with the analysis of the 1930s depression offered by Schedvin, who claimed that the expansion of investment in manufacturing was not sufficiently significant to explain recovery; if anything, productivity gains were made in the traditional export industries, he argues, not in the import substituting manufacturing sector. So while the economic historians see structural change in the 1930s consolidating the industrial change of the 1920s, they seem to be arguing that the wage constraint (Arbitration) and the artificial nature of the temporary incentives (tariffs and related import barriers) did not achieve a sustained and self-sustaining industrialisation.

We should, however, exercise considerable caution in accepting their analysis (their facts seem somewhat more soundly based). Firstly, the theoretical categories of most economic historians are hostile to non-market political intervention, even where these interventions were recommended at the time by academics, financiers and bureaucrats. So market failures are always to be explained by necessarily undesirable political interference. Secondly, the economic historians deal in statistical averages and physical data and indeed market-priced asset values (that swing dramatically during a depression and recovery). Their statistical categories and market concepts are notoriously incapable of detecting precisely what we need to know: were there important changes to the technical and social division of labour not reflected by aggregate investment statistics?

It is therefore plausible to accept that so-called traditional manufacturing—such as food, drink and clothing—expanded in the 1930s but used traditional (that is, non-innovative) production techniques, while the new manufacturing industries, such as steel making and metal fabrication, electrical generation and supply, electrical appliance makers, chemical industries and motor car assembly, were based upon new organisation and production methods. During the depression, mergers and take-overs resulted in larger ownership and production units in these industries, while dispersal and new entrants typified the older industries. For example, BHP expanded from its Newcastle plant by acquiring and then modernising the Port Kembla works in 1935. Some of the newer companies were branches or subsidiaries of large British or occasionally American companies. Whatever their national origins, they brought with them new technological, assembly-line and management practices. Scientific management and a growing technical division of labour were used, although the Australian interest in scientific management was rather more unsystematic than American experience. Ford began vehicle assembly while General Motors went into partnership with the Adelaide-based coach and vehicle assembler Holden. It seems reasonable to conclude that the institutional context placed some powerful constraints on employers' freedom of manoeuvre and divided the workforce in several ways. While a substantial group of long-term unemployed workers became either resigned to their misery or disillusioned with mainstream Labor politics and gravitated into the Unemployed Worker's Union or its mentor, the rapidly growing Communist Party of Australia (CPA), other employed workers became locked into bitter industrial conflict. The bulk of the employed maintained their living standards and their (probably unenthusiastic) loyalty to the labour movement and Laborism at the cost of anxiety about possible future unemployment and the intensification of work itself. Women workers were treated especially badly since the labour movement, most male workers and employers shared many assumptions about the gender order in society. Another pattern of segmentation, even hostility, within the working class was thereby exacerbated during the depression. As we can now appreciate, both Fitzpatrick and Macintyre captured part of this confusing and contradictory reality. It remains now to examine the pattern of workplace industrial relation to further test this hypothesis.

Workplace industrial relations

It therefore followed that shopfloor industrial relations in the 1930s took on a wide variety of seemingly irreconcilable characteristics. In 1938, over 610 000 Australians were factory workers and yet more than 40 per cent of factories employed fewer than five workers. Throughout Australia (though more than two-thirds were in Victoria and New South Wales), nearly 1000 factories employed over 100 people. For many workers, hours were long, work was tedious, backbreaking and often dangerous. Workers, especially women, were still exploited in sweatshops while doing outwork at home. Neither the Commonwealth nor State arbitral systems had the resources to effectively police the regulations governing workplace conditions and minimum rates of pay. Unions tended to favour the larger employers and their introduction of scientific management on the grounds that they were better and more secure bosses than the myriad small capitalists. The retention of the small entrepreneur and the concomitant poorer working conditions makes it difficult to claim that Australia was a mature industrial nation. A more concentrated effort by the state or by a coherent industrial or financial capitalist grouping was required. This was not possible in the circumstances of the 1930s. Nor was it consistent with the 'semi-colonial' status of Australia's primary, secondary and financial sectors.

Shopfloor industrial relations included the craft aristocrats, like the printers who weathered the depression but not *without* some significant cost. Wages were cut, some workers in smaller firms were paid below-award wages and there was greater use of juniors and women. Unemployment grew to 16.8 per cent in 1931–2 and union membership fell from 16 000 to 13 000. As the depression ended in the mid-1930s, new investment in technological innovation, speed-up and new work practices were introduced. But—and this is the crucial fact—the union was preserved, the Award process maintained and the union leadership mildly revitalised. But juniors and women were both integrated and excluded in the process; women were fired from some firms to retain jobs for men, women were concentrated in the deskilled section of the workforce, and juniors were similarly treated.

In the metal industries, a similar situation emerged. The Amalgamated Engineering Union (AEU), the largest and most powerful union, was well placed to benefit from industrial expansion in the 1920s. Its 1928 membership of 23 000 enjoyed relatively high wages, a well-developed union organised, an extensive benefit system and comparatively low levels of unemployment. The union had the financial resources, organisation and strategic position to combine its recourse to the arbitration system with direct bargaining and regular demonstrations of militancy towards recalcitrant employers. As the Federal Court become less sympathetic towards the AEU after 1922, the union relied on its industrial strength to protect conditions and placed its hopes for longer-term improvements on the return to government of the ALP. By 1930, this hope was shown to have been completely misguided. From 1927, the Court was pressing the union to accommodate itself to employer demand to reorganise awards and thus to accept the full implication of mass production techniques. Paradoxically, by acceding to the drift of employer demands, the union secured employer preference for its members. Again, this brought unions and the larger and modernised employers together. Nevertheless, the union started to lose members (by 1933 membership declined to 18 400, 20 per cent fewer than five years earlier), and militant members were especially discriminated against by their bosses. Award conditions deteriorated, tensions between the skilled and unskilled intensified, while managerial control was enhanced. The union's structure emerged from the depression relatively unscathed; its financial reserves were, however, greatly depleted and its political outlook chastened by its experiences in supporting what emerged as an incompetent labour government.

The New South Wales Teachers' Federation provides another useful example of the effects of the depression. In this case, a responsible, well-integrated organisation representing the bulk of school teachers in New South Wales found a section of its membership affected by unemployment, wage reductions and the spread of radical ideas. The Federation flirted with oppositional politics but soon came to adopt a 'responsible' posture. For some teachers, wage cuts in line with federal and State Arbitration decisions were considerably greater than cost of living reductions. For example, between 1929 and 1934 a senior headmaster's salary fell some 24 per cent. Yet despite these and other real declines in salaries, the overall implications were limited. Membership fell, though the organisation remained. Within the Federation, the number who espoused or supported radical, even socialist, ideas grew, but few represented a serious threat to property or the state. A further example to illustrate this point was the unions that represented the salaried and manual workers in the New South Wales Water Board. Together these unions covered those workers whose livelihood depended directly on Government public works. Again the depression saw cutbacks in the construction of sewerage and drainage works as revenues declined and retrenchment of public servants became common. The Salaried Branch passed relatively unscathed as it contained the organisers and managers of the bureaucratic state. The manual workforce was reduced in size, while the skilled and experienced managed to maintain their position. The unskilled and recently employed suffered more directly. Unemployment was of course rather more serious than wage reductions or increased work pressures caused by retrenchment. Again, we can observe the separation between a large, if declining, strongly unionised and continuously employed workforce, and the long-term and powerless minority. In these unions, the power of the conservative Laborist tradition remained relatively unscathed.

In the transport industry, a different pattern occurred. Though the increased use of motorised transport in Australia was dramatic in the inter-war period, the position of the workers and unionists was very considerably weakened. What began as a phase of greater militancy after the Great War and growth in union membership, peaking in 1926 following amalgamation, degenerated into a severe decline in membership and an almost complete loss of industrial initiative. The union accepted the State and federal industrial relations system despite a dramatic fall in financial membership (from 2003 in 1927 to 838 in 1933). But many transport workers indicated widespread disquiet and dissatisfaction with their union leaders as they experienced almost no protection when forced by employers to leave the union and accept below-award individual contracts and the casualisation of employment. Meanwhile, to withstand the pressure, the union developed an increasingly bureaucratic and thus unresponsive outlook, a militantly anti-communist ideology as it strongly identified with the conservative end of the Laborist spectrum. With economic recovery, membership recovered, industry coverage grew and wages and conditions improved. But the fragmentation of the industry and its workers, an effect of the union's depression stance, took longer to overcome. In 1937–8 the union managed to press for new awards, new areas of coverage and a new name. The Transport Workers' Union, as it was now to be called, demonstrated that the union's survival and with it the preservation of the Laborist tradition could be achieved in the most difficult times but at a very high price.

Elsewhere in the industrial system, the waterside workers and timber workers had seen their unions collapse in the strikes of 1928–30. These were the unions where the left had already made major inroads and where leaders and unionists accepted 'class-struggle' ideology and the need to respond vigorously to the employers' industrial offensive. It was especially important for employers and the state to disarm the radical and militant end of the labour movement spectrum. It was here and in the CPA that a hegemonic challenge to capitalist production relations was taking form. The coal miners faced similar pressures as employers attempted a lock out in the Northern Collieries, pushing for lower wages to compensate for falling world coal prices. Despite an intelligent campaign by the miners to pursue political, industrial and legal avenues to regain employment and maintain their wage, the use of police violence in December 1929 and a realisation that the state was against them forced a strategic capitulation. But again the union survived despite lingering bitterness, while the union leadership moved significantly to the communist left. Amongst rural workers, the Australian Workers' Union (AWU) maintained its stronghold, despite rank-and-file radicalisation and attempts by the left to establish a competing union, while in the new manufacturing industries the reality was new technique and a slow undermining of many of the traditional skill classifications that Awards had previously protected. But at the grassroots and through the Labor Councils, and in the Australian Council of Trade Unions (ACTU), which was established in 1927, the union movement remained a powerful presence preventing overt employer reaction and widespread worker repression. As we have observed from these examples, generalisations about workplace industrial relations are not clear-cut; further examples would only add to this heterogeneous picture. Nevertheless, we have enough detail to suggest a conclusion.

Conclusion

Industrial relations in the 1920s and 1930s were substantially deadlocked. This is evident at all three levels of industrial relations— in the workplace, in the wage-fixing bodies and at a political level. Neither capital nor labour was able to pursue other than defensive strategies because neither had the resources, organisation or ideology to overcome an 'aborted passive revolution' (Gramsci 1971, pp. 105–20). A society that had a generation earlier been noted as a 'social laboratory' was degenerating into a society bereft of social policy and political imagination. None of the established political, economic or industrial actors had been able to seize the initiative. The radical left and the radical right made their debut, but their effectiveness was limited. The mainstream conservative side of politics failed to re-invigorate the economic and social processes. If anything, the conservative commitment to an increasingly outmoded Imperial order and ideological fixation with sound finance and deflation betrayed an astounding insularity. The reign of the pastoral and financial connection with Britain was too obdurate for the industrialist, the modernisers and the liberals to overcome. The conservatives were not even especially good at being reactionary despite occasional genuflections to European fascists. Ideologically destitute, they merely regained office when labour demonstrated its own failings. They were not yet a ruling class capable of constructing or imposing an independent and coherent national hegemony.

In the very depths of the depression, Labor gained office in the Commonwealth and in most States. But it failed to provide the necessary coherence and leadership. Labor cabinets—but probably not the vast weight of labour opinions in the Party and the unions—became beguiled by the conservative political and industrial relations agenda. They exercised greater restraint and humanity but introduced policies similar to those of their political adversaries. Their willingness to sacrifice the unemployed, the majority of women workers and many of the young was inconsistent with labour ideals. The communist and socialist left of the labour movement had a more hard-headed analysis of the situation but a rather fanciful strategy for its resolution. The generation of radical intellectuals of the Great War and the early 1920s tried to reconcile with growing despair their sense of disillusionment with parliamentary reform and the Laborist tradition, and the dogmatism and strategic pragmatism of the CPA. The labour movement was unable to offer much real hope to its constituents. Those in the factories, including their bosses, were likewise perplexed by their incapability to find sensible leadership and adequate solutions to a national crisis. Conservatives created semi-fascist armies to protect their property rights because they feared an impending class war organised by socialists. But defence of material interests in the face of a real or imaginary threat is not the same as resolving a social crisis. As Gramsci had noted in another context, the system of fortresses and earthworks of civil society—the extended institutions of the state— were strong enough to sustain a modern capitalist system through a severe economic crisis (1971, p. 238). This protective structure in Australia could withstand the crisis but could only offer a purely defensive program and thus maintain only a fragile hegemony. Neither capital nor labour were hegemonic in the dynamic and creative sense of the concept, thus neither social class was able to resolve the crisis decisively. Industrial relations were thus left in an unstable but continuous stalemate. Many workers suffered because of the indecisiveness of their leaders. It would take the trauma of a world war to create the necessary circumstances to break this stalled passive revolution.

6 Post-Second World War labour relations in Japan

Kazuo Nimura

Until only ten to twenty years ago, most Japanese felt that their country was behind the times in international terms. As a late developer, Japan looked to foreign models in all sorts of fields and sought to catch up with more advanced countries. In the area of labour relations, employers, bureaucrats and trade unionists looked for models to America, Germany, Britain or the Soviet Union. But from the late 1970s, the situation changed and increasingly people began to look to Japan for labour relations models. A great number of papers and books appeared on the theme of Japanisation, or on something that was held to be virtually identical with it—flexibility. Certainly it testifies only too well to the pace of change in Japan that, whereas most Japanese once felt that Japan was behind the times, they now feel that it is one of the most advanced nations, at least in the field of economy.

The modern history of Japan as a whole has been one of prodigious change, and after the Second World War the pace of change was at its most frenetic. The Japan of the 1940s was in all aspects—politically, economically, socially and culturally—a different country from the Japan of today. A glance at union membership figures, one of the main indicators of labour relations, shows that in the early 1940s membership was zero, all unions having been disbanded, yet in 1992 membership stood at 12 541 000. In qualitative terms, the changes were also enormous. The union movement of the late 1940s and 1950s was confrontational to a degree unimaginable when measured by the standard of today's labour-management cooperation.

It is impossible to present the full complexity of the scope of such dynamic transformation in this short chapter. I shall therefore deal with this fifty-year period in four stages, describing the broader changes in Japanese labour relations, their characteristics and historical background. My tentative conclusion is that there are two main reasons why Japanese labour relations have differed from those of the West, in which I include Australia. The first is that Japan has lacked a tradition of craft unionism, and the Japanese artisans' guilds of premodern times had little sense of autonomy. Secondly, Japanese blue-collar workers felt no particular pride in being members of the working class and constantly sought to escape working-class status. That they were able to succeed in this was due to the democratisation policies of the post-war Occupation which enabled them to demand equal treatment with white-collar workers.

The war years, 1940–45

The dissolution of trade unions and the Sanpo (industrial patriotic) movement

In July 1940, Japan's largest national labour organisation, *Sôdômei* (Japan General Federation of Labour) reluctantly resolved to disband itself. This was followed by the forced dissolution even of ultra-right-wing unions, which had been at the forefront of the industrial patriotic movement and advocates of the 'Nipponism' labour movement. All unions were thus disbanded and merged into the *Sanpô* Federation. The Federation was soon superseded by the *Sanpô* Association, an official government organisation under the jurisdiction of the Welfare Ministry.

The aim of the *Sanpô* movement was to ensure that workers cooperated with the war effort. But the origins of the *Sanpô* Federation, which was organised by the semi-governmental organisation *Kyôchôkai* (Harmonisation Society), lay in the bureaucrats' and management's intention to prevent any labour upsurge in the post-war period. Drawing on their experience of labour unrest at the end of the First World War, and determined to prevent a similar scenario, Interior Ministry officials thought up the idea of the *Sanpô* Federation. It was believed that, during wartime, when the nation's attention was fixed on the performance of the armed forces, it was relatively easy to suppress workers' demands, but that there was a danger of these flaring up again after the war was over. To prevent this from happening, it was thought necessary to thoroughly uproot all traces of autonomous labour organisations during wartime. As we will see later, the relative effectiveness of the government's policy is shown by the fact that there was a period of nearly two months immediately after the end of the war when there was virtually no labour movement.

Each plant was reorganised as a branch of the *Sanpô* Association headed by a president or factory director, and the workers were thus mobilised for the war effort. Indeed, the *Sanpô* not only brought about the break-up of autonomous labour unions, but it also introduced measures to ease the frustrations which Japanese workers had harboured for decades. For example, it emphasised that blue-collar workers, who until then had been referred to as *rôdôsha* (labourers) or *kôin* (factory hands), were just as essential as producers for the Greater Empire of Japan as managers and white-collar workers, and were thus redesignated as *sangyô senshi* (industrial warriors). In such ways, labour policy during the war years was more inclined toward providing a spiritual palliative than it was in improving workers' material welfare. Nevertheless, it must be said that these measures were by no means meaningless or ineffective; they were to a degree successful in stimulating workers' spirit and motivation. As will be seen later, their effects were clearly reflected in the post-war trade union movement.

At the same time, the government took various steps to boost productivity and stabilise labour relations. In order to guarantee the labour power necessary to meet military demands, one piece of legislation after another was passed to restrict workers' job changes, to draft men to work in factories, and to organise students in higher education into various groups that could serve the war effort. The most significant impact of these measures on post-war labour relations was the way in which the government actively intervened to determine wage levels. Government bureaucrats fiercely criticised wage payments by the hour as un-Japanese and sought to replace them with the concept of the *seikatsukyû* (livelihood wage), a minimum wage that would guarantee the livelihood of workers' families. This meant doing away with hourly or day rates in favour of age-related wages and benefits paid in accordance with the size of the family. The concept of the livelihood wage was accepted by companies and supported by workers. It will be seen later that the adoption of a monthly wage payment system for blue-collar workers in the post-war period can be traced to the weakening, during the war years, of the notion of payment for a fixed amount of work.

The post-war period 1945–55

The rapid growth of the labour union movement

The various reforms carried out by the Occupation authorities changed labour relations in Japan considerably from what they had been before the war. Japan's first Trade Union Law was passed, under which the existence of trade unions was legally recognised. A Labour Standards Law and a Labour Relations Adjustment Law were also enacted at this time. The Trade Union Law provided for the establishment of central and local Labour Relations Commissions, independent of central governmental bodies, which were to arbitrate and mediate in cases of industrial disputes. Each of these commissions was made up of representatives from labour, management, and impartial third parties. The commissions gave labour unions a public space in which they could make their views known to labour administration authorities. A new labour ministry was also established as the government body with overall responsibility for labour relations. The legal framework for labour relations thus created was strongly influenced by American and European models, but the actual practice of labour relations in Japan since then has been markedly different.

In the period immediately after Japan's defeat, those who had experienced the labour movement in the pre-war years set to work to rebuild it. Yet the first post-war union did not appear until October, nearly two months after the surrender. Ex-union leaders and socialists, who had been repressed for so long, could not immediately find the courage to restart their activities openly. Also, the experience of defeat was a new one; people felt bewildered and waited to see how the Occupation forces would act. The largest of the pre-war unions, the Seamen's Union, was the first to reform and organise publicly after it was learned that the formation of unions had been allowed in occupied Germany. The seamen were followed by municipal tram workers, who had had a comparatively solid organisation in the 1930s, and by coal and metalminers, large numbers of whom were concentrated in particular areas. Following stories on employers' responsibility for the war and on their wartime activities, newspaper workers throughout the country began to organise their own unions, which in turn had a great effect on workers in other industries. By the end of 1945, nearly 600 000 workers were organised in 843 unions. This was only the beginning of what was to become a tidal wave. By the end of the following year, there were 4 400 000 union members; in June 1947, 5 700 000, and in June 1948, 6 700 000 (53 per cent of the total workforce). Union organisation was especially vigorous in the first half of 1946 when the monthly average was 500 000 new members. 1 100 000 enrolments were recorded in the peak month of March that year.

Two national labour organisations emerged in August 1946. *Sôdômei* (Japan General Federation of Labour), with 850 000 members, was re-formed under the leadership of socialist activists who had been engaged in the pre-war labour union movement, while the more left-wing *Sanbetsu-Kaigi* (Congress of Industrial Unions), with 1 630 000 members, was an alliance of twenty-one industry-wide union federations mainly in the media and mining. With its dynamic campaigning, it quickly became the vanguard of the post-war labour movement. While *Sôdômei* was the basis of support for the Japan Socialist Party, most of the leadership of *Sanbetsu-Kaigi* were either members of, or else sympathisers with, the Japan Communist Party, and followed the lead set by that party.

Meanwhile, the Occupation authorities refused to allow the formation of strong nation-wide employers' organisations, fearing that they would prevent the growth of the labour movement. Employers' groups therefore began to form on local or intra-industry lines. A liaison organisation was set up in 1947, and in the following year, with the formation of the Japan Federation of Employers' Associations (*Nikkeiren*), a national employers' organisation finally emerged which was intended to take on the labour movement.

Why did so many workers rush to join unions in such a short space of time? Various factors were involved, but the main one was political. The new masters of Japan, the Occupation authorities, had decided on a policy of encouraging and promoting the growth of trade unions. The wartime allies felt that labour unions would act as a break on any tendencies in Japan to return to militarism and therefore adopted the objective of promoting the growth of unions. Furthermore, many of the General Head Quarters Labor Division staff who were responsible for implementing the policy were themselves former labour activists, and went on tours of Japanese factories and mines promoting the formation of unions. That this political factor lies behind the rapid growth of the post-war Japanese labour movement is borne out by the fact that on 10 October 1945, GHQ directed the Japanese government to promote labour unions. The government responded with the Trade Union Law, which was passed by the Diet in December 1945 and became law in March the following year. It will be remembered that the formation of labour unions began in October 1945, rapidly accelerated in December, and reached a peak in March 1946.

There were of course also economic reasons for the growth of labour unions. Inflation, which had begun during the war, worsened rapidly after Japan's defeat. In 1946, prices were six times higher than those of the previous year. Everybody understood that wage rises were a vital demand for workers and that unions were necessary to achieve them.

However, there were also social factors at work in the rapid unionisation of so many workers in this period. Unionisation did not proceed in the normal way, that is, by persuading individual workers to join; rather, almost the entire company workforce would join together *en masse* to form a new union. In that sense, apart from the few who were actively engaged in leading the process, the majority of workers did not join as a result of a freely made individual decision, but rather, simply 'followed the crowd'. In any society, those who take a stance different from others in their group come under pressure, but in Japan the emphasis on conforming with one's peers is particularly strong. Given such a situation, it would naturally have been hard for those who had little interest in unions or who in some cases opposed joining to have refused to join when most of their peers seemed to be moving towards forming a union. This was one of the reasons why a remarkable number of workers were unionised in such a short period.

This social atmosphere was felt throughout the whole society and not just in individual companies. When other workplaces and companies were forming unions, both workers and managers in remaining non-unionised workplaces were inevitably affected. To hang back would be to 'miss the unionisation boat', to be left behind by the rest of society. Above all, when it became clear that GHQ, the highest authority in the land, was seeking to promote unionisation, employers, who had for decades been opposed to legalisation of labour unions, were forced to realise that their position was untenable and began actively to promote the kind of unions that they themselves could control.

Characteristics of post-war Japanese labour relations

The key characteristics of Japanese labour relations from 1945 to the present emerged in the post-war years. Of these, the most notable is the extremely small number of occupational-based unions or industrial unions as against the vast majority of plant unions or enterprise unions. Industrial unions were formed, but they were only loose federations which were unable to exercise much effective leadership for their member unions. National umbrella organisations linking these federations were also formed, but the management of their member unions—decision-making powers as to personnel appointments, finances and union policy—was left to the individual unions themselves.

The second major characteristic is the fact that the membership of most unions include not only blue-collar workers, but supervisory and managerial staff—in fact virtually the entire workforce. There have been not a few examples where literally everyone except the factory manager belongs to the union. Before the Second World War, there were no unions in Japan to which both blue- and white-collar workers belonged, and there have been very few examples of such unions in other countries at any time.

It has not been a matter of white-collar staff simply joining unions. Rather, in the process of the formation of a union, employees at the level of section or department head would be appointed to important union posts, such as chairman or secretary, where they were in a position to exercise control over the union's affairs and direction. It might seem from this that post-war Japanese unions have been little more than tools of management, but in fact many unions of this type have fought hard for substantial wage rises and for democratisation of management.

In the period immediately after the end of the war, a great many blue-collar-only or mostly blue-collar unions were formed, notably in the mining and shipbuilding industries, as well as in municipal transport. These industries all consisted of large-scale plants with mostly male blue-collar workforces in which there were still a number of union activists left over from the pre-war era. But even here, where blue- and white-collar employees started out as members of different unions, after a few years they invariably got together in a single plant union. The exception was the mining industry, where blue- and white-collar workers continued to stay apart in their own unions. Again, in fields where white-collar workers were in the majority, white-collar-only unions were formed. This was especially the case in the tertiary sector, such as education, finance and the civil service, and in fact union density in this sector is higher than that in blue-collar-centred industries.

An important and unique feature of Japanese labour-management relations in the post-war period has been the fact that managements have frequently provided their unions with various facilities, such as the use of company property and buildings, free of charge, or the opportunity to have one's union dues automatically docked from one's pay (the 'check-off' system). This was already the case in the period under discussion. Many full-time union officials were allowed to go about their union duties, while receiving a full salary, without doing any work for the company, and it was quite acceptable for union meetings to be held during working hours.

The reason for the emergence of plant unions and joint 'blue- and white-collar' unions

Why were most post-war unions of the single factory or workplace type and not in the form of craft or industrial unions? Various factors play into this, but the most important are the constraints of the situation in the early post-war years when most unions were formed. On the way, the state had abolished unions altogether, so that when, after the war's end, Japanese workers tried to restart the labour movement, there were no organisations which could serve as the nuclei around which workers could unite. At that time, workers' demands for wage rises and democratisation were legion, but the only way to achieve them was to pressure individual managements. It was entirely natural that one should feel solidarity with fellow-workers whom one met every day and with whom one worked. For their part, management was loathe to negotiate with anyone from outside the company and sought by various means to ensure that unions were restricted to individual companies. The wider historical dimension also ought not to be overlooked in considering this question. There was no western-style craft-union tradition in Japan, no custom of regulating working practices beyond the framework of the single company. Prior to industrialisation, what workers' organisations there were had been formed at the behest of the political authorities for the purpose of making tax-collecting more effective. There were none of the autonomous craft guilds such as had developed in the free cities of western and central Europe.

Why then have most post-war Japanese unions been able to organise blue-collar and white-collar workers in the same union? Before addressing this question, we must first ask why it was that white-collar workers, who had never before been unionised, sought to join unions. This was because white-collar workers found themselves in the same state of economic privation as blue-collar workers as a result of post-war inflation, food scarcities and the damage wrought by the wartime bombing, and they felt that the only way to tackle their problems was through unionisation.

Lower-ranking white-collar workers—those educated to junior high school level—also harboured a deep sense of frustration about the discrimination between themselves and university graduates. They joined with blue-collar workers in calling for workplace democratisation. University graduates, for their part, while they all had the possibility of becoming managers, were dissatisfied with their low wages and had to live with feelings of insecurity about their company's future. They felt more committed to the company than blue-collar workers. They were also in a better position both to gain and to understand information about the company's condition and prospects. Most companies had been engaged in military production, which stopped with the war's end, and it was assumed that plant and equipment would be sequestrated in lieu of reparations. Many university graduates accused their bosses of war crimes or else called for the resignation of managers who had lost their confidence as a result of defeat. The younger men had received their higher education in the late 1920s and 1930s when the influence of Marxism on college and university campuses had been strong. This was another reason why, after the war, these former university graduates actively participated in the union movement and provided many of its leaders. Their bitter wartime experiences had also heightened their social conscience and stimulated them to seek meaningful social change.

Why did blue-collar workers accept white-collar workers both as fellow union members and even as leaders? Firstly, there was little sense of a tradition of class solidarity among Japanese blue-collar workers. They were far from harbouring any feelings of 'them and us'. Even in the pre-war union movement, many top leaders had been university-graduated intellectuals. There had been some opposition to leadership by such men, but it had been very limited. This was no doubt because Japanese workers had no particular pride in belonging to the working class; on the contrary, they sought rather to escape from it. Secondly, the suppression of the union movement in the years prior to and during the war had severely damaged the movement's traditions. As a result, there were few blue-collar workers with the necessary knowledge and experience to be able to handle the written formalities and other problems involved in the formation of unions. They were therefore forced to rely on the better-educated white-collar workers. Also, due to their ease of access to information about their companies, white-collar workers were able to speak and write more persuasively than blue-collar men.

Blue-collar workers could easily understand that white-collar workers were also badly off, and they found the argument for joint rather than separate action in the pursuit of pay claims only too persuasive. Furthermore, a blue-collar worker would have found it more difficult to gain the support of the whole plant than a white-collar worker, because blue-collar workers were not in a position to get to know men in sections other than their own, whereas white-collar workers, and especially section heads, had many men under them and could easily communicate with a wider range of employees. If a certain section chief had a good reputation, then union support for him would in turn bring the union many supporters. This was the reason why there were many examples, during the period when unions were being formed, of blue-collar workers asking white-collar section chiefs to join them and help in the process.

The struggle for the control of production

Despite the large number of unions and union members, there were surprisingly few industrial disputes in the period immediately after the war: a mere 810 disputes involving 635 000 workers in the whole of 1946. Due to employers' confusion and lack of authority in the immediate post-war period, workers were easily able both to secure recognition of their new unions and to obtain their demands.

A notable feature of the disputes in 1946 is the fact that in many disputes workers took over control of production. In that period of rampant inflation, owing to the lack of food and other goods, employers did not suffer even if workers went on strike, because the price of raw materials was continually spiralling upwards, and employers were able to make a profit simply by selling unworked raw materials. This practice was obviously threatened by the struggle for workers' control of production, which was a severe psychological shock for employers. Also, at a time of chronic shortages of consumer goods when the whole of society was suffering from a lack of articles of all kinds, workers felt that their control of production and increased output would gain more public support than strikes, and the participants in such disputes were thus able to engage in them in good conscience. The reason why the Japanese government and the Occupation authorities did not move immediately to outlaw such disputes—which, after all, touched on the fundamental principle of private ownership of property—was that there were those at GHQ who also felt that such tactics were more constructive than recourse to strikes.

It must not be overlooked, however, that what made such tactics possible was the fact that the unions were organised on a plant-by-plant basis and that they included virtually all workers, from the shop floor up to the higher, white-collar echelons of the technical staff and section chiefs.

The significance of the demand for 'democratisation of management'

The significance of the labour disputes of this period for the later development of Japanese labour-management relations lies in the demand for the 'democratisation of management'. This demand was strongly supported by union members as a whole, but it meant different things according to union members' place in the company hierarchy. For blue-collar workers, it meant doing away with the discriminatory practices they had had to endure owing to their lower educational background—a demand for which was the outcome of the strong resentment of such practices felt by workers over the years. For lower-ranking white-collar and supervisory staff, it meant an end to discriminatory practices between them and university graduates. For section chiefs, it meant confrontation with the generation of wartime managers and the demand for a share in higher management responsibilities, notably in personnel management.

Pre-war Japanese companies, with a few exceptions, operated the following kind of in-house status system: *shain* = regular staff were recruited from university and senior high school graduates only. Junior high school graduates were known as *jun-shain* (semi-regular employees). Between them and regular employees, there were marked differences in wage levels, bonuses and housing benefits. Those who had received only elementary education, such as office boys and janitors, were called *yatoi* (hired hands) and were treated as blue-collar workers. Foremen were promoted from the blue-collar workforce and were classed as semi-regular employees like junior high school graduates; they were looked down upon by white-collar staff. Factory workers were recruited from among those with an elementary school education and their conditions of work differed considerably from those of white-collar workers in various ways. While white-collar workers were paid a monthly salary, for instance, factory workers were paid by the day, which meant that if they were absent from work for a day or two their pay was immediately docked, which was not the case with salaried workers. Factory workers were in general under much stricter supervision and control than salaried employees. They had to use a special entrance to get into the plant and, on leaving, were subjected to body searches to check if they had pilfered any company equipment or tools. Only salaried staff received the normal twice-yearly bonuses. Factory workers regarded all this as discrimination on the grounds of status. In particular, they bitterly resented having to subject themselves to the body searches which were carried out in full view of everyone and with a degree of arrogance by the company security staff.

With the Occupation, democracy became the supreme value and numerous Japanese social customs were branded as feudal, pre-modern or undemocratic. Responding to this new social mood, blue-collar workers began to demand the removal of discriminatory practices on the grounds that they were undemocratic. The result was that the more crass forms of discrimination, such as separate factory entrances and body checks, soon disappeared. Status designations such as 'factory hand' (*shokkô*) and labourer (*rômusha*) were abolished and replaced by the more egalitarian-sounding 'employee' (*jûgyôin*) or 'company man/staff' (*shain*). There could be no change, however, in the difference between manual and desk work and, effectively, demarcation remained between manual and office workers. Those new university graduates who were marked out for future management positions continued to be selected and posted by company head offices, while high school graduates and below were employed at company plants. The speed of and limits to promotions continued to be determined by the employee's education record. Industries and companies where there had been a lot of piece-rate work were slower to introduce monthly salaries for blue-collar workers, but by the 1950s most companies had done so. In the 1960s, there was a fundamental shift in that companies began to draw the majority of their new blue-collar employees from high school rather than junior high school graduates. Promotion prospects were opened up equally to both blue- and white-collar workers, and the number of companies that removed all limits on promotions for blue-collar workers increased markedly.

This equalisation of treatment meant the end of the resentments against discrimination which Japanese workers had harboured for decades. These resentments had surfaced again and again in labour disputes, especially in those which took a particularly violent turn. These were by no means merely disputes about economic grievances. They were invariably accompanied by moral and emotional confrontations which reflected the workers' intense anger at the high-handed manner in which employers and supervisors treated them and ignored their feelings. However, it must not be overlooked that while Japanese tend to resent discrimination and demand to be treated like everyone else, their demand is not based on any concepts of human rights or human equality. They are not opposed to discrimination in itself; they just want to be treated as proper members of the community to which they belong. This can be seen clearly in the nature of Japanese discourse. When Japanese speak to each other, they are always making internal judgements of the state of the relationship between themselves and the other. Society requires them to pay very careful attention to the way they select forms of personal address, for example. Social relations in Japan simply cannot be maintained if occupation, status, age and the male-female relationship is ignored in any form of discourse. At the risk of pressing the point, it could be said that for Japanese, there is no one equal to oneself; everyone else is either of higher or lower status. It is only natural that there should be discrimination in a situation where there is no equality. However, it is not a fixed form of discrimination as in a caste system, but rather is fluid and ever-changing according to the different levels of social relationship into which one enters. Furthermore, such relative social relationships are determined not by a single criterion, but by a complex of interwoven criteria: occupation, status, age and sex.

In a society which is based on relative differences in social relationships between oneself and others, people resent unreasonable discrimination (that is, discrimination that is perceived to be unreasonable), but at the same time recognise reasonable discrimination. A problem arises here with respect to the social criteria for judging what is perceived to be unreasonable or justified. These social criteria change with time and place. In the status-determined society of pre-Meiji Restoration Japan, discrimination on the basis of occupation was the basis of the social order. Such status-based discrimination was legally abolished after the Restoration, but although people did not cease to judge their social status vis-à-vis others in social relationships, the criteria for judging changed. As a result of the introduction of the universal school system, educational achievement and ability came to be strongly emphasised. In other words, it came to be thought natural that if one is recognised to be possessed of ability, one should be rewarded by a high-ranking occupation and by a high salary. However, the cause of blue-collar workers' resentments with regard to educationally based discrimination before and just after the Second World War was that one's educational record was determined by one's parents' financial circumstances and not by individual ability alone.

The new meritocratic influence was what lay behind companies' decisions to introduce examinations for junior high school graduate blue-collar workers wanting promotion to white-collar jobs or for high school graduate employees who sought to get on to the elite managerial track. The examination system came in at the same time as the equalisation of the treatment of blue- and white-collar workers. Japanese regard rankings which are determined solely by ability as unfair. They feel that it is only right that commitment and age (length of service) also ought to play a part in assessing ranking. Indeed, it can be said that the criteria for ranking in the Japanese workplace are a mixture of length of service, ability and aptitude.

Management changes

The character of management, the other side of any labour relationship, also underwent far-reaching changes after the war. Until 1945, the norm had been for ultimate decision-making powers in Japanese business to lie with the owner's family and relatives. However, owing to the large number of pre-war owners who were found culpable of dubious wartime activities, most were purged from their positions by order of GHQ. Suddenly 2210 top company managers lost their jobs and were replaced by younger managers chosen from amongst the staff. Since then, the pattern in large Japanese companies has been for university graduates to join the company immediately on graduation and to work their way up the career ladder, gaining experience of various sides of the business for some thirty years until they come to the position of being eligible for selection to the board of directors. In the first ten to fifteen years of their career, they are members of the labour union of the company and many of them gain experience as union executives. According to statistics of a survey conducted by *Nikkeiren* in 1981, of 313 member companies which responded to the survey, it was the case that in 232 companies (74.1 per cent), former union executives went on to become company executives; of the 6121 company executives, 992 (16.2 per cent) had had experience of serving as union executives.

In the public sector, there were no such unions in which career officials and non-career officials belonged to the same organisation, because the career officials are selected through the public examination system prior to taking up employment, and subsequently would not usually join a union. Non-career officials hardly ever rise beyond the level of section chief. This is one of the reasons why labour relations are more tense or confrontational in the public sector, where workers do not have the right to strike, than they are in the private sector where unions cooperate more with management.

The change in GHQ policy and the employers' counter-attack

Labour unions' successes in the immediate post-war period did not last long. The peak of union activity was the attempted general strike of 1 February 1947, which was prohibited by the Occupational forces. With MacArthur's order removing the right to strike from public-sector unions, which had been at the centre of plans for the February general strike, the labour movement suddenly began to falter and retreat. The movement was also weakened by conflict within the ranks of its national organisation, *Sanbetsu-Kaigi*, where there was dissension over the issue of leadership of the Japan Communist Party. Meanwhile, employers encouraged by GHQ's change of policy, moved onto the offensive by refusing to recognise previous labour agreements which had stipulated that unions must give their consent to any personnel changes. Employers were also opposed to managerial staff joining union posts on the grounds that it was 'abnormal'. For example, in 1948 *Nikkeiren* called for 'clarification of the line between ordinary staff (clerks) who can join unions and managerial staff who are not allowed to be union members' and also 'for management to make clear that they will not help unions in any way' (by the free use of company property, payment of wages to full-time union officials, etc.). They succeeded in having their demand that union membership be strictly limited to 'representatives of the interests of the members' incorporated into the 1949 amendment of the Trade Union Law. This had the effect of causing many section chief-level union members to withdraw from membership. Sub-section chiefs and supervisory staff remained, however, and union leadership gradually passed into the hand of foremen and supervisors who were promoted from blue-collar workers and who worked alongside them.

In 1950, GHQ manoeuvring brought about the formation of *Sôhyô* (General Council of Trade Unions in Japan) from the former *Sôdômei* and from individual groups which had broken away from *Sanbetsu-Kaigi* after opposition to its Communist Party leadership. The new organisation sought to join the International Confederation of Free Trade Unions (CFTU), but soon after its formation it adopted the so-called Four Peace Principles, namely, it opposed the re-arming of Japan, it opposed Japanese support for American military bases, it opposed the signing of a peace treaty which excluded China and the Soviet Union and it formally adopted as fundamental union policy strict adherence to neutrality. At the same time, it sought to accompany all this with a reactivation of the union movement. These developments, completely unforeseen by GHQ, owed very much to the fact that *Sôhyô* was then under the leadership of militant socialist Minoru Takano, but he himself enjoyed wide support amongst the Japanese people who were extremely alarmed by GHQ's move to amend the Constitution in order to provide for Japanese rearmament. Their feelings were based on their vivid experience of the recent war. Until 1941, the Japanese had had hardly any experience of warfare against foreigners in Japan itself, but during the Second World War, they had had to ensure daily bombing. The unforgettable horror of the atomic bombs above all had burned itself into their collective memory. In the 1950s, that memory was much fresher and more vivid than it is today. The fact that Japan was the forward military base for UN forces during the Korean War made the Japanese keenly aware that the dreadful prospect of nuclear war was by no means an impossibility.

The period of economic growth, 1955–74

Twenty years of sustained growth

The Japanese GNP grew at an average 7.6 per cent between 1955 and 1959 in real terms and at an average 11 per cent between 1960 and 1970. The number of those in employment almost doubled from 17 420 000 in 1955 to 34 440 000 in 1975. The increase was particularly vigorous—1 000 000 a year—in the 10-year period from 1955 to 1965. On the other hand, there was a corresponding decrease in the self-employed workforce in the farming, forestry, and fishing industries from 15 050 000 in 1955 to 6 900 000 in 1975.

In 1955, 59.3 per cent of industrial output had been in light manufacturing, notably textiles, but by 1960 this situation had already reversed to the point where heavy industry and chemicals accounted for 55.2 per cent, and by 1973 the figure had risen to 71.4 per cent. The growth of the automobile, electric and engineering industries was particularly marked. These three sectors accounted for only 13.5 per cent of total output in 1955, but 37.4 per cent in 1973. Labour productivity improved sharply during this period, from a base index of 100 in 1960 to 284.3 in 1970. Such rapid improvements were made possible by companies' fierce competition for market share and by massive capital investment in plant and equipment.

Anti-rationalisation disputes

In the first half of this period, there were major labour disputes in most industries, and the majority of them were related to company rationalisation programs. The 1952 Electric Industries dispute, the 1953 Nissan Motor Co. Ltd dispute, the eleven strikes by the Steelworkers' union *Tekkô Rôren* in 1957, the 1958 Oji Paper Manufacturing Co. Ltd dispute, the 1960 Mi'ike Coalmine dispute, and the 1964 Mitsubishi Shipbuilders' dispute at Nagasaki—all these were disputes in leading companies in their respective sectors. They were, of course, not all of exactly the same pattern, each had its own specific problems, but they all shared similar features. As the pace of competition stiffened, the relatively beneficent working conditions in these leading companies began to have an adverse effect on their profit margins and they turned to rationalisation to solve the problem. In a growing industry, those companies which arrived on the scene later sought to cut the market share of older, more established companies by investing in new equipment, paying comparatively lower wages, and thus boosting their competitiveness. Unions in the older leading companies had been able to maintain high wage levels by appealing to the company's prestigiously high-wage profile. Drawing on this experience, many unions in the older companies which had built up considerable organisational and bargaining strengths opposed rationalisation plans. In every one of those disputes, the companies involved strove to shut out union leaders and activists, which often led to splits in the union and the founding of new unions. But however strong, none of the unions, precisely because they were enterprise unions, was able to maintain a long strike, because during the period of the strike, the company's market share would be eaten into by other companies, profits would fall, and in the worst cases, lay-offs would follow. Another problematic consequence of enterprise unions was the fact that even those 'elite course' men who were clearly marked out for managerial posts in the future belonged to the union for ten to twenty years after joining the company and often became union officials. Many of them were inclined towards management thinking on issues like wage rises and rationalisation. In other words, even within the union there were groups which tended to share the same thinking as the management.

When there was a split in the union, it was also related to the nature of plant unions that those who broke away first tended to be white-collar workers and then supervisory staff and foremen. Amongst the university-educated white-collar workers, there were many who had experience of student activism and had gone on to become union leaders. When they quit their union activities after a relatively short while, their experience was taken as evidence of leadership quality and would often buy an advantage in the company promotion race. But if they continued to take a non-cooperative attitude towards the company, they were sure to lose when it came to promotion time. Blue-collar workers too had to be resolved to put up with various discriminatory practices, such as transfers to undesirable locations. Those who remained with the original union were usually Communist Party members or belonged to the left wing of the Socialist Party. They would find themselves increasingly isolated at work and would eventually have to choose between either joining the more compliant 'second union' (*daini kumiai*) or else leaving the company. One of the main reasons why workers invariably lost their struggles with management was because their unions were all organised on a company basis.

When it was a matter of getting rid of a troublesome union, employers in some industries and firms (shipbuilding, electrical engineering; Tôshiba, Hitachi etc.) would often form secret informal groups aimed at combining efforts to shut out the more radical union activists. They set up systems whereby their members could monopolise union posts. During this period, the leadership of unions in Japan's major private corporations gradually passed into the hands of men who could be counted on to be 'cooperative'. The basic policy of unions led by such men was to cooperate with the company to ensure that it did not lose in the struggle for increased market share, and thereby union members would be guaranteed a greater cut of the pie during the distribution of the profits that would result.

However, although the workers indeed lost most of their disputes in this period, they did come away with something to show for their efforts. Employers realised the damaging effects of disputes both on the company's economic performance, and on morale when rival unions clashed. They therefore determined to avoid the tactic of encouraging rival unions in the future and opted instead for a policy of encouraging unions to work in partnership with the management. The price they were prepared to pay to obtain union agreement to this was recognition of the effective 'right' to 'lifetime employment'. What made it possible for managements to do this was the increased profitability which had resulted from the long period of sustained high growth. The downside of this was that it institutionalised the practice of using temporary workers to enable the company to cope with periodic fluctuations in demand. These employees, while working alongside regular workers, shared few or none of the benefits of regular employment, but had to work long hours when business was good, and were promptly shed when they were no longer needed.

Shuntô

The Japanese labour movement developed its own unique form of campaigning in this period—*Shuntô* (Spring struggle). Following a prearranged schedule, groups of unions in one industry after another would put forward demands for wage rises and various fringe benefits, and if these were not met, would simultaneously stage a series of repeated short-term disruptive strikes. When all unions in a particular industry went on strike together, they did not have to worry about their companies losing market share to competitors during the strike period, and since the strikes were all short-term, they would not cause the collapse of the company either. Strikes by single enterprise unions had been found to be largely ineffective, and *shuntô* was a strategy that sought to make up for that weakness. The key element in the *shuntô* campaigns was the decision as to which industry's unions would take the lead. Normally, these were unions in industries which achieved high profits and could afford to meet wage demands. Unions in other industries would then regard such wage rises as a yardstick, a goal at which to aim. In the middle of the *shuntô* campaign period, the railway unions, whose actions always have a significant social impact, would then simultaneously come out on strike. At that point, the Central Labour Relations Commission would step in to mediate, and its actions would usually result in the establishment of criteria for wage rises in other industries. These criteria were perceived to be 'a fair judgement by an impartial third party'.

After 1955 when the *shuntô* campaigns began, and during the period of high growth, profits throughout industry as a whole were good, companies could afford wage rises and the increasing labour shortages during the period all worked in the union's favour. Moreover, although the participants in *shuntô* campaigns represented only a portion of Japan's total labour force, the benefits of the wage rises they achieved flowed over to other groups of unorganised workers and the result was a broad increase in Japanese wage levels as a whole.

However, younger workers gradually began to feel frustrated by this system of demands for higher base rates, because the average rate of increase which was the publicly declared result of the campaign was often quite different from the amount workers actually received. The average amount of the wage rise represented only the increased proportion of company wage costs and not the actual amount distributed to each worker. It was only natural that workers should feel frustrated when they received only Y500 of a declared Y2000 average increase. Neither companies nor unions could afford to ignore the disquiet among the younger workers whose skills in operating new high-technology equipment were responsible for boosting output and profits. The result was the broad adoption of the so-called *fixed-raise-plus alpha* formula. This provided for a uniform amount of increase for all union members and thus ensured that younger workers would at least always get a certain set amount. With each passing year, this system led to a narrowing of the gaps between the wages of younger and middle-aged workers and between those of blue- and white-collar workers. Graph curves of wage profiles show the wages of blue-collar workers increasingly approximating those of white-collar workers, but this was, after all, also due to the fact that both groups of workers invariably belonged to the same unions which had presented the same wage demands. In wage terms, the period thus saw a considerable 'whitening' of blue collars.

The consolidation of the *shuntô* system also saw a change in the basic unit of union organisation. Union decisions had previously been taken at plant level, but now there was a move towards company level organisation. All the major labour concerns—wage rises, bonuses, severance pay etc.—were increasingly negotiated and decided for the company as a whole rather than at the individual plant level.

In some industries, such as steel, wages at *shuntô* time were increasingly determined by agreements among employers in the same business rather than in single firms, and collective bargaining between union and management at the plant level became an empty formality. It was superseded by ongoing discussions between the union and management prior to the *shuntô* season. From the beginning, in labour relations at the plant level, there had been no clear distinction between labour-management joint consultation and collective bargaining. There had also been a tendency to move to collective bargaining only when joint consultation had failed to agree. This tendency now became even stronger. The reason there was no clear distinction between joint consultation and collective bargaining was that there were no German-style industry-wide unions which appointed union officials in each plant and who could thus take part in discussions with management.

In Japan, the participants at joint consultation and in collective bargaining discussions were invariably the same people. Furthermore, owing to the infrequency of clashes of views between management and unions, management conferences usually consisted of descriptions by management of plans for production and equipment to which the union representatives would merely add their opinion.

The period of power economic growth, 1975 to the present

The diffusion of flexible manufacturing systems

With the oil crisis of 1973, Japanese manufacturers were suddenly faced with a steep rise in production costs. Employers responded by investing even more heavily in new equipment and by introducing flexible manufacturing systems which could adjust to market demands for different types and quantities of product. It was during this period that the rest of the world began to take notice of the efficiency of Japanese industry. Previously, people had believed that Japan's competitiveness was due to its relatively low wages and inferior working conditions, and they had tended to brand Japanese labour relations as pre-modern and outdated. Behind the *volte-face* in such views lay the rapid progress that was made at this time in micro-electronics technology and its swift application by Japanese industry as a whole. The new technology made possible continual upgrading of productive techniques. For example, the 'Just in Time' system developed by Toyota and widely adopted by other firms facilitated the frequent reformation of the production process, and as a consequence workers were often moved about and had to be able to adapt themselves to new jobs. An indispensable element of this kind of production system was the worker who was not attached to one job only but who could flexibly apply himself to working with new technology. This was why Japanese productivity and the 'Japanese-style labour relations' that underlay it drew increasing attention.

The high quality of Japanese products was also focused on at this time, as well as small group activities, such as Quality Circles which began in the early 1960s. Motives other than improving quality and cutting costs underlay these latter. Through the Quality Circle movement, employers hoped to bind all their workers into groups that would cooperate with management. The unique feature of the practice is that workers 'voluntarily' cooperate with the company in reviewing and evaluating their work and thus contribute to cutting costs. In the history of labour world-wide, there have surely been few such examples of workers voluntarily cooperating in activities that might eventually undercut their own work. Why did this happen in Japan? Yet, the question could equally well be put the other way around: why has it not happened elsewhere? Indeed, the question in this form is actually easier to answer.

The answer lies in the fact that in the West the archetypal form of labour movement was the craft union, the historical predecessor of which was the craft guild. The guilds' basic aim was to control the labour market in their own interests by regulating the number of apprentices and the working hours of their members. Guild members regarded their familiar acquired skills as all-important. This way of thinking passed on to craft unions, which fiercely opposed the introduction of new technology on the grounds that it would reduce the value of their skills. Furthermore, unions were organised on an industrial, supra-company basis and sought to determine working conditions throughout the industry. If one company tried to introduce new technology, this was then seen as a problem not only for the workers at that company, but for workers throughout the industry, and attempts to prevent it were also made on an industry-wide basis.

Why then did Japanese workers not only not oppose new technology, but actually cooperate with its introduction? Some elucidation of the historical background is required to answer this question. Prior to industrialisation, the kind of autonomous, self-governing guild organisation that emerged in Europe had no chance to develop. Such artisans' organisations as existed were created by the domain authorities for the purpose of facilitating tax-collection. This is why craft unions failed to emerge in Japan. Related to this, another difference between Japan and the West lies in the contrasting attitudes towards competition between workers.

The aim of the western guilds was precisely to reduce competition between workers in terms of working hours, output, and wages, but in Japan, there has been a deep-rooted feeling that those with ability who do their best ought to be well-rewarded. Materials and sources are insufficient that would allow a reasonable judgement as to whether this feeling worked against the emergence of craft guilds, or whether it resulted from the lack of craft guilds. Also, in craft guilds and unions, job demarcation has been confirmed and reinforced socially, but there is comparatively little of this in Japan; the distinctions between skilled, semi-skilled, and unskilled work have been more vague. This is one of the reasons why Japanese workers have not been averse to transfers to different kinds of work.

Another factor which helps to explain why Japanese workers have been so cooperative in working to boost productivity is that during the 20-year period of high growth, workers came to feel that the bigger the pie, the more there would be in it for them. They reckoned that short-term sacrifices in cooperating with the company were acceptable if they led to a greater distribution of company profits in the long term. Employers had learned from the big disputes of the 1950s and made it clear that regular workers' positions would be secure in any rationalisations. These workers were thus able to feel that the introduction of new technology presented no threat to their employment. The introduction of robots did mean, of course, that there was a high chance that some workers' acquired skills would be made redundant. But the Japanese company had never hired its regular employees in order to train them to do only a single job but rather as workers who would be able to handle a variety of jobs and skills. Companies thus employed workers without any particular skill, frequently rotated them within the company and built up their skills by on-the-job training. Rotations often meant promotions, which was another reason why there was little opposition to them. Blue-collar workers were not moved as often as white-collar workers, but they too were not kept at only one job and, as their career with the company developed, they were moved on to more skilled jobs. Nor was it unusual for a worker to be engaged alternately in a number of different jobs at the same workshop at any one time. Hardly any workers thus felt attached to a particular job or skill. Also, even if a relocation might mean a lower-skilled job for a time, the practice of seniority-based wage payments meant that the worker's wages would likely be unaffected by the move.

One reason why Japanese unions did not offer any opposition to new technology was because they were company-based unions. To oppose new technology would have meant that one's company would lose in competition with its rivals, which could only lead to lower wages and, in the worst-case scenario, company closure and mass redundancy. Within the company, Japanese workers felt no sense of 'them and us', but it is no exaggeration to say that in those industries where marketplace competition was especially fierce, Japanese workers did indeed come to regard people in other companies as 'them' and all members of their own company as 'us'.

For some individual workers, of course, job relocation did indeed mean disadvantage. A worker's family would be greatly affected by a company decision to 'scrap and build', which often required families to move to a completely different location. At such times, it fell to the union to try to minimise the effects of such decisions. Nevertheless, even in such cases unions rarely offered strong opposition to the management's decision.

Revision of the seniority system—the introduction of meritocratic management

Japanese employers have always considered company-based unions to be one of the most important components of Japanese labour relations and have done all they could to ensure the continuance of the enterprise union concept. They have not given the same wholehearted support to the 'lifetime employment' and 'seniority wage' systems. The establishment and maintenance of the 'lifetime employment' system owes far more to pressure from the unions. For their part, employers would obviously prefer a system which allowed them to freely adjust their labour complement to meet the changing demands of the market.

Nor were the automatic increases in pay and status guaranteed by the seniority system in the interest of employers. With job security and such automatic pay rises and promotions, the number of employees who did not put their all into their work was bound to increase. From the late 1950s through the 1960s, companies enjoyed the benefits of the seniority wage system in that they were able to recruit new graduates of good quality at rock-bottom wages. For their part, workers had accepted the system because, in the grinding poverty which almost everyone experienced after the war, automatic age-related increments enabled them to meet their increasing family and social commitments.

But with the gradual tightening of the labour market during the high growth period, starting rates for new recruits began to show substantial rises. Under the seniority system, this obviously pushed up wages for the entire workforce and thus led to a rapid rise in company wage bills. This was what lay behind the calls for a reassessment of the seniority wage system that came to be heard increasingly from the mid-1960s onwards. Many employers stressed the need to revise the seniority wage system and replace it by a more meritocratic system. Meanwhile, younger workers had themselves begun to feel their own misgivings about the seniority wage system. The result was that a meritocratic element, in which workers' pay and promotions were assessed on the basis of results achieved, was grafted onto what had been until then a basically age-related system. Thereafter, the age-related component of the worker's total wage gradually diminished in proportion, while the meritocratic, ability assessment-related component increased.

This meritocratic way of thinking affected not only employers but society as a whole during the 1960s and early 1970s. Higher education rates increased dramatically at the end of the 1960s. In the early 1950s over 40 per cent of schoolchildren had gone on to senior high school. This figure rose consistently from 70 per cent plus in the 1960s to 80 per cent plus in the 1970s and 90 per cent plus in the 1980s. Today it stands at around 95 per cent. A senior high school education has thus become in effect compulsory. In 1960 10 per cent of those eligible went to university and college. By 1973 the figure had passed 30 per cent and stands today at 38 per cent. Behind these increases was the greater prosperity of individual households as a result of the high growth period and also the decreasing birth-rate. The rise in the number of those going on to higher education and the wide difference in ranking of the various universities fuelled a fierce competition for school places. Educational achievement was no longer dependent largely on parental finances. Academic ability was what counted in the entrance examinations; those with ability, it was thought, ought to receive their due reward—a literal meritocracy had clearly become the dominant value in Japanese society. This was reflected in company management.

More and more companies also came to emphasise meritocracy rather than just length of service in considering promotions. There had from the first been a certain contradiction between the concepts of lifetime employment and the seniority wage. Positions of responsibility obviously decrease the further up the hierarchy one goes, so one cannot be guaranteed continual automatic improvements in one's position. This contradiction was not so conspicuous when companies were growing rapidly and expanding their managerial echelons. But with the onset of low growth in the 1970s, the problem soon became obvious. This was partly due to the move over to 'meritocratic' wages, because the attempt was made to solve the problem by introducing a ranking system (*shikakuseido*) which was not directly connected with the worker's actual job. However, it must not be overlooked that whereas the meritocratic element in school education was assessed by examination points—which, although one-sided, are nevertheless objective—the 'meritocratic' element in company assessments included not only the worker's results at his job, but also his age and subjective factors such as his ability to get on with colleagues and his sense of loyalty to the company.

While the seniority wage system was undergoing these changes, the lifetime employment system could not remain unaffected. Those members of the company's 'elite course' who were not marked out for the highest positions were normally transferred to head the boards of affiliate companies about ten years before their retirement. After the oil crisis of 1973, Japanese companies moved to a policy of cost reduction management and took steps to cut excess staffing by emphasising even more than before the principle of meritocracy. The result was an even greater degree of competition for pay and promotion among the workforce. Under the cost reduction management regime, what had hitherto been tacitly understood to mean the promise of a job for life was now broken. Many unions had no effective means of opposing these changes, and the result was a loss of faith by the members in their unions, as is only too clear from the statistics of union membership. From a peak of 55.8 per cent in 1949, membership continued steady at around 35 per cent from 1953 until 1975, after which there was a gradual annual decline for seventeen years. In 1992 the figure stood at 24.4 per cent, which is itself an overestimate in real terms in that since many Japanese unions are organised on a union-shop basis, all company employees have to join the union whether they want to or not. Consequently, although they may be union members in the formal sense, they may have little or no consciousness of being such. The figure of 24.4 per cent is thus not a real estimate of members' commitment to unions or of the union movement's actual strength.

Japanese labour relations—the present situation and future prospects

Several keywords that can throw light on the factors that are likely to have an effect on Japanese labour relations in the near future. These keywords are: the ageing society, the higher-education-oriented society, the increasing employment of women, the service economy, microelectronics, and internationalisation. All these issues are already having a significant social impact; indeed, they are important issues that are necessary for any understanding of Japanese labour relations today, rather than being issues that enable predictions about the future. They are issues that are common to all the advanced countries, but their effects vary according to national conditions. The two which I believe contain the most potential for changing Japanese labour relations are internationalisation and the increasing employment of women.

Internationalisation has already had a significant impact in the form of the export of Japanese goods, imports of raw materials and direct overseas investment. So-called Japanese-style management practices are also having an effect on foreign labour relations in countries where Japanese companies have set up operations. The emphasis on flexibility, the introduction of Quality Circles and single-union agreements are all evidence of this influence.

On the other hand, the spiralling high yen of recent months is bound to have its own considerable impact on Japanese labour relations in the near future. The export industry, and especially the automobile industry, which has been the locomotive of the Japanese economy for the past twenty years, has been hit hard and is losing competitiveness. One way around this problem will no doubt be sought in recourse to overseas relocation. This will in turn invite the de-industrialisation of Japan, which will then be following the same path as America. However, unions and government, and even some employers, have grave misgivings over such a change of direction, and it is unlikely that it will be assented to completely. If this path is rejected, the only way to maintain international competitiveness will be to effect a drastic reduction in costs. But rationalisation in the manufacturing industry, right down to supplier level, has already been pursued to a point often described as 'trying to wring out a dry towel' and there is little scope for more. Any further rationalisation will thus more likely occur on the administrative, indirect side of industry. Japanese offices have long held to their own uniquely Japanese ways of decision-making, and the productivity has often been described as low in comparison with that of the shop floor. But with the pace of computer technology, the rationalisation of Japanese offices is likely to take off soon. The possibility of large-scale redundancies among white-collar workers, especially middle-aged ones, is very real.

An obvious question is whether the already weakened labour unions will be able to respond to this situation and uphold the principle of 'lifetime employment'. It is hard to be able to answer 'Yes' to this question.

Another element of internationalisation that is likely to have a major impact on Japanese labour relations is the issue of foreign workers coming to Japan. This issue rapidly gained prominence in the late 1980s when the effects of the high yen were percolating through the economy. A marker was the amendment of the Immigration Law in 1990 to allow descendants of Japanese emigrants (foreigners of Japanese ancestry and their spouses) to work freely in Japan. The number of Japanese Brazilians and Peruvians arriving rose sharply and in 1992 stood at 170 000. If one includes undocumented workers, the number of 'new foreign workers', apart from Chinese and Koreans who have been in Japan since before the Second World War, is now over 500 000. In view of the ageing demographic profile of Japanese society, an increase in the number of foreign workers will be unavoidable. To date, companies have not taken on any such foreign workers as regular employees and have only employed them as temporary workers, while the unions have not been very positive in their efforts to organise temporary workers. On present trends, union membership is therefore likely to continue to decline. Japanese unions have thus far shown only opposition to the employment of foreign immigrant workers and have taken virtually no positive steps in formulating any policies towards them.

The increasing employment of women has become a conspicuous trend in recent years. In the 1980s, the number of women employees rose to 5 000 000, whereas today (1992) it is almost 20 000 000, or nearly 40 per cent of the total workforce. Most of the increase, however, is accounted for by so-called non-regular workers, that is, by part-timers, temporary workers and personnel agency staff. For a long time, female workers, even those who are regular employees, have been treated within their companies as second-class citizens. Most women workers only worked for a few years until marriage, and they were subject to discrimination in that, even if they were doing the same work as men, they were paid less and had almost no chance of promotion to managerial positions. Since the enactment of the 1986 Equal Opportunity in Employment Law, many companies have recognised the right of their regular female employees to the same advancement prospects as men, but there still remains a gap between recognising the letter of the law and fulfilling its spirit.

In reviewing the past half-century of Japanese labour relations, one cannot but be struck both by the considerable achievements of the union movement during that short period and also by the equally conspicuous weakness of the unions at the present time. The first of the achievements has been that of a substantial rise in real wages. Of course, this was not due simply to the union movement but also to the rapid growth of the Japanese economy and to the fact that for much of the period the Japanese labour market was a seller's market. Yet it is certain that without the labour movement, and in particular *shuntô*, such gains would not have been possible. It was also the unions which contributed most to the second achievement: the *de facto* right to job security for their members. The third major achievement was the raising of the status of blue-collar employees within the company to the point where they were able to consider themselves as members of the middle class, although they had for decades been regarded as the lowest of the low in Japanese society.

Yet at the same time it is clear that it has been just these achievements that have led to the marked decline of the union movement. While the strength of Japanese companies has grown over the years and is now widely recognised around the world, that of the unions has faded proportionately. As the statistics of steadily declining membership make clear, the unions' influence over workers has weakened, and workers today show a conspicuous lack of interest or lack of faith in their unions. Individual workers no longer feel that unions are something to rely on when the going gets tough. In a recent survey on union leaders carried out by the Ohara Institute for Social Research, it was clear that union officials thought that unions had little influence on their members. Other surveys have also shown that a wide cross-section of people feel that the union's influence has waned.

Will Japanese unions be able to come through this situation and recover their lost energies? It is my own view that this is unlikely in the near future, but in the long term, it is not impossible that the union movement will revive.

The history of the Japanese labour movement has been one in which those at the bottom of society have demanded full membership in companies in which they were previously only second-class citizens. Looking into the future from this perspective, I believe it is likely that the best possibility of reviving the currently floundering union movement lies with women. I do not know when or how that change might come about. The ones in the best position to set the ball rolling are probably the women of Japan, but what stirs them into action will probably be external influences. I am thinking of the feminist movement world-wide and also of something related to it, namely, changes in Japanese government policy. At any rate, if the Japanese labour movement does manage to revive sometime in the future, it will not likely be a revival of the present form of single company-based unions, but rather a movement with a completely new form of organisation.

7 Labour relations in Australia, 1940–90

Tom Sheridan

The fifty years from 1940 to 1990 cover more than half the life of both the Australian federation and its regional and national arbitration systems. They witnessed great changes in the structure of the economy, of the workforce and of the union movement—as well as noticeable swings in the attitudes of unions and employer groups towards each other and towards the utility and purpose of the arbitration tribunals. Along with the central dynamic of economic change was a complex series of overlapping shifts in social and political parameters which closely affect labour relations. Because of the complexity of these changes only the main issues can be touched upon here. This chapter is divided into two sections. In the first, the bare contours of historical change will be outlined. In the second, the more important shorter run fluctuations—some of which appeared as permanent trends to contemporaries—will be briefly considered.

I

At the beginning of this period there was minimal unemployment; when wartime manpower restrictions were lifted, male workers could pick and choose between jobs. By the end of the 1940s, women too were enjoying a demand for their services unparalleled in peace time—although the return of servicemen saw them again barred from the skilled and higher status 'male occupations' which some had entered during the wartime emergency. The economy was subject to unprecedented regulation during the war. With the advent of peace, the federal government eased back only slowly on the major controls.

92

Prices rose moderately but at a quickening pace after 1945. No balance of payment or overseas debt problems troubled the economic planners. The victorious USA was imposing a new order on the world economy in which freer trade was a major objective, but everyone, including all parties to industrial relations, expected an eventual slump.

The Australian workforce in 1939 was overwhelmingly of Anglo-Celtic descent, containing some two million employees, three quarters of them male and only 44 per cent working in the tertiary sector. The world war ushered in thirty years of unprecedentedly stable full employment. This allowed for the social acceptance and eventual economic absorption by 1990 of over 3.5 million immigrants (net), who came not only from traditional Anglo-Irish sources but increasingly from continental Europe and, from the 1970s, Asia. *Pari passu,* attitudes towards females working altered drastically. The extent of the changes in the supply and nature of labour is indicated by the fact that a workforce survey in 1993 revealed that of a total workforce of 8.7 million, 42 per cent were female, 23 per cent were part-time workers, 15 per cent came from non-English speaking countries and 71 per cent worked in service industries. Significantly the workforce participation rate had risen from below 50 per cent in 1940 to over 60 per cent in 1993.

During the three decades of the 'long boom', the state and employers successfully sought to restrain the unions' bargaining power. The Chifley ALP government (1945–49) set the pattern by tightening control over unions by moral suasion, by continuing its wartime wages freeze, by suitably amending the Arbitration Act, and, finally, by retrospective repressive legislation and direct use of force against the vanguard coalminers' union. The Menzies government (1949–66) picked up the baton by clarifying, improving and enforcing the penal sanctions and union-regulating mechanisms initiated by Chifley.

In the 1940s, private enterprise was on the defensive as it endeavoured to withstand world-wide criticism of its pre-war failures. Most companies—including the largest, BHP—had little knowledge and scant recourse to public relations techniques or advanced personnel practices. In times of over-full employment and faced with a spontaneously aggressive workforce, employer groups gave fervent support to the centralised wage-fixing system and to increased government regulation and restraint of the union movement. Most firms sought to avoid direct bargaining, whether enterprise- or industry-based.

Australia was a full participant in the world-wide swing to the left. The pre-war record of private enterprise and of conservative governments endeavouring to sustain it contrasted miserably with the full employment flowing from wartime government intrusion into every sector of the economy. The democratic political imperative of peacetime full employment, supported intellectually by the 'Keynesian revolution', demanded continued government intervention. It was widely felt that the time of the 'little man' had arrived. Public opinion was clearly sympathetic towards workers and unions moving to take advantage of the demand for labour and was highly sceptical of private mass media industrial reportage. Only at the very end of the decade did Cold War fears begin to alter public perceptions of the cause of industrial disputes.

Most areas of public policy reflected the swing to the left: the electoral tide favoured the ALP. In state management, the policy-making levels of the mushrooming bureaucracy were swollen by young public servants imbued with the prevalent left-liberal philosophies. In the new area of economic planning, Keynesians dominated. The many regulatory agencies reflected the firm belief in market intervention. The new intellectual respectability of unions' century-old instincts sat easily with ALP governments. In addition to the ideological green light, the war gave the federal government clear *de jure* and *de facto* pre-eminence in macroeconomic policy making. The ALP ministries which ran most States after the war were only too pleased to accept Canberra's leadership. Dominated by J.B. Chifley, the prime aim of Cabinet and Treasury was to restrain inflation. This entailed holding down real wages. The government envisaged no redistribution from profits to wages. Workers' standards would improve through the maintenance of high employment and improved social welfare provisions. The wage-fixing system must not be decentralised; rather, union bargaining power must be restrained. Sanctions and, if necessary, force and repressive legislation must be deployed against them. In this, the arbitrators and industrial regulators wholeheartedly concurred.

The ACTU was not highly regarded by the federal Labor government. Its affiliates—overwhelmingly blue-collar—accounted for only one-third of unionists in 1945 and perhaps 40 per cent by 1949. The ACTU had only one full-time official and no research staff. Most affiliates saw the metropolitan Trades and Labor Councils as more significant—but in any case they usually acted independently of peak councils in pursuit of their own short-run ends. A strong radical strand—not simply confined to members of the Communist Party of Australia (CPA)—ran through the labour movement. Equally, workers' determination to make advances after long years of restraint during depression and war was not confined to a few militant unions. In the 1940s, it was manifest in many normally pacific areas of the workforce. The post-war years constituted one of the historical peaks in working days lost through industrial disputes. The militant vanguard, frustrated by the centralised arbitration system, increasingly looked for means of direct bargaining whereby their market strength could be exercised.

Faced with tight labour markets, the federal arbitration tribunal acted as a sea anchor, restraining the movement of official wage rates. The Metal Trades Award, covering metal manufacturing workers, was acknowledged as the key piece in the federal award system. The traditional minimum adult male rate, the basic wage, became less significant as the payment of extra 'marginal' rates spread down the wages pyramid. The set-piece basic wage cases heard at irregular intervals remained an important means of lifting the wage rate floor, but the 'margin' of the engineering fitter, the archetypal craftsman, and of the semi-skilled metals process worker became equally important pivots upon which the elaborate and interrelated system of national wage rates rested and moved. Given the reluctance of the tribunal to acknowledge market forces, the skilled metal workers led the way in direct bargaining with employers for 'over-award' payments. Wages paid began to 'drift' away from award rates—but at a slower rate than would have been the case without the curb imposed on unions by the penal sanctions.

The possibility of united union resistance to the state's restraints was weakened by several factors. Most notable was the internal ideological division of the Cold War years which produced clear, opposed factions at ACTU Congresses and on its Executive, as well as a 'split' in the ALP which helped keep the party out of office federally until 1972 and in the States of Victoria and Queensland until even later. In addition, technical change reduced the significance of traditional vanguard unions such as the coalminers and wharf workers, while the Menzies government courted and promoted the status of the 'moderate' ACTU leadership. At the same time as penal sanctions forced militant unions to rethink their tactics, the prosperity of the long boom altered workforce attitudes towards militancy—not least through increases in employees' fixed financial commitments through house mortgages and improved credit facilities.

In the national arbitration arena, the metal trades firms proved the most dynamic employer group. In the mid-1960s they persuaded the federal tribunal to abandon the notional dual wage structure of basic wage and margins in favour of a single occupational wage. This induced the tribunal to propose investigating the 'work value' of specific metal trades occupations. This dubious procedure brought protests from unions and employers alike, but led to the bench trying to end wages 'drift' by encouraging employers to 'absorb' existing over-award payments in its new metal trades award. The employers met the consequent outbreak of disputes across the industry in 1968 with what proved to be an over-use of the penal sanctions. Such was the spontaneity and extent of unionists' indignation that the use of the 'penal powers' was all but abandoned for the next two decades. The immediate result was a progressive switch to direct negotiations in the private sector.

Female minimum rates in federal awards rose from 54 per cent of the male rate in 1940 to 75 per cent in 1951 and to nominal 'equal pay for equal work' in 1969. The segmentation of labour markets along gender lines dampened the effect of this. Not until 1974 was the gender differential in minimum rates removed. While the ratio of female to male rates rose from 74 per cent in 1970 to 94 per cent by the end of the decade, the ratio of actual earnings moved only from 65 to 86 per cent. While it was clear in the 1940s that a married woman's place was in the home, by the 1970s this was being contested.

The swing to direct bargaining was checked by the end of the long boom and the importation of 'stagflation'. As unemployment began to inch upwards, the rate of inflation soared, fuelling pessimistic price expectations among the unions, with consequent effect on wage claims. The new ALP government (1972–75) abandoned its original view that direct bargaining was desirable and the arbitration tribunal resumed its position at the centre of wage fixation. Having, in 1953, abandoned cost-of-living adjustments to the basic wage because of their allegedly inflationary effect during the Korean War commodities boom, the tribunal re-introduced 'indexation' of wages in 1975 to dampen workers' inflationary expectations. It had earlier moved to ensure more conformity between industries by dividing the awards for which it was responsible between 'panels' of its members headed by senior personnel. The conservative Fraser government (1975–83) provided employers with a new sanction by amending the Trade Practices Act to allow the Federal Court to penalise unions which used secondary boycotts in industrial disputes.

Indexation, in diminishing form, lasted six years. As real wage rates fell, the stronger unions reverted to bargaining. At the end of 1982 the conservative government initiated a six-month wage freeze. By this time, full employment was only a memory. Manufacturing shrank and the construction, transport and oil refining industries began to replace metals as wages leader. The metal unions began to look favourably on the concept of a 'social wage'. Unions in general belatedly became interested in a range of non-wage benefits pioneered in Europe and North America. Superannuation, pensions, redundancy and severance allowances and occupational health began to appear on the stronger unions' agenda. Reinterpretations of long-standing definitions by the federal tribunal and by the High Court of Australia made more feasible the inclusion of such items in awards and widened federal award coverage.

The new economic depression exposed divisions among employers. While larger, capital-intensive firms saw advantage in making concessions in return for higher productivity, small firms found it harder to pay for newly granted benefits. For them, inflexible award conditions, industrial legislation in the States, and workers' compensation schemes seemed ever more irksome as profit margins were squeezed. A trend began for regular employees to be nominally engaged as self-employed 'subcontractors' in order that firms could avoid paying all these 'on-costs'. This helped the decline in the proportion of workers covered by awards—particularly federal ones. Changes in technology, industry structure and in social attitudes all stimulated the rise of part-time work, where females predominated.

Complaints about employers' public disunity helped bring about the establishment in 1978 of a new employers' peak council, the Confederation of Australian Industry (CAI). But the divisions widened. While, on the union side, the ACTU could usually present a united front on major issues, the employers were unable to follow suit. The 1980s saw a procession of important affiliates secede from the CAI. A separate Council of Small Business Associations was formed in 1982. The leading executives of big business, dissatisfied with the influence of the State-based employer associations, imitated North American and British initiatives to form in 1983 their own Business Council of Australia to promote their interests directly in the national political arena. A strident 'New Right' pressure group, demanding complete deregulation of the labour market and urging employers to take common law damage suits against unions, gained many adherents, particularly among small businesses and primary producers. Other associations were more cautious and the traditional pace-setters, the metal employers, preferred to work within the emerging corporatist framework.

In the 1980s the ACTU reached an unparalleled peak of prestige. As tertiary industries expanded, its influence, and the moderation of its policies, were heightened by its absorption of the private- and public-sector white-collar peak union councils in 1979 and 1981 respectively. A change in leadership image which began under President R.J.L. Hawke (1969–79) was confirmed and consolidated by subsequent leaders, who were formally well educated and articulate. Although the ACTU's first attempt to organise a national 24-hour stoppage—on the political issue of the dismantling of the public health insurance system—had proved only a partial success in 1976, the deepening economic depression lent it greater authority as weakened unions, particularly in manufacturing, turned anxiously to the ACTU for support. New white-collar ACTU affiliates with little tradition of direct action were even more amenable to long-run planning and corporatist modes of thought. The ALP's personnel, policies and active membership also had long been reflecting social and economic changes. Parliamentarians with blue-collar work experience were a decreasing minority. Even before former ACTU advocate and president Bob Hawke became Labor's federal leader, the ACTU and ALP were working out an 'Accord' whereby restraint was offered in return for efforts to maintain real wages and to dismantle the Fraser government's anti-union legislation. When the ALP was returned to power in 1983, the social contract of the Accord became the cornerstone of its economic policy.

The years of the Accord were quite unprecedented in terms of union policy. Organised labour adopted a long-run outlook, agreed to endure real wage erosion, abandoned many jealously preserved craft demarcations, moved to reduce greatly the number of unions and sought to initiate improvements in labour productivity while pressing employers to lift their efficiency. Significantly, the metal workers were in the van, working closely with their employers' association. Dissent was rare, but labour's representatives wholeheartedly supported the harsh treatment handed out by the state to the militant Builders Labourers' Federation and to the Federation of Air Pilots. The reaction of rank-and-file unionists to the Accord was harder to judge. The public popularity of unions remained low and union density fell back towards the levels of the 1930s, the previous period of consistent unemployment.

As industries, occupations and awards were 'restructured' under the Accord, most employer leaders could not but privately applaud. Nevertheless, anti-union and anti-regulatory sentiments mounted in many quarters as employers—particularly smaller ones—reacted in similar fashion to the vanguard unions in the long boom by agitating to be allowed to shake off the trammels of the award system in order to take advantage of favourable market forces. By 1990 the corporatist ALP–ACTU thrust was towards bargaining at the enterprise level above a 'safety net' of basic conditions guaranteed by the tribunal. The next decade would, *inter alia,* reveal both the feasibility of bargaining in the hundreds of thousands of small enterprises in the private sector and the future of the traditional arbitration system.

II

The aim in this section is to emphasise that there was no inevitability, no simple, smooth progression over this half-century. Rather, there were fits and starts and some important swings and reversals—and hence a number of false dawns and mispredictions of where industrial relations were headed. The choice of six sub-periods as presented below is open to debate. Only three dates—1945, 1969 and 1983—seem to mark clear turning points. The other dividing lines are much more watery and are placed loosely in the middle of the 1950s and 1970s respectively.

Second World War

As already stressed, the command economy demonstrated to workers the desirability of federal government immersion in macro-economic policy. With specific regard to industrial relations, the federal tribunal was explicitly and directly subordinated to government strictures. There would never be in future any outright rejection of federal government views such as occurred with the 1931 basic wage cut. (Conversely, however, no federal government would in future dream of departing from the orthodox economic wisdom of the day.) Similarly, the wartime subjugation of State tribunals to the federal Arbitration Court was the emergency *de jure* implementation of what became the *de facto* post-war case. Other enduring wartime legacies were the multiplication of arbitral personnel through the emergency appointment of conciliation commissioners and the establishment of special tribunals and/or regulatory agencies in certain key, bothersome industries like coal, shipping and stevedoring. Management and labour drew their own conclusion from the need to limit the hours individuals worked, the use of 'dilution' (adult retraining) schemes to boost the reservoir of key skills rapidly and the extensive use of new mass-production techniques. While employees restrained most of their industrial impatience until the war was won, employers rid themselves of their long-standing fears concerning the federal arbitration system. Rather, they improved their own federal organisations and threw their weight behind Curtin's and Chifley's determination to keep the unions restrained within an unprecedentedly centralised system.

Industrial labour's attitude went through two distinct phases. At first it looked askance at the conservative government's attempts to put the economy on a war footing. The more powerful unions continued to assert their independence. Early in 1940 coalminers pressing for shorter hours went on strike for ten weeks. The sense of emergency caused by Germany's victories in France helped end this dispute, but exaggerated estimates of the communists' role in the strike helped persuade the government to suppress the CPA. The government had asked the ACTU to represent unionists on a number of new wartime committees and panels. But the ACTU, established in 1927, still had only a little over 10 per cent of union members affiliated to it. Powerful unions such as the Amalgamated Engineering Union (AEU) and the unaffiliated Australian Workers' Union (AWU) insisted that they would cooperate only if given separate representation on the bodies concerned. In May 1940, the AEU independently reached a self-protective agreement with the government to allow a carefully controlled expansion of the skilled workforce in essential war industries through adult training schemes. A rapid growth in the supply of tradesmen was essential for the war effort, but such was their suspicion of the Menzies government's motives that union spokesmen from right and left combined to attack the AEU 'sell-out'.

The second half of 1941 changed everything. When Germany invaded Russia in June communists suddenly embraced the war effort. In October, Labor took office in Canberra after ten years. In December, Japan's attack turned the war into one of direct defence of Australia. The union movement swung fully behind an all-out war effort. Tight manpower regulations directed workers into essential jobs. Wages were pegged, the campaign for shorter hours was abandoned, working hours were increased, and shift work became common; skilled workers dropped their objection to dilution of their trades by adult trainees—and even, eventually, women.

The more assertive groups of workers had begun to elect communists to union positions in the 1930s. The CPA, re-legitimised by Curtin, reached a peak of public popularity in the late war years when, for example, Stalin's portrait once decorated the cover of *Women's Weekly*! However, seamen, coalminers, wharfies and skilled metal tradesmen all continued to demonstrate their independent militancy by frequent spontaneous resort to direct action despite their communist officials' pleas not to endanger the war effort.

War hastened Australian manufacturing industry's growth in scale and complexity. Especially important was the growth of the female workforce. Alarmed unionists feared that women would retain in peacetime jobs hitherto regarded as being exclusively men's. Confident of their own higher value to employers, male unionists mounted towards the end of the war a campaign for equal pay, while warning that in peacetime most females would have to withdraw from the workforce. The campaign for equal pay failed; employers resisted it, and the Labor government feared it would jeopardise its policy of price stabilisation. By the end of the war, only a few skilled women approached equality of pay, and then only temporarily. Clothing and rubber workers were on 75 per cent of male wages, but overall female rates averaged only about 60 per cent of male awards.

1945 to the mid-1950s

It is important to emphasise the essential post-war continuity in macro-economic and wage policies, despite the change of government with the election of R.G. Menzies' conservative coalition at the end of 1949. Both Chifley and Curtin were determined that union bargaining power was to be constrained by penal sanctions. Important regulatory legislation of 1947, 1949 and 1951 was consolidated and confirmed in comprehensive 1956 legislation which formally separated the arbitral and judicial powers of the federal tribunal.

While unsuccessfully endeavouring again to ban the CPA and to remove its members from union office, Menzies was less prepared to use the naked power of the state than his two immediate predecessors. A fairly ineffective airlift of a handful of troops to a remote sugar port in 1953 hardly matched the deployment of servicemen in the 1940s, let alone Chifley's draconian retrospective legislation of 1949. Menzies was, however, much more anxious to encourage the ACTU and to use it as the bell-wether for its labour policies. Diplomatic courtship of President Albert Monk set the ACTU off on its thirty-year climb towards the innermost economic councils of state.

Record twentieth-century inflation in the Korean War boom seemed fully to justify anxiety about the effects of wage increases—hence automatic quarterly indexation of the basic wage was abolished in 1953 and the Catholic Chief Judge of the Arbitration Court suggested a strange, un-Australian, neo-corporatist accord emphasising wage restraint and productivity improvements. Despite the tribunals' roles as sea anchors, continued full employment and the willingness by militant unions to risk sanctions meant certain industries and individual employers were forced to concede above-award rates. Similarly, it became easier for less skilled employees to persuade tribunals to award them 'margins' above the basic wage.

The tight labour market enabled the Chifley government to sell to unions the idea first of mass immigration and then of including continental Europeans in the inflow. Some employers such as BHP saw ethnic diversity in their workforces and immigrants' experience of communist rule in Eastern Europe as helping hamper the appeal of militant unions. Later surveys, however, suggested that foreign-born workers were more likely to be union members than their Australian equivalents. In the 1950s and 1960s, immigrants were Australia's main source of skilled workers. Non-British immigrants were directed to certain industries and for a long time virtually everyone accepted that these 'New Australians' should come bottom of the industrial pecking order.

The ACTU's resistance to expansion of incentive pay schemes was progressively overcome and the more dynamic firms turned to greater use of overseas 'time and motion' and other quality engineering techniques. A smaller minority even began to ponder if 'them–us' attitudes might be altered by enterprise bargaining. Unions were increasingly diverted and factionalised by the communist issue, particularly with the growth in importance of the ALP's Industrial Groups, established in the mid-1940s within certain unions to fight the communist influence. In some cases anti-communist 'Groupers' sought to demonstrate their own militancy by urging direct action. However, if not originally antipathetic to the tactic, the expelled rump of Groupers became ideologically opposed, after the ALP 'split', to taking other than the path of arbitration and welfare legislation to improve conditions. Similarly, communist support for union organisation at the enterprise level caused right-wing and 'moderate' union officials to distrust shop committees and to disapprove of active shop stewards—thus fortifying the de-emphasis of enterprise bargaining already inherent in the industry award structure and the fixing of minimum wages and hours at the national level. Refusal of the tribunals to allow hard-won blue-collar gains to 'flow on' to white-collar workers moved white-collar unions in the private sector to form a coordinating peak council (ACSPA).

Immediately after the war, unions campaigned for shorter hours, higher pay and more annual leave. The claims were spontaneous and, after the general experience of wartime austerity, enjoyed widespread public support. The unions had every reason to be confident. Apart from the high demand for all kinds of labour, the 1943 ALP Conference had decided that the federal government should, within six months of the war's end, use its emergency powers to implement both a higher basic wage and a 40-hour week—the latter plank placed in the ALP platform by John Curtin himself. With peace, disputes broke out in all sectors of the economy. Workers with no previous record of militancy moved to make their gains while the going was good. In 1945 major stoppages occurred among printers and power workers, while coalminers, seamen and wharfies showed constant readiness to take direct action. For fifteen weeks at the end of the year, the steel industry experienced one of the largest stoppages in Australian history.

Faced with this explosion of unrest, Chifley conducted a skilful rearguard action by ignoring the 1943 ALP Conference decisions and by diverting claims into the arbitration system, with its ponderous pace of decision-making. He refused outright to decentralise the arbitration system and make it more responsive to market forces. He did reduce legalism somewhat and increased the number of conciliation commissioners, but his Arbitration Act of 1947 failed to abolish the role of the judges, as the unions hoped. Instead it ensured that judges alone determined the basic wage, standard hours, holidays, overtime and shift rates.

Union anger with the Chifley government reached its peak late in 1946 and early in 1947, when the ACTU almost called a general strike. A six-month Victorian metal trades dispute begun by an employers' lockout eventually broke Chifley's wage freeze, and AEU gains flowed on to most workers by the beginning of 1948, when the national 40-hour week was also at long last inaugurated. Wage gains were, however, soon eroded by inflation. Union wage campaigns and opposition to the abolition of basic wage indexation were hampered by internal friction as the Cold War intensified. With peace, communists' traditional industrial militancy allowed them to ride and sometimes lead the spontaneous aggression of workers. Some ALP leaders falsely branded such major disputes as those in steel and the metal trades as communist plots to wreck the ALP and the economy. A climax came in the winter of 1949 when an industrial dispute in the coalfields threatened to breach Chifley's economic policy. The government introduced unprecedentedly harsh retrospective legislation against the miners and anyone who supported them, gaoling union leaders, levying fines, freezing union funds, and sending troops into mines. One bank even refused to let a coalminer withdraw his own savings. Menzies banged the anti-communist drum even louder. Apart from seeking to ban communists from union office, they were kept under constant surveillance by the Australian Security Intelligence Organisation (ASIO), which also infiltrated the militant unions.

Eventually the communist issue provoked a split in the ALP between 1954 and 1957, which further distracted union energies and made easier the use of penal sanctions against industrial action. The insertion of penal clauses into federal awards prohibiting work bans and stoppages had begun in the Chifley era and became more common under Menzies. Unions challenged the practice, and had their case upheld by the Privy Council. Menzies then restructured the arbitration system in 1956 by creating an Industrial Court to police the awards of the new Arbitration Commission. Fines were virtually automatic once employers demonstrated breaches to the court; the rights and wrongs of an issue could not be considered. Employers did not always need to proceed to the court; the threat was usually enough. Union tactics changed, with brief rolling strikes and lightning stoppages replacing the old set-piece disputes.

Mid-1950s to 1969

The years 1947–69 constitute the only lengthy period in Australian industrial history in which penal sanctions were continuously used. The subdivision in the mid-1950s is chosen for three main reasons. Around this time community expectations began to accept full employment as the norm—witness Menzies' cliffhanger win by a single seat in the 1961 general election when the official unemployment rate reached 3 per cent for the first time in twenty years. Secondly, the intensity of the Cold War diminished—although the 'red menace' was still trailed across the stage in most major industrial relations debates. The CPA itself began to split and fade. Nevertheless, thirdly, the wounds opened by the ALP split kept the unions' party away from federal power and prevented union coordination on a number of major issues. Notable advances in workers' conditions largely stemmed from New South Wales ALP governments' initiatives. A vanguard employer group set the pace in strategic thinking. Only its eventual over-use of penal sanctions sparked off an industrial confrontation which eventually broke the hobbles on union bargaining power.

The character of industrial disputation was affected by technological change on the traditionally turbulent coalfields and wharves. They remained the most disputatious industries but, with mechanised coal-cutting reducing the number of miners, the public spotlight shifted to stevedoring which, *inter alia*, saw two major national strikes (1954 and 1956), three major inquiries into the industry (1951, 1954–56 and 1965) and four major amendments to the Stevedoring Industry Act (1954, 1956, 1961 and 1965), each made with the specific intention of curbing the union's bargaining power. From the mid-1950s on, the aim of the Waterside Workers' Federation (WWF) was to engage in meaningful direct bargaining with employers. The latter, however, saw their best course to be an insistence on formal arbitration of all differences. Employer attitudes were changed only in the mid-1960s by the imperative of containerisation and the associated need for replacement of the traditional casual workforce with permanent employees. A massive showdown was averted at the eleventh hour in 1965 when all parties sat down to an 18-months bargaining conference, conducted in a novel atmosphere of give and take. The WWF leaders were always mindful of the necessity to maintain support from the ACTU. Isolation would free the government for another, long-threatened attack on WWF control of labour supply. The final 1967 agreement and the associated switch from arbitration to bargaining proved in retrospect satisfactory to all wharfies, but at the time a strange alliance of extreme left-wingers and former 'Groupers' vigorously opposed it. The employers' initial mistake in favouring employees permanently attached to their own individual company over those in the holding pool helped the wharfies' renowned group loyalty to triumph easily over any incipient company loyalty.

None of the waterfront campaigns or disputes of the 1950s ever induced stevedoring companies to offer over-award payments to wharfies. Wage leadership rested rather with the metal craftsmen. The AEU wage victory of 1947 confirmed the pace-setting importance of the metal trades award. For the next quarter century, fears of inevitable flow-on made employers reluctant to concede ground in this industry. Their stance encouraged the militancy of the major skilled engineering unions, which began to coalesce around the AEU in what eventually became known as the Amalgamated Metal Workers' Union (AMWU). On the employers' side the lead was taken by the Metal Trades Employers' Association (MTEA), which, through a series of amalgamations with other associations, eventually constituted the Metal Trades Industry Association of Australia (MTIA). In 1959, prompting by the MTEA persuaded the leading employer groups formally to pool their research resources. The new think-tank thus created was, by the early 1960s, arguing that the dual wage structure of a basic wage plus margins was outmoded and gave the unions two bites at the same cherry.

Pressed by governments and employers to contain inflation by keeping wages down, the Arbitration Commission zigzagged inconsistently in an effort to reconcile its own changing notions of the national interest with the realities of the industrial marketplace. Public attention was often diverted by the commission's window-dressing reasons for judgment and, from 1959, also by the fiery advocacy of ACTU research officer R.J.L. Hawke. Essentially, however, the commission was reluctantly, and with a lag, following market forces demonstrated by deals struck with employers by those unions prepared to brave the penal sanctions. The 'shunter's law' of comparative wage justice ensured that gains by metal unions and others flowed on to the bulk of the workforce. In 1961 the higher grades of white-collar employees found a major route to salary increases when an assessment of the 'work value' of professional engineers led the commission to grant substantial pay rises. This immediately stimulated other white-collar groups to mount their own work value cases, citing the engineers as the benchmark.

State Labor governments helped improve work conditions either by granting pace-setting concessions to their own employees or by legislating for all workers under state awards. Unions used the precedents to apply pressure on private sector employers, state arbitration tribunals, non-Labor governments and the federal Arbitration Commission. The New South Wales Labor Government led the way on many issues, including annual leave (two weeks in 1944 and three in 1958), long-service leave (1951) and equal minimum pay for men and women (1958). These initiatives spread to workers in other States at differing speeds. For example, Western Australians employed in the private sector waited a further seven years for long-service leave; women on federal awards waited eleven years for a decision promising 'equal pay for equal work', fourteen years for 'equal pay for work of equal value', and sixteen years for equal minimum wages.

Significant federal award decisions came between 1965 and 1967, when the employers succeeded in getting the 60-year-old dual structure of basic wage and margins abolished. In moving to a national wage case which determined a total wage, the Arbitration Commission also announced that it would make 'work value' studies to discover whether specific occupations deserved wage changes. It did not get far along this hazardous track. The bench used its first work value decision to try to end the wages 'drift' in the metal trades by encouraging employers to 'absorb', in existing over-award payments, pay rises it was now granting in the award. In the first two months of 1968, there were 400 separate stoppages of work, and on 6 February, 180 000 metal workers went on strike for twenty-four hours. A compromise settlement was reached, whereby the tradesmen's formal rates were reduced, but over-award payments continued. More importantly, the employers invoked the penal powers so often as to create an unstoppable tide of unionist determination to break the hobble. The ACTU was persuaded to declare that no union should henceforth pay fines. In May 1969, Clarrie O'Shea, secretary of the Victorian branch of the Tramways Union, was sent to gaol indefinitely for refusing to hand over the union's books after it had failed to pay previously imposed fines. On the morning of O'Shea's arrest 5000 shop stewards demonstrated in Melbourne, and over the next few days an estimated one million workers were involved in stop-work meetings of protest. O'Shea was released after six days when an anonymous benefactor paid the fines. The industrial turmoil forced the federal government to negotiate on the penal provisions. In 1970 the Act was amended to allow the tribunal to make some inquiry into the merits of the situation which had given rise to a strike before applying the sanctions. In March and December 1971, confrontations on the issue were avoided by other anonymous benefactors paying outstanding fines. After that, no union paid a fine, with the exception of two metal unions which wanted to ensure amalgamation with the AEU to form the AMWU. The door to direct bargaining was open at last.

1969 to the mid-1970s

This short period at first seemed to mark the end of the traditional centralised wage-fixing system. A spurt in prices induced accelerating inflationary expectations among the unions. Incorporated into wage demands, these further fuelled the domestic ingredients of inflation.

The end result was that all parties settled, more or less gratefully, for re-centralisation of the system. Simultaneously, manufacturing began to take a pounding from overseas competitors while the tertiary sector, including the public service, expanded. The first ALP federal government in twenty-three years offered many reforms but upset manufacturing unions by its lack of consultation in cutting tariffs 25 per cent across the board. The shifting balance between white- and blue-collar unionism was symbolised in 1969 by the appointment of Rhodes Scholar lawyer R.J.L. Hawke to lead the ACTU. These years were the last to see left-radicals confident about the immediate future. The experience of the Vietnam protest movement flowed naturally into other 'street politics', which saw, in particular, building unions allying themselves with residents and conservationists against developers.

Once the penal powers lapsed into disuse, workers were free to use their bargaining power in full employment for the first time since a very brief period at the end of Chifley's wage freeze. The metal trades award was determined by agreement. Over-award deals began to be incorporated in 'going rates' awards. The monolithic centralised wage-fixing system was fragmenting. By 1973 less than half the increase in male adult federal award rates could be attributed to national wage cases. A change in outlook seemed to be required from those unions long used to letting other, militant, bodies persuade the Arbitration Commission of the need for improvements. Simultaneously, their rank and file faced the disturbing possibility that long-established 'relativities' might be altered in the new world of market forces. No longer might an engineering fitter's rate be a pivot for *pro rata* movements in all awards.

The Whitlam ALP government (1972–75) introduced paternity leave for federal public servants, increased their annual leave and maternity leave, and greatly increased their unions' size by threatening to give improved conditions only to members. Other developments boosting white-collar unionism included closed-shop agreements negotiated in retail, banking and insurance industries. Female workers were aided further. The 1969 'equal pay for equal work' decision caused bitter dissension between employer groups, whose proportion of female employees varied greatly between industries. It was strengthened by an 'equal pay for work of equal value' decision in 1972 and the removal in 1974 of the long-standing differential in minimum wage fixation. The special problems of European immigrants also began to be belatedly realised. In 1973 a riot followed the narrow adoption by a mass meeting of a joint-union recommendation to return to work at Ford Motors' Broadmeadows plant. Militant metal union officials were particularly shocked when thus alerted to their long-standing neglect of the growing section of their membership to whom English was a foreign language.

'Green bans' and political strikes over Vietnam, old age pensions and other social issues all added to an upsurge of participatory street politics. Left-radicals sensed a new social era in the offing. Then 'stagflation' arrived from the international economy and, as in the 1930s and early 1950s, most economists concluded that wage costs were the major problem. Inflationary expectations were incorporated in wage claims, so that in 1974 the rate of wage increases was higher than ever and blamed for rising unemployment and high prices. The Whitlam government abandoned its original view that direct bargaining was desirable, and the Arbitration Commission resumed its position at the centre of wage fixation. With the government's qualified support, it moved in the 1975 national wage case to reverse the 1953 decision and to index wages for inflation. For each quarter of 1975, wages were increased by a proportion equal to the increase in consumer prices.

The mid-1970s to 1983

The 1975 election of the Fraser government, which amended the Arbitration Act to make more explicit the commission's responsibility to consider the likely effects of awards on levels of employment and inflation, increased pressure on the new system of cost-of-living adjustments. From 1976 the commission gave full indexation for lower-paid workers only. Later this 'plateau' indexation gave way to 'partial' indexation whereby all wages were adjusted at a rate lower than the rise in prices. When real wages fell, the stronger unions reverted to bargaining. Unemployment dipped to 6 per cent at the height of the business cycle, but the 'resources boom' failed to eventuate. The inflation and unemployment rates each reached 10 per cent in the 1981–82 slump—with conservatives attributing all the blame to the unions' wages campaign. In 1981 indexation was abandoned. At the end of 1982 the nervous government initiated a six-months federal wage freeze.

Many workers saw technological change as a major cause of unemployment. The silicon chip and computerisation seemed to threaten scores of jobs. Those groups and occupations strong enough moved to protect their own positions, and the weaker went to the wall. Weakest of all were the school-leavers, with neither bargaining power nor cohesive organisation. Public concern with their plight ensured considerable sympathy for calls, enthusiastically initiated by employers, to reduce junior award rates. Other calls for cutting real wages included proposals to abolish weekend penalty rates in the leisure and tourist industries.

The sectional character of unions was clearly revealed. While deploring high unemployment among young people and supporting the idea of a shorter week to spread available work, each union moved to protect its own members. From outside, the increasingly influential supporters of 'free market' economics criticised the centralisation of the arbitration system—yet the more powerful unions felt hampered, if not blackmailed, by Arbitration Commission 'guidelines'. With manufacturing in trouble, the construction, transport and oil industries emerged as wage pace-setters. Following the world-wide trend, hours were gradually reduced towards 35 a week, despite the resistance of the federal commission. Unions also now became interested in a range of non-wage benefits common to northern hemisphere democracies. The MTIA applauded the 1981 agreement it negotiated with the metal unions which guaranteed no further claims for twelve months and established clear grievance procedures. Two months later, in February 1982, AMWU leaders declared that the most realistic prospect for advances rested in the government improving the 'social wage' by lowering taxes, interest rates and health charges.

Elsewhere, there were growing divisions between employers differentially affected by the slump. The new peak council, the CAI, had no sooner been created than the differing requirements of large and small, rural and urban, and manufacturing and other industries led, first, to public squabbles and then to a series of damaging secessions from it. Regional rivalries also impeded unity among employers. The independent assertiveness of the Victorian Chamber of Manufactures, which changed its title to 'Australian' in 1985, helped persuade the CAI to reorganise itself and give manufacturers a national forum through a new CAI manufacturing council. A trend towards a greater nominal cohesion did appear within several states where the umbrella organisations moved closer to merging, but in New South Wales plans to merge the Employers' Federation and the Chamber of Manufactures in 1985 broke down at the last moment.

From the 1960s, Western Australia had begun to figure more prominently in news of national industrial relations. This trend was aided by the belated separation of the political and industrial wings of the labour movement. Until 1963 the ALP itself was the Western Australian branch of the ACTU, but in that year the two were separated and the new WA Trades and Labor Council affiliated to the ACTU. In the Pilbara region, which became Australia's major source of iron ore, there was much unrest as mining companies and their employees evolved a pattern of bargaining suited to the particular problems of this new industrial location. The conservative government of Sir Charles Court introduced repressive legislation limiting public assembly which resulted in the arrest of AMWU officials in 1979 for addressing workers on a vacant lot. The ACTU responded by calling a national protest stoppage on 21 June. Other legislation in 1979, making it unlawful for anyone to obstruct or hinder development projects, brought conservationists, nurses, teachers and church leaders before the courts. In 1980 a union ban on transport to a proposed mining operation on an Aboriginal site at Noonkanbah was broken by a security firm acting in concert with private firms and the State police.

Faced with hostile media reporting and diminishing public support, certain unions in the 1970s began at last to take their public relations seriously. White-collar workers usually led the way, but Telecom technicians and Victorian railway workers devised a popular means of pressuring their employers, not by withdrawing labour but by refusing to charge the public. The Trade Union Training Authority established by the Whitlam government in 1975 helped widen the horizon of many rank-and-file unionists.

Despite its threatening posture towards unions, the Fraser government did surprisingly little to change industrial relations. The much-vaunted Industrial Relations Bureau, supposedly created to clamp down on unions, in fact behaved mildly; and so, usually, did Fraser's Ministers of Labour. The government, however, did withdraw some of the public service leave concessions granted in the Whitlam years, and introduced tough provisions for dismissal and stand-down. Fraser also tightened still further the regulation of internal union affairs, widening the scope for deregistration from the federal arbitration system and adding Section 45D to the Trade Practices Act, which provided employers with a new legal procedure for ending disputes involving secondary boycotts.

1983 to 1990

While stressing the proviso that apparent trends may be reversed in future, it is difficult at present to gainsay the view that the 1980s witnessed the most pronounced changes in twentieth-century industrial relations. Certainly the changes on the union side were unprecedented. The status of the ACTU, its closeness to the federal government and the discipline of the union movement have been noted. The AMWU best personified the dramatic change. From being for at least thirty-five years the major seeker of short-run gains through direct action, the AMWU became the prime advocate of a long-run strategy resting on wage restraint and cooperation with employers to improve productivity. Despite an occasional contretemps, the metal industry employers actively supported this vision of the future. Some other employer groups were impatient for deregulation of the bargaining system. As enterprise bargaining appeared towards the end of the decade, smaller firms and unions alike experienced difficulty in coping with the actual mechanics of the process. When the ALP was elected to federal office in March 1983, it had already reached an 'Accord' with the ACTU. The idea of a prices and incomes policy guaranteeing a fair social wage proved particularly appealing to the stricken manufacturing unions. The ALP had been negotiating with the ACTU on and off for three years. The deal was clinched during the 1983 election campaign. In all, there were five Accords reached in this period. In summary, the wage freeze was converted in September 1983 to indexation, which lasted nearly three years. For the first two years full indexation saw 96 per cent of all award increases coming from national wage cases. Only in the building industry did bargaining bring significant increases outside indexation. Business recovery proceeded apace, but yet again the international economy intruded as balance of payment problems soared and the dollar nose-dived. The ACTU therefore accepted a 2 per cent discounting of the 4.3 per cent price rise in the second half of 1985. In return the government promised compensating tax cuts and provision of a national safety net superannuation scheme to force contributions from employers failing to provide schemes for their employees. The latter point dovetailed with the ACTU log of superannuation claims upon which, the High Court now ruled, the commission had the power to arbitrate. The Commission saw the mushrooming of superannuation bargains as analogous to over-award payments. Hence, while refusing to arbitrate, it was anxious to help conciliate and to ratify and coordinate suitable agreements.

In March 1987, three months after dropping indexation and with the basic agreement of all parties, the Commission introduced a two-tier wage system whereby a basic amount was awarded to all employees, but the second-tier increase—limited to a 4 per cent ceiling—was to be determined on a decentralised, industry-by-industry, or award-by-award basis. The second-tier criteria were restructuring changes to improve efficiency. The emphasis from henceforth was clearly on micro-economic reform to lift productivity. Second-tier bargaining revealed the difficulties for those managements and unions which had relied the most on arbitration and consequently lacked expertise in local bargaining. By the end of 1987, only one-quarter of the workforce had achieved second tier increases.

In 1988 came the structural efficiency principles which promoted extensive workplace reform through reducing the multitude of job classifications common to most awards, making workers more adaptable and offering them skill-related career paths and enhanced training facilities. In the event, negotiations often centred at the industry level, with details of implementation sorted out at the workplace. Given the lack of interest shown by most private firms in training schemes, the federal government moved to force their involvement through its Training Guarantee Act (1990). The Accord had originally promised full indexation and tax concessions for wage restraint. Deregulation of the currency and of the financial sector dynamically aborted such simple equations.

The net result was a restoration of profit's share of income from its low point of 1983 and a decline in real wages. Some of the stronger unions, notably in building, made their own wage gains. All workers benefited from the Medicare national health system and from State legislation in the areas of equal opportunity, unfair dismissal, sex discrimination and occupational health and safety—some of which prompted or induced the federal commission to take an interest. While a landmark 1983 High Court decision allowed such occupations as teachers, academics and nurses to enter the federal jurisdiction, structural change, particularly the decline of manufacturing, produced a decline in the proportion of employees under federal award coverage.

Outside of the tribunals there were several significant industrial confrontations. Nurses had become noticeably more militant in the 1970s, but the six-week strike of the Victorian nurses in 1986 still came as a considerable culture shock to most members of the public. Despite such a notable wage gain, women still trailed behind men. At the end of the decade they earned on average only 78 per cent of males' full-time total earnings. If part-timers are included the figure drops to 65 per cent.

The more radical employer associations, such as the National Farmers' Federation, urged all employers to emulate the Mudginberri meatworks and the Dollar Sweets company, which respectively used the Trade Practices Act and common law to defeat unions' direct action—bringing an award of $1.8 million damages plus costs in the Mudginberri case. The New Right, as the more militant conservative and free-market liberals were called, also applauded the Queensland government both for its use of special legislation enabling it to sack 800 striking power workers and for its provision for Voluntary Employment Agreements, which allowed for a break-out from the award system by authorising enterprise agreements without any trade union involvement.

The federal government, after establishing a major inquiry, passed an Industrial Relations Act (1988) which, while affecting little change to the fundamentals of the system, swept away the encrustations of the old Act, encouraged enterprise bargaining and union amalgamation and took application of sanctions for breach of bans clauses away from the Federal Court, placing it clearly in the hands of the renamed Industrial Relations Commission.

In the 1970s the BLF and its federal leader, Norm Gallagher, occupied the place in popular demonology previously held in succession by coalminers, wharfies and metal workers and their various 'red' leaders. By the late Fraser years, however, other unions increasingly objected to the BLF's roughshod approach to inter-union affairs. In a throwback to the Cold War, when leading communists were imprisoned on what in retrospect appeared to be flimsy grounds, Gallagher himself was gaoled in 1983 for contempt of court. It was a measure of his isolation that no other union took official industrial action in his support.

After a Royal Commission investigated allegations of corruption in the BLF, Gallagher was found guilty, in 1985, of taking bribes in the form of building work and materials for his own and his son's beach houses. He was sentenced to four years in gaol and automatically lost BLF office for five years under the 'Norm Gallagher Act' introduced by the Fraser government to disqualify union officials from holding office if found guilty of dishonesty. Four months later, his conviction was quashed and a retrial ordered by the Criminal Appeal Court. Gallagher returned to the helm of the BLF as it resumed its independent campaign to wrest concessions from building employers. In 1986, supported by an alliance of building trade employers, the ACTU, and State and federal ALP governments which passed enabling legislation, the deregistration of the BLF succeeded in destroying its power. Its members in the major States were forced to join other building unions.

An even harsher fate awaited the Australian Federation of Airline Pilots (AFAP). The highly paid pilots had tried as long ago as 1959 to escape the clutches of the centralised system. Their initial success had seen the Holt government force them back through special legislation in 1967. Since then they had been able to bring their considerable bargaining power to bear at regular intervals to make gains from their employers. In the late 1980s, the Accord prevented pilots from matching the gains made by private sector executives, their usual reference points. When they took limited industrial action to force wage concessions outside the Accord guidelines, the federal government plunged immediately into the fray. It subsidised the employers, authorised international airlines to carry domestic passengers on internal routes, used RAAF planes to supplement services and short-circuited normal immigration procedures to allow use of strike-breaking foreign pilots. The airlines refused to negotiate and moved to implement common law sanctions, forcing AFAP members to resign their jobs to limit potential damages suits. The Industrial Commission offered no shelter, cancelling the old awards and later making new awards based on individual contracts accepted by the strikebreakers which, *inter alia*, greatly increased pilots' flying time. Completely overwhelmed, the AFAP finally was hit with a civil court decision for $6.5 million damages to the employers. When the union was finally granted respondency to the new awards, it represented less than 100 employed pilots compared with 1700 at the beginning of the strike. While the ACTU cheered the government and the airlines on, few unionists seemed to be at all concerned for the precedents set for future conservative administrations by the 'boots and all' intervention of the Hawke government.

Conclusion

The collapse of the Soviet bloc and its centrally-planned economies seemed clear indication of the 'victory' of private enterprise. In English-speaking countries, ideological trends dating back before the apparent discrediting of Keynesianism in the 1970s came to dominance in the 1980s. Extolling the efficiency of economic self-interest given free play in the marketplace, they influenced politicians and planners, conquered universities and entered popular culture in such catch-phrases as 'level playing field' and 'greed is good'. Government regulation was seen as harmful; 'natural' market forces must be untrammelled. Trade unions were regarded by many as obsolete hindrances to structural change, labour mobility and individual freedom. Their popularity was low, strikes were widely regarded as intolerable, and union density fell. The small minority of left-radicals, also concerned with peace, the environment, feminism and racial discrimination, made little impact on the central economic and labour market debates.

Labour management was most sophisticated at the larger end of the size range where human resource management skills, deployed by better-trained personnel, sought to change ingrained 'them and us' attitudes in the workforce. But while enterprise productivity and teamwork were thus encouraged, the enormous tail of firms employing a handful of workers chafed under the restrictions of arbitration awards and States' labour legislation. While most employers sought to shake off these regulatory shackles, the dynamic metal industry group, together with some other manufacturing industries, saw continued cooperation with their unions under the ACTU umbrella as offering the best path forward.

By the end of the 1980s, everyone accepted that the prospect of regaining full employment was remote. Part-time and casual work were an integral part of working life. The more racially, and gender-diverse, workforce was healthier, wealthier and, in terms of formal education, also 'wiser' than their parents and grandparents of the 1940s. Workers had more leisure, more mobility and owned more property. The average working life was shorter, with longer education at one end and earlier retirement or redundancy at the other. The social welfare safety net was much higher and wider. Social change influenced attitudes to workplace change. As the higher participation rate demonstrated, fewer homes depended solely on male breadwinners. The old, enduring, two-parent families were less common. The triumph of the suburbs, the changing entertainment format and the decline of extended families tended to make for greater social isolation and diminished experience of participation in group activities.

Thanks to technical and structural change, to state legislation and to changing management views, workplaces themselves were, on average, cleaner and healthier. By international standards their size was still very small and their workers had low levels of formal training. Vocational training in Australia had again overtaken immigration as the main source of skill. The multitude of tiny enterprises makes generalisation difficult, but, apart from the obvious improvement in human resource management skills in most large private and public enterprises, management characteristics must also have reflected the improved education levels and, partially, the changing ethnic mix and the increased proportion of female workers.

8 The labour movement and the government in Japan

Ryuji Komatsu

Formation of Modern Labour Relations

In June 1992, 12.5 million Japanese workers were organised by trade unions, about one quarter of the total number of workers. This rate of unionisation may be contrasted with a membership as high as 55 per cent in 1949. Gradually it has decreased to half that percentage currently, though the absolute number of organised workers has not decreased.

In the fifty years since the Second World War, trade unions have organised workers in big enterprises and in the public sector. In other words, they were run mainly by workers employed in stable companies or organisations, and not by those from medium- and small-sized enterprises. Despite this big fall in union density, unions' social status and power have not weakened proportionately.

In contemporary Japan, labour relations are generally based on an equal and independent relation between labour and management. On the surface, it is extremely rare for the government to intervene directly by force or power in labour relations. It is particularly so with labour relations in private sector enterprises, where government intervention is rarely observed. Over 85 per cent of the number of trade unions and 79 per cent of union members are employed in the private sector.

Thus, ordinary activities of trade unions are not undertaken at close proximity to the government. It goes without saying, however, that government policies and guidelines are reflected in the labour relations in government offices and amongst local authorities. But even there the government does not have direct contact with them. In view of the fact that members of trade unions in government offices and local authorities are only 20 per cent of the total union members and that few studies have been undertaken over the role of the government, it is difficult to identify and evaluate the role of the government. Thus, the role of the government in labour relations does not seem significant.

A governmental institution, the Labour Relations Commission (LRC), does intervene, however, when failure to reach collective agreements or consensus in labour relations occurs. This conciliation and arbitration system, generally speaking, owes much of its success to judgements and responsibilities on the part of labour and management. Insofar as the LRC was established and operates under state law, the government takes on responsibility for the smooth running of the system itself, but under normal circumstances it does not in reality interfere with its actual management. In recent years, the tendency has been for both the number of disputes and the number of participants to decrease. This system, moreover, is not used as frequently as in the past.

Japanese labour relations are mainly organised in each enterprise and function accordingly for the most part. Trade unions are, generally speaking, independently established in each enterprise. Collective bargaining and negotiation of labour agreements are the main functions of trade unions; collective bargaining takes place within each enterprise. In other words, the basis for trade union formation is the independent initiative of employees in individual enterprises.

Consequently, workers tend to limit themselves to seeking improvements within each enterprise. The main issues for collective bargaining are also problems which can be solved within the enterprise. Issues such as wages, working hours, overtime labour, holidays, working environment and the like become the principal matters of concern for trade unions and workers, while discharge, unemployment, employment exchange, introduction of new jobs or training are not of direct interest. Particularly in this respect, there is little need for the government to intervene in day-to-day union activities or indeed in labour relations as a whole.

Only recently in the history of trade unions, however, have free and equal relations between unions and employers been established. Therefore, labour relations in Japan are more dependent upon and supported by laws and regulations than is perhaps desirable.

Origins of Labour Relations

It was not until the Second World War that workers in Japan were legally granted basic labour rights to organise trade unions and to engage in collective bargaining with employers. In this respect, the Japanese government lagged behind development in other capitalist states in its willingness to respond to the trade union movement.

Previously, the government sided with employers rather than keeping a neutral position. This became most apparent after an economy based on capitalist principles was established in Japan. At an early stage in the development of Japanese capitalism, the Japanese government and employers were viewed as a single body with little difference perceived to exist between their interests and aims. Needless to say, laws, policies and institutions reflected this close relationship. Subsequently, however, successive Japanese governments have come to understand the importance of a more balanced approach and have positioned themselves towards the middle ground between employers and trade unions.

In the early phase of Japanese capitalism, trade union or organisational activities amongst workers did not exist, while attitudes towards labour reflected the ideology of laissez-faire economics at a fairly early stage. The government was tolerant of these attitudes towards unions. Possibilities for workers to promote union activities were still scarce, so the government did not fear the introduction of trade unions or even undertake research on them.

What attracted government attention was not the possibility of workers forming a union, but rather the problem of how to obtain a labour force and how to make the best of it on the job. Workers lacked group consciousness and identity, and thus remained unorganised. Since they were considered idle without rules and commands, employers and the government were more concerned with how it was possible to keep workers employed for long hours and on low wages, rather than considering the protection of workers' rights.

In 1897, after the Sino-Japanese War and during the Industrial Revolution, the first continuously operating trade unions came into existence in Japan. The government did not initially suppress unions or unionists, but as trade unions became increasingly active, the government soon turned oppressive.

In 1900, the government enacted two oppressive security laws, namely the Security Police Act and the Administrative Execution Act. With these Acts, the government strengthened its oppressive attitude toward the labour movement. The Security Police Act did not deem the existence of organisations illegal, but collective or group activities were subject to government control. In addition, this Act gave hardly any consideration to women's participation in social activities.

Following the enactment of the Security Police Act, the labour movement suffered more and more oppression and almost disappeared.

However, in 1911 when Japan was proceeding with industrialisation, the Factory Act, the first law for workers' protection, was enacted, whereby the government began to protect the working conditions of children and women. The items subject to protection and the imposition of standards were, nonetheless, few. The government was still in close cooperation with employers and workers suffered severe treatment through legislation and its enforcement.

Regularisation and oppression of trade unions

Trade unions were reorganised after 1912. Yûai-kai was the first National Centre, and was formed by fifteen persons, including one intellectual graduating from Tokyo University. Soon the First World War broke out; this accelerated industrialisation, and provoked labour movement growth.

However, a Trade Union Act was yet to be enacted; workers were free to organise unions but were without legal protection. Rank-and-file workers lacked the incentive to join trade union movements under these circumstances.

Notwithstanding this situation, Japan affiliated to the International Labour Organisation (ILO), which was established in 1919. Through its participation in ilo, the government had to change its attitude gradually. It altered trade union policy, partially accepting labour unions, in keeping with the international trend. Trade unions were not accepted as workers' rights, but more freedom was given to their activities.

From about this time, trade unions whose activities were job-wide or industry-based were augmented by those based on enterprises; enterprise-wide trade unions or labour relations began to appear. This was a result of the growing life-time employment and seniority-order wage system which employers or big enterprises had introduced around the time of Russo–Japanese War (1904–05). This system in particular was applied mainly to white-collar workers, who were guaranteed life-time employment. For this reason, white-collar workers did not join trade unions in principle and instead maintained a sense of unity with employers and companies.

Around this time, progressive government officials attempted to introduce some labour legislation, including the Trade Union Act, or to establish collective agreement in order to protect society during times of economic depression and worsening work conditions. This ended in failure due to strong objections from employers' circles. Taking just this issue, it is clear that the government was under the control of employers on matters related to labour policy, such as working conditions, labour market policy and trade unions. There were government officials who were concerned with the conditions under which workers were placed and showed readiness to listen to them, but when the matter was taken up at a higher level in government, it was dropped.

The more deeply Japan involved herself in the war, the worse became her economy, including financial institutions and labour market conditions. The government began to assume leadership over labour policy in addition to economic policy. In these circumstances, it became extremely difficult for trade unions to undertake free activities, until finally in 1940 all trade unions were forbidden to organise.

Thus, the Trade Union Act did not come into existence before the war, and workers were not granted their basic rights.

Democratisation and labour relations after the Second World War

After Japan lost the war in 1945, the Trade Union Act was the first enactment of labour policy. In 1946, the new Constitution was also established. The occupation army instructed the Japanese government to grant basic rights to workers as an important first step towards Japan's democratisation. The Japanese people were finally granted basic human rights, and workers were also granted, for the first time, three basic worker rights: the right to organise, the right to engage in collective bargaining and the right to engage in labour disputes. Immediately following the proclamation of these three rights, the guarantees of basic human rights embodied in the constitution provided the foundation for several other Acts, including the unemployment insurance system. These Acts settled the labour policy as a whole. As for labour relations, its main function became collective bargaining, undertaken by labour and management and based on enterprise-wide agreements. In the event, such an endeavour should have ended in failure, but the Labour Relations Commission was instituted (Labour Relations Adjustment Act), and given power to administer the system of mediation, arbitration and conciliation. In contrast to its role before the War, the Labour Relations Commission functioned and stabilised as a democratic and neutral institution. Consequently, the LRC has contributed greatly to the democratisation and stabilisation of Japanese labour relations.

In collective bargaining, which is the major function of trade unions, economic concerns such as wage, term-end allowance, working hours and the like are raised as main issues. The timing and the method of bargaining have come to be institutionalised. In other words, activities tend to peak during the spring labour offensive, or *Shuntô*, which takes place at the beginning of the new fiscal year. Matters not taken up then will be subject to bargaining at different times. For example, it is general practice to hold separate bargaining for term-end allowances two or three times a year.

Thus, labour relations gradually reached stability; the number of labour disputes decreased. Labour–management reconciliation was stabilised. The Labour Relations Commission was not employed as frequently as previously. With all these factors, the government's contact with labour relations on an individual basis is seemingly decreasing, while its role with regard to labour policy in general is increasing.

Government and the stabilisation of labour relations

Together with the establishment of democracy and stability of labour relations, it is becoming more and more common for the government not to have direct contact with labour relations individually nor on specific matters.

In the history of the Japanese labour relations, the government tended to stand very close to employers—particularly so before the Second World War but also afterwards—and it often placed itself in a competitive and oppressive position toward trade unions. Needless to say, it could not help but appear to keep a neutral position after the war, which it did insofar as the system was concerned. But in reality, as the government showed interest in capitalist or employer-oriented economic growth, it stayed even closer to employers.

There are several reasons for this. Firstly, in an underdeveloped country such as pre-war Japan, the government took on responsibility for sustaining capitalist development. Secondly, the government was in the hands of conservative parties, which were supported almost without exception by employers. Lastly, Japanese business management was dependent on cooperation and assistance from the government or public agencies. But trade unions, in contrast, claimed socialism as their ideology and this ran counter to the agenda of a government committed to capitalist ideas.

Furthermore, as one of the characteristics of labour relations after the war, together with the generalisation of enterprise-wide labour relations, there has been an increase in the roles of state and local public servants in their labour movements. In the former enterprise-wide labour relations, bearing in mind industry-wide development, economic activities on the enterprise level were more important.

Despite these changes, the government has not taken direct charge of labour relations in government agencies, but its role is significant. Here, in contrast to the private sectors, government policy based on economic, financial and labour market perspectives becomes the base of all agreements and decisions on working conditions. However, the government does not have direct dealings with labour organisations, but acts through official institutions, such as the Labour Relations Commission of public-sector enterprises or the National Personnel Authority.

Finally, from the point of view of historical development, the Japanese government first showed contempt towards the labour movement, and then hostility; subsequently came acceptance, and, finally, partnership. The development of labour policy or law after the war contributed to the increased status of workers as a whole; this promoted equality among Japanese people as a nation.

Japan has at last entered an era in which labour and management can work as equal partners. However, there are still problems. Unfair treatment of workers and failure on the part of employers to observe labour acts, as well as a disregard for the organisation of trade unions, remain as issues to be addressed. This need continues to characterise labour relations in Japan.

9 Australian labour relations: the influence of law and government

Andrew Frazer

I t has long been recognised that law has exerted a strong influence on Australian industrial relations. This influence is greater than in most developed capitalist societies and is certainly far more extensive than in other developed English-speaking countries. The importance of legal doctrines and processes in twentieth-century Australia has usually been attributed to the compulsory industrial arbitration system. From its inception, compulsory arbitration has been blamed for creating a rift between employers and their workers, replacing personal ties with impersonal legal obligations. More recently, similar though more sophisticated claims have been voiced: the intervention of arbitrated industry-wide awards has institutionalised class struggle, encouraging solidarity between workers, exacerbating tensions between workers and their employers, while relieving workers of personal commitment and responsibility to the enterprise.

The legalism of Australian industrial relations is usually equated with inflexibility and over-regulation, but this seems to confuse form with content. Australia is not so unusual among the developed capitalist economies in having labour relations highly regulated by law, when we take into account both the individual and collective levels of regulation. What is most distinctive about Australia is the concentration of legal regulation in the compulsory arbitration system. This system constitutes and processes employment relations through quasi-judicial institutions which produce formal and codified rules by way of awards. Many European legal theorists studying labour law have recently concentrated on the effects of legal regulation under the banner of 'juridification'. This term is used to describe the process of bringing social relations within the sphere of legal power, resulting in their increased formal regulation. It is the range, intensity and combined effect of legal regulation that is most significant in this process, not the outward appearance of the institutions and other sites in which it occurs. Seen in this perspective, compulsory arbitration is but one of the sources of legal regulation of labour relations which have developed since the nineteenth century. The character of this ensemble of legal relations is closely related to the peculiar development of Australian society. Rather than concentrating solely on the effects of law on employment relations, we should recognise that law is but one aspect of the culture of work, one which both mediates and reinforces the society's values, norms and power relations.

Nineteenth-century state and law

Following the end of convict transportation in the mid-nineteenth century, the role of government in the Australian colonies was limited. In the labour area, it was largely confined to assisting the expansion of the labour market and maintaining the conditions for a productive workforce. British immigration was encouraged, while half-hearted attempts were made to develop apprenticeships and technical education. Intervention in employment and labour relations, however, remained firmly within the classical liberal conception of the state: intervention was countenanced only to protect those workers unable to best care for their own interests, or minimally to support a free market in labour. Pressed by the union movement, governments gradually adopted legislation which regulated the labour process and employment relations of able adult males, but the pace of such reforms runs contrary to Australia's reputation as a social laboratory in the late nineteenth century. Australian colonial parliaments were decades behind Britain in adopting legislation dealing with factory and mine safety, employers' liability for accidents and schemes for workers' compensation. The impetus for this kind of interventionist legislation only came with the formation of labour parties in the 1890s. In fact, the political activities and aspirations of the early labour movement were largely circumscribed by legislative changes. These reforms were invariably branded by conservatives as interventionist 'class legislation', which unfairly catered to a sectional interest. Initiatives that were not so closely related to the labour market were less controversial. Assistance was also given to the development of 'responsible' trade unionism by donating land for the building of trades halls, or by legislating to give unions the right to hold property.

Although government intervention in industrial relations was limited, the legal system played a crucial though frequently invisible role. Before the advent of compulsory arbitration, legal disputes over the employment relationship were handled by the ordinary courts administering criminal and common law. The most frequent legal actions were brought before magistrates under the Masters and Servants Acts. The operation of these statutes has commonly been assumed to follow the pattern observed in Britain, where the legislation was used mainly by small employers against workers, especially unionists. Certainly the legislation in Australia followed its English antecedents in treating employer and worker as both formally and substantially unequal before the law. The masters and servants legislation saw a servant's breach of contract as a crime punishable by fine or imprisonment, while a master's breach was considered a less serious civil claim for recovery of wages. The legislation was a common method of disciplining recalcitrant or absconding workers. Yet however unequal before the law, both master and servant often used this legislation as a way of shifting the locus of individual conflict from the shop or shed floor into the public arena of the courtroom. Pastoral workers especially used the Acts with frequent success to recover unpaid wages, while in return employers defended themselves by accusing their workers of sheep-stealing. Conflict was articulated and rationalised in a legal discourse which, if not recognising equality between the parties, at least admitted elements of mutual obligations. Besides this, the conflict was no longer subject to pure force, but was mediated by a third party in the form of the magistrate. However, by remaining within the sphere of the employment contract, the conflict always remained categorised as purely individual conflict, whatever its source.

The courts were also used in rare, though highly controversial, prosecutions of union leaders for various 'industrial crimes' such as criminal conspiracy. The prosecution of striking shearers during the Queensland 'shearing wars' of 1891–94 and the imprisonment of six unionists during the Broken Hill strike in 1892, convinced even moderate unionists that the judges and the legal system were hostile to the labour movement. In the climate of the early 1890s, when the very existence of trade unions was under threat from implacable employers keen on enforcing 'freedom of contract', combined with a severe economic depression, the legitimacy of the legal system itself was questioned by many labour leaders.

Compulsory arbitration

It may seem paradoxical to us in retrospect, but compulsory arbitration was introduced to Australia in order to encourage collective bargaining. The debate on Australian industrial relations over the last decade has tended to treat the two as polar opposites, but the liberal lawyers who devised the arbitration system believed that, in the industrial relations climate of the 1890s, collective bargaining could only be achieved by allowing unions resort to special courts having the power to make legally enforceable awards. The arbitration Acts all had, as a key feature, machinery for registered unions and employers to make legally binding agreements. The power of the tribunal to conciliate disputes was also seen as an encouragement to the making of collective agreements. Alfred Deakin, when introducing the Commonwealth bill in 1903, said that:

> . . . the very existence of such a court will form a strong inducement to considerable bodies outside of its judicial operations or even of its conciliatory intervention, to make as between themselves agreements in regard to the conduct of the particular trade or business in which they are engaged. Then this Act will bind them. (Deakin 1903, p. 2861)

The drafters of the first arbitration legislation sought a solution to a problem which faces all systems of collective bargaining in the Western legal tradition: if collective agreements are to be given the force of law, how is this to be achieved? The principles of classical contract law could not properly conceive of a binding agreement between a group of workers on the one hand and an employer on the other, since the workers collectively had no legal status. In continental systems of collective bargaining, the answer has been to give unions special legal status and to make the agreements enforceable as a normal contract in the ordinary courts. After a long period of uncertainty, a similar conclusion was reached in the United States in relation to agreements made under the National Labor Relations Act (*Lincoln Mills* Case 1957). In Britain, the answer was to steer away from legal involvement altogether, and from the 1850s legislative schemes of extra-legal conciliation and bargaining were adopted. The policy of legal abstention from industrial relations was continued from 1876 to 1906, when trade unions were given immunity from criminal and civil liability.

In juridical terms, the Australasian system of compulsory industrial arbitration represented a third method: adjudication and legal enforcement by tribunals independent from the ordinary legal system.

In the wake of the 'great strikes' of the 1890s when employers, supported by the colonial governments, used the criminal law to repress trade unionism, the labour movement was in no mood to subject itself to the existing courts which were regarded as hostile to trade unionism and unsympathetic towards the working class. Faced with this legitimation crisis, the liberal reformers (who depended on the Labor Party for power) devised an approach which was supposed to create an altogether new system of labour law, one independent of the existing law of master and servant and administered not by common law courts but by 'a special tribunal outside the present law.' (Wise 1900, p. 648)

So the specific form adopted by the state for the regulation of labour relations at the turn of the century owed much to the collectivist philosophy of its liberal proponents, and to the political power of the labour movement, but it also rested on a hegemonic acceptance of the importance of legal issues as well as a faith in the neutrality and just outcomes of judicial processes. Compulsory arbitration resolved the legal problem of making collective agreements enforceable by giving unions a special though limited legal status. This approach satisfied the concerns of the labour movement by promising to encourage union growth through preference to unionists, and protecting unions from the prejudices of the existing legal system. This interventionist approach depended greatly on a faith in legal forms and processes, in the belief that, however unjustly the law may be administered, at its core the notion of legality carried with it value-neutral concepts, such as those embodied in the notion of the 'rule of law'.

While the expected aim of compulsory arbitration was intended to be legalised collective bargaining, the result was quite different. Within a few years of their establishment, the State systems in particular were regularly producing awards which extended as a 'common rule' across the whole industry. Collective bargaining took place on an unprecedented scale, and a large number of agreements were registered. Many agreements between unions and specific employers were also embodied in consent awards which were presented to the arbitration court in draft form for ratification and translation into law. The development of collective bargaining was stifled by a series of decisions by the High Court and state Supreme Courts which limited both the autonomous powers of the parties to make agreements and the capacity of the arbitration courts to supervise the agreements, even if the parties themselves wanted it. These legal decisions, for example, prevented an agreement from being varied by an arbitration court, prohibited a common rule award being made on the basis of an existing industrial agreement, and limited the making of industrial agreements in the federal sphere. At least in part, these restrictions were applied because the judges of the superior courts regarded collective bargaining as something altogether different from arbitration, which was limited to the judicial determination of a particular existing dispute. As the federal sphere in particular was constitutionally limited to conciliation and arbitration, the arbitration court and even the parties themselves could not participate in bargained agreements which went beyond this narrow view of dispute resolution.

To these purely legal restraints must be added the limited capacity of the parties to engage in collective bargaining in the early decades of the system. The union movement was often minutely fragmented along craft lines, so that demarcation disputes often hindered agreements. The lack of organisation among employers also prevented widespread industry-based collective bargaining; indeed, particular employers or fractions of an industry often conspired with unions to subject their competitors to award regulation by seeking to have an agreement or specific award extended across an industry in an application for a common rule. Such attempts to use the arbitration system were often fought in the courts with funds raised by the newly formed employers' organisations. David Plowman's research has shown how employers' associations only developed in reaction to arbitration, and spent most of their time trying to prevent award regulation by legal challenges and political lobbying, rather than by seeking to influence the outcomes of the system through participation in the bargaining and conciliation process (Plowman 1988, 1989).

Government and labour relations

When the Commonwealth Constitution was enacted in 1901, the federal parliament gained no powers to legislate directly on matters of wages, conditions or union organisation; Section 51(XXXV) allows it only make laws for 'conciliation and arbitration for the prevention and settlement of industrial disputes extending beyond the limits of any one State'. No such restrictions exist in relation to State governments, yet all have until recently adopted systems which have ceded direct regulation to arbitral tribunals or wages boards. The federal parliament also withdrew from exercising those powers of direct regulation which it could legally exercise in relation to its own employees, when the Fisher Labor government gave the federal arbitration system jurisdiction over public servants in 1911. With such an approach, the government became a supplicant party to the tribunals along with organisations representing unions and employers.

In general, this model of indirect intervention by government has remained the rule in Australia. Notable exceptions to the tendency towards regulation by central arbitral tribunals, such as the federal Hughes government's Industrial Peace Act in 1920 and the creation of the federal Coal Industry Tribunal in 1946, followed this pattern by creating specialist tribunals, often headed by an arbitration court judge. Even the Stevedoring Industry Commission, which began as a consultative council headed by a government official in 1942, was presided over by Judge Kirby of the federal Arbitration Court from 1946, although the government continued to issue it with directives. The exception was the Maritime Industry Commission, which was also established in 1942 and, though initially chaired by a judicial arbitrator, operated by direct tripartite negotiation until its abolition in 1952 (Sheridan 1989, pp. 167, 162). The pattern of arbitral regulation continued in the post-war period with the establishment of specialist tribunals, until these were absorbed into the Australian Industrial Relations Commission in 1988 following the Hancock Report's recommendation for a single federal tribunal.

Despite following this pattern, governments have attempted to influence the tribunals in several ways. Tribunals have been forced to take into account specific matters by amendment of the objects of the legislation and by legislative directions to consider the public interest and the state of the economy. Matters of general importance, such as national wage cases and standard hours, must be heard by a full bench, a requirement originally designed to restrict the federal tribunal's activism. Public criticism has also been a common tactic.

Governments have occasionally also intervened directly in the regulation of the labour market and working conditions. At the federal level, the outstanding example occurred during the Second World War, when manpower planning regulations vested the executive with extensive powers to control both employers and workers. Special commissions were also established to direct problem industries. State governments have also continued to exercise powers over working conditions through legislation for annual holidays, long-service leave and factory sanitation. The New South Wales government went further when in 1922 it legislated for a 44-hour week, and again in 1947 when it introduced the 40-hour week by statute, forcing the federal tribunal to follow suit (Larmour 1985, p. 184).

The system and its constraints

Despite criticisms levelled against it, the arbitration system has not entirely betrayed the aspirations of its designers. In many respects it has operated as a highly formal system of legalised collective bargaining.

This has mainly been accomplished by consent awards which in the early 1970s comprised around 70 per cent of all federal awards made (Cupper 1976, p. 345). The vast majority of disputes are settled by conciliation, and few cases are resolved by adversarial arbitration. Seen in this way, legal rules have both hindered and masked the true processes by which the arbitration system resolves disputes. The main function of the system has become one of industry regulation through the resolution of often artificial 'paper disputes'. The securing of awards has become a major objective of trade unions, not least because the respondency to an award effectively gives a union a field of recruitment from those workers covered by it. The rules for union registration also entrenched existing divisions within the labour movement between general, industry and craft unions.

Thus, once the arbitration system was established, it began to function and develop according to its own internal dynamics, as well as influences from the existing legal structures, the demands of particular fractions of labour and capital who represented its clients, and the policies of governments. One of the most significant of these external forces was, as has already been noted, the individual and concerted opposition of employers to regulation by awards. In both New South Wales and the Commonwealth, the arbitration courts faced constant legal challenges to their powers. The superior courts which heard these challenges restricted the jurisdiction of the arbitration courts not merely because the judges were ideologically opposed to extensive state regulation of managerial prerogative, but also because the legal system itself found it difficult to accommodate the new tribunals and the juridical form of regulation which they represented. They were, in truth, among the first administrative tribunals performing what is now called a quasi-judicial function. But at the time they were established, these bodies were practically unique among the organs of the state. The inability of the legal system to fully accommodate this novel form of state regulation reached its high point with the *Boilermakers* case in 1956, when both the High Court and the Privy Council determined that the federal Arbitration Court could not impose a penalty for disobedience of its award or order, since that involved the exercise of an exclusively judicial power which the Arbitration Court did not possess. Even conservative judges like Barwick later admitted that this decision carried the division of powers further than was required by the constitution and hindered the processes of government.

Since the arbitral tribunals were empowered only to arbitrate in matters involving an 'industrial dispute', the employers' legal challenges concentrated on the meaning of this phrase. A succession of decisions by the High Court established that the federal tribunal could only intervene in a dispute in a productive industry or business carried out for the purpose of making profits. Many employees in the public and service sectors, such as firemen and teachers, were therefore excluded from federal award coverage. This restrictive interpretation was taken because many judges did not regard it as the proper province of the state to intervene in employment relations except to maintain the peace and prevent harm to other, 'innocent', parties. Conversely, judges who took an expansive view of the meaning of the constitution also believed that compulsory arbitration represented an extension of the state's functions beyond the classical liberal formulation such that the state now had a direct interest not only in keeping the peace but in securing industrial justice.

The effect of these decisions was to complicate enormously the process of obtaining an award. This required the union to serve individual employers with separate demands and to prove it had members employed by each of them. Union advocates needed to present a case which addressed legal arguments in support of the commission's jurisdiction, as well as evidence of skill, industry wage standards and capacity to pay. The financial and organisational burden of such demands quickly resulted in greater bureaucratisation of unions. In particular industries, such as meat processing, the struggle over federal arbitral jurisdiction has dominated industrial relations between the union and employers.

Beginning in 1983, the immense edifice of complex constitutional law has been systematically simplified, giving the federal commission greater powers. In that year, the *Social Welfare* case swept away the special pleadings that had developed over the meaning of the phrase 'industrial dispute'. Essentially, the court decided that the commission itself was best able to determine what constituted an industrial dispute (*Social Welfare* Case 1983, p. 312). This tendency away from legal formalism has continued, resulting in a reduction in the legal restrictions on the commission's powers and a curtailment of the ways in which employers can challenge awards on constitutional grounds. The new realism has also given the commission new powers. In the period of high legalism by the Barwick High Court, the federal commission was held unable to order the reinstatement of dismissed workers, since that involved the determination of existing legal rights and therefore an exercise of judicial power. Since the 1980s, the current High Court has expanded the federal commission's jurisdiction by giving it the power to determine whether a dismissal was unfair, and to order the reinstatement of dismissed workers in the process of settling a dispute (*Ranger Uranium* Case 1987; *Boyne Smelters* Case

1993). The effects of this new jurisdiction have not yet become apparent, but it may result in greater *direct* involvement in individual employment relations by the federal commission as reinstatement disputes take over from the more abstract issues of award-making. Recent amendments to the federal Industrial Relations Act may have even wider ramifications, since the federal commission's jurisdiction over unfair dismissals has been extended to cover all employees, even those not covered by an award.

The influence of arbitration tribunals

Statutory awards and agreements largely determine the legal conditions of a large majority of the workforce, but the incidence is declining and is concentrated at the 'lower end' of the labour market (in terms of status, wages and security). In 1990, 80 per cent of the employed population was covered by an award or collective agreement, a decline of about 6 percentage points since 1983. There are significant differences in terms of sector, gender, industry and occupation. Public sector workers have a higher incidence of coverage than those in the private sector, where the late 1980s saw award coverage decline from 76 to 68 per cent for male workers and from 83 to 78 per cent for female employees. Women workers have higher overall coverage than men and tend to be covered by State rather than federal awards (58.4 per cent State, 23.2 per cent federal). Casual and part-time workers have a much lower incidence of award coverage than full-time workers. White-collar workers have a lower incidence of coverage than blue-collar workers, and for both categories coverage is higher for lower status occupations (labourers and plant operators, clerical and sales workers) than for higher status levels (trades, professionals and para-professionals) (Australian Bureau of Statistics 1990).

Another statistical measure of the effect of arbitration tribunals on employment relations is the series on methods of settlement of industrial disputes, which has been collected since 1913 (Oxnam 1968; Wooden and Creigh 1983, table A23; Australian Bureau of Statistics 1992). These statistics, which are summarised in Table 9.1, show that in terms of the number of workers involved and the number of working days lost, until the 1930s direct negotiation between the parties and private mediation by a third person remained the dominant forms of dispute resolution, while intervention by federal and State industrial tribunals exerted only a minor influence. From the 1930s, arbitration developed as the leading dispute resolution method; private mediation has become almost insignificant and state intervention has remained fairly stable in significance. In recent years, the relative incidence of dispute resolution by state intervention has wavered, but its overall significance has increased during the 1980s.

Table 9.1   Dispute settlement methods: incidence by workers involved and working days lost, decennial averages, Australia, 1913–90

Decade	Negotiation %		Mediation %		Intervention %	
	Workers	Days Lost	Workers	Days Lost	Workers	Days Lost
1913–20	49.9	23.5	14.2	43.4	8.8	8.5
1921–30	46.8	49.4	7.7	22.5	8.1	11.1
1931–40	52.6	32.4	3.0	8.3	13.4	45.7
1941–50	25.5	19.5	8.5	9.6	18.4	48.0
1951–60	10.0	18.2	0.4	0.9	13.4	29.3
1961–70	9.0	16.9	0.1	0.2	16.5	30.8
1971–80	10.8	18.7	0.4	0.7	14.2	32.5
1981–90	14.4	16.8	0.0	0.0	18.3	37.6

Source: Labour Reports; Oxnam, 'The Changing Pattern of Strike Settlements in Australia, 1913–1963', *Journal of Industrial Relations* 10 (1968); Wooden and Creigh, 'Strikes in Post-War Australia', *National Institute of Labour Studies Working Paper* no. 60, 1983, table A23; ABS Industrial Disputes, cat. 6322.0

However, we should not forget that since the Second World War, the most important means of ending a dispute has been by workers resuming their employment without change to their conditions. The high score for unilateral resumption of work seems to reflect the frequently commented fact that the large majority of disputes in Australia involve workers 'going out on the grass' or attending a stop-work meeting. Such disputes, moreover, tend to be short in duration. This pattern of strike activity has been attributed to the existence of the arbitration system, which has evolved a pattern of initial demands by a union (usually by way of an inflated ambit claim), rejection by the employers with little negotiation, a short stoppage by union members to demonstrate their genuineness, then involvement by the commission through conciliation and ultimately arbitration resulting in an award or variation (Dabscheck 1989, p. 127).

The effects of the arbitration system on individual attitudes and relations are more difficult to gauge. Several commentators have noted the persistence of collectivist notions through the influence of the arbitration system and industry-wide occupational awards. One study, which directly compares similar Australian and American firms and their employees, concluded that compulsory arbitration may reduce competitiveness and innovative motivation, but Australian employees tend to have stronger satisfaction and commitment to their organisation (Drago 1988).

The persistence of general law

While the arbitration system has become the dominant form of legal regulation of labour relations, the common law has also exerted a strong if sometimes imperceptible influence. Compared with other common law countries, legal issues involving the individual employment relationship have remained relatively undeveloped in Australia. Because both unions and employers have been so willing to submit industrial disputes to arbitration, the common law of employment has largely remained in a 'time warp' located some time around the turn of the century. The Australian courts have retained with few alterations a formulation of the contractual duties of employers and employees which rests ultimately on the pre-industrial relationship of master and servant. Awards apply only to employees as defined by the common law 'control test', which has often been criticised as unrepresentative of current industrial practices. As the recent *Troubleshooters* case highlights, awards may be evaded by shifting to contract work and outsourcing (*Troubleshooters* Case 1991). The federal government responded to such developments in 1992 by giving the federal commission the power to adjudicate over unfair contracts made by independent contractors (*Industrial Relations Act 1988*, ss.127A–127C).

Apart from the contract of employment, there are the various industrial torts, which were devised by the English courts at the instigation of a concerted employer onslaught on trade unionism in the 1890s. These torts—conspiracy, intimidation and interference with contractual relations—apply anomalously to industrial relationships. In Australia, they have been used rarely, but a few cases such as the *Dollar Sweets* case in 1986 and the *Airline Pilots* case in 1989 have had an impact disproportionate to their frequency. Unlike Britain, the protection of unions from civil liability in legitimate industrial disputes was adopted only by Queensland (between 1915 and 1976) and currently by South Australia.

Since the 1960s, the British courts have progressively expanded the reach of these torts by reducing the limits on their application and even by creating new torts. The Australian courts have been keen to follow these developments, without giving any consideration to whether they are appropriate to this country. The overall effect of the industrial torts has been to reaffirm the labour movement's view that the ordinary courts are both inherently and overtly biased against trade unionism, to renew the self-confidence of aggressive employers and their organisations, and to increase the uncertainty of the legal rights of industrial disputants. In the *Airline Pilots* case, the greatest disruption occurred after the union advised its members to resign, because the union's lawyers had informed it that pilots who remained employed could face civil actions in tort.

Apart from the ordinary law which may apply in violent disputes, criminal penalties still exist in the industrial arena in the form of essential services legislation in Queensland, New South Wales and Victoria. Such legislation has been a fixation of conservative governments, and is usually promulgated in the name of the 'rule of law', although the selfsame legislation bears all the hallmarks of rule by decree unchecked by parliamentary or judicial scrutiny. The International Labour Organisation has held that these laws exceed restraints on industrial action permissible in international labour law. Despite their range and prominence in political rhetoric, they are rarely used. The use of the Masters and Servants Acts has also continued in the twentieth century—in New South Wales between 1901 and 1920, there were on average 420 workers charged and 250 convicted each year. This legislation has continued to be used in more recent times, and was repealed in New South Wales only in 1978.

Conclusion

The state's role in twentieth-century Australian labour relations has remained strongly interventionist, although the pattern has been one of intervention at the collective level, mediated by quasi-judicial institutions and processes rather than by direct governmental regulation of individual employment relations. The arbitration system, which enshrines collective rights and third-party mediation, has displayed remarkable endurance for nearly all of this century. Yet compulsory arbitration has not replaced pre-existing forms of legal regulation. Indeed, in many respects the arbitration system has become dependent on, and been colonised by, the institutions, processes and discourses of the general law. Labour relations in Australia have been subjected to a double legal effect, at both the individual and collective level.

Only in the last few years has the compulsory arbitration system been subjected to fundamental alteration. The most obvious recent changes have been designed to reduce industry-wide collective regulation by promoting individual rights and encouraging bargaining at the workplace level. Since 1986 the federal Industrial Relations

Commission has developed policies designed gradually to transform the character of industrial relations and award regulation. The federal government has entrenched these principles by legislative amendments which reduce the ability of the federal commission to scrutinise enterprise agreements and allow such agreements to override award conditions. Under principles of structural efficiency, award restructuring and enterprise bargaining, both the aims and content of awards have changed. Many awards now concentrate less on prescribing outcomes (wages, hours and conditions) through substantive rules, and instead set procedural rules which describe processes of consultation between unions and employers at the workplace level.

These attempts to decentralise industrial relations have achieved only limited success. Most enterprise agreements merely supplement existing awards, leaving most of the general industry provisions intact. Many employers appear reluctant to invest significant time and cost in enterprise bargaining, a process which may have uncertain or illusory benefits. It is difficult to say whether the reluctance of employers to embrace enterprise bargaining is a vote of confidence in the arbitration system or a sign of innate timidity. However, the clamour for deregulation of only a few years ago does appear to have receded, partly as the result of transformations achieved within the arbitration system itself and partly from disappointment with the results of enterprise bargaining in practice. Experience so far suggests that the current system of enterprise bargaining and award restructuring does not represent a diminution of legal regulation, or juridification. Instead, formal and therefore relatively ascertainable rules of determinate application are often being replaced by a variety of rules, many of them informal or procedural. The whole collection of rules governing a particular workplace increasingly originates from a number of sites and may carry different, possibly conflicting, meanings. A common cry of personnel managers is the difficulty of coping with the increased complexity and uncertainty of this volume of law.

At the same time, the level of government regulation shows prospects of increasing both formally by way of direct legislation and more informally through labour market programs, the social wage, and industry restructuring. Recent federal government initiatives, such as the training guarantee levy, fringe benefits tax and compulsory employer-funded occupational superannuation, represent a shift towards direct regulation of employment relationships with little mediation by third parties.

The most recent reforms, introduced at the end of 1993, represent a dramatic shift in the focus of the federal industrial arbitration system. By implementing international conventions and extending enterprise bargaining to non-unionised workers, the Industrial Relations Reform Act directly introduces international law as a source of labour regulation in Australia. It also adopts concepts drawn from European and American labour law systems, which are based on labour courts and privatised collective bargaining (*Industrial Relations Act 1988*, Pt 6A; McCallum 1994). The new laws on unfair dismissal in particular involve a shift from the collective determination of conflicts to the handling of individual grievances. The unfair dismissals procedure which evolved within the arbitration system relied on collective rights and union representation of workers before an arbitral tribunal. However, under the recent reforms, individual workers now have standing to bring an action before a specialised court. Other reforms introduced in 1990 and 1992 have given individual employees the right to enforce awards and recover unpaid wages, when previously only registered organisations had standing to appear in such matters (*Industrial Relations Act 1988*, ss.178–79).

Since the advent of compulsory arbitration, the state's influence on employment relations has been most strongly felt at the collective level, mediated by arbitral tribunals. However, legislation and initiatives in the last few years indicate that the mode of legal regulation may be shifting back towards the individual level. Such changes may well have a serious effect on the power of industrial organisations, as both unions and employers' associations are increasingly bypassed in favour of direct approaches to the arbitral tribunals and courts. These changes are all the more surprising because they emanate from a Labor government.

10 Legal regulation and managerial practice in Australia

B.M. Noakes

This chapter gives one perspective on the interaction of managerial practice with labour market regulation in Australia. This perspective will focus on the change in managerial style from authoritarian to participative, on the growth of cooperative rather than adversarial models of workplace organisation, and on changes to legislative frameworks to facilitate these developments.

There have been barely two hundred years of European settlement in Australia. Both before and since that settlement, Australia has not had a peasantry, has not known feudalism, has never had an indigenous nobility, and lacked European-style class structures. These forces that shaped the cultures of many other countries have been marginal to this country. The foundations of Australian society are therefore different from the foundations of many other societies. Relationships within the world of work, including those between management and labour, have also been different. The beginnings of European colonisation were distinguished by authoritarian rule and harsh relationships between the governing and the governed.

While these relationships became ameliorated with time and with different forms of settlement in different areas, throughout Australian history relationships between management and labour have been consistently adversarial in nature.

Early hardships, isolation and cultural background bred a tradition of *individualism* which militated against management–labour cooperation. Australia is not a communitarian society in the Asian sense; it is not a society in which the individual good is routinely subordinated to the collective good, or in which labour submits easily to the will of management.

The early years of settlement were marked by extensive managerial prerogative, few rights for workers, and minimal statutory regulation of labour. The common law and the law of master and servant were the dominant influences (Quinlan 1989). The history of state intervention in labour relations is, however, a long one in this country. Extensive statutory regulation became accepted in the late nineteenth century. The establishment of wages boards led to the adoption, first at State level and then by the Commonwealth parliament, of systems of compulsory arbitration. Workers also turned to parliaments for the realisation of their aims, and their increasing parliamentary representation resulted in an even greater degree of state intervention.

The early systems of compulsory arbitration were bitterly opposed by employers who waged war through the courts against what they saw as unacceptable interference in the running of their businesses. Every conceivable form of legal action was mounted in an attempt to defeat compulsory arbitration (Plowman 1989).

At the same time, legislative encouragement was given to the formation of trade unions, and the arbitration systems fostered these unions. The mainly occupation-oriented unions further divided management and labour in individual enterprises. Almost a century later, there are still virtually no enterprise-based unions in this country, unlike many other countries. This preservation of traditional union structures has been a consequence of preserving labour market regulation.

Management learned to live with and be comfortable with compulsory arbitration. In part, this was the result of the link forged between arbitrated wages and tariff protection, in part the realisation that arbitration often worked against employee's interests, and in part simply an abdication of one area of managerial responsibility. In this latter respect, it was often easier to pass decision-making on difficult issues to a tribunal rather than to take a managerial decision. The decline of the owner–manager and the rise of the professional manager was also a pertinent factor. Owners found it easier to take hard decisions and accept responsibility than did managers.

The overall impact of compulsory arbitration was to entrench adversarial and conflict-based relationships between management and labour and to inhibit the development of constructive relationships based on mutual commitments.

The search by Australian management for a different basis for its relationship with employees began in the 1960s, when management commenced to show an interest in employee commitment and participation. Some of the early experiments in this direction were unsuccessful and foundered because of entrenched attitudes. However, this interest was maintained, influenced in part by overseas developments, particularly by 'Industrial Democracy' in the United Kingdom ('The Report of the Royal Commission on Trade Unions and Employers' Associations' 1968; 'The Report of the Committee of Inquiry into Industrial Democracy in the United Kingdom' 1977).

In the 1970s, greater interest developed both at national and State levels, and among individual managers, but progress remained slow. In 1978 the federal government established the National Employee Participation Steering Committee, a tripartite body which published two important booklets designed to arouse interest in participative management styles—'Employee Participation: A Broad View' (1979) and 'Employee Participation—Ways and Means' (1980). Also in 1978 the Confederation of Australian Industry (CAI) published a comprehensive guide entitled 'Involving Employees in the Enterprise (Workers' Participation)—A Guide for Employers'.

In 1983, the National Labour Consultative Council established an Employee Participation Committee. In 1984 this Committee published 'Guidelines on Information Sharing', a document which continues to have contemporary relevance.

In 1986 a joint statement between the CAI, the Business Council of Australia (BAC) and the ACTU was issued. This statement urged the adoption by management of more participative styles. It was the first such statement to recognise deficiencies in management practices needing to be addressed. It was also suggested that more emphasis be placed on workplace resolution of these issues ('Issues Related to Productivity Improvement'—Joint Statement between Confederation of Australian Industry, Business Council of Australia and Australian Council of Trade Unions—24 September 1986). In April 1987, the CAI released a publication entitled 'Employee Participation: A Guide to Realising Employee Potential and Commitment'. This publication contained the first comprehensive commitments by Australian employers to fundamental changes in management styles and practices:

If an enterprise is to survive in a climate of rapid technological change, increasingly competitive markets and continuous shifts in the economic and social influences of the external environment, then it is essential that the enterprise develops new skills and flexibilities to which all of its members can be committed. The development and maintenance of employee commitment is one of the most pressing priorities confronting Australian management today.

The involvement of employees in the identification and resolution of organisational issues provides a positive and constructive approach to the generation of shared responsibility and commitment. The general acceptance of organisational solutions and their effective implementation is largely dependent on the process employed in developing the changes to be undertaken.

The responsibility rests with management for initiating the development of processes which enable employees to contribute to the full extent of their skills and to participate constructively in the decisions affecting them and the effectiveness of their workplace. Without a positive and cooperative approach to employee relations on the part of management, employee cooperation and commitment cannot be expected to materialise unaided. The old belief that free enterprise cannot peacefully co-exist with organised labour to their mutual benefit must be abandoned.

The next important step was the reaching of an agreement in April 1988 between the CAI and the ACTU, resulting in a 'Joint Statement on Participative Practices'. This statement was, at that time, probably the only agreement of its type in the world, that is, an agreement between a peak trade union body and a peak employer body on the controversial issue of employee participation.

The first paragraph of that joint statement reads:

> The CAI and the ACTU share the conviction that the cooperation of management and the workforce is critical to the development of more efficient enterprises and industries in Australia.

On the role of management the joint statement said:

> Communication, information sharing and consultation should be integral components of the management process of any organisation.

Throughout this period, legal regulation of the labour market continued unabated. In fact, in the 1970s and early 1980s the general trend was for enhanced centralised control through arbitral tribunals. A particularly curious example was the adoption, in the name of controlling inflation, of systems of wage indexation which effectively paralysed interaction between management and labour. When this system was temporarily abandoned in the early 1980s, the unleashing of forces which had been inhibited by this centralised system resulted in a resurgence of adversarial relationships and a wages explosion.

Concurrent with these developments, Australia became more exposed to international economic pressures. A series of decisions was taken to liberalise the economy through the floating of the currency, financial deregulation and the elimination or reduction of tariff protection. These decisions have created a more open and liberalised economy, and have exposed industries and enterprises to greater international competition. This has led to increased pressure for efficiency and productivity gains in an effort to obtain and retain markets.

Since efficiency and productivity can best be improved at the micro-level, that is, at the level of the enterprise, the result has been a much greater emphasis on enterprise-level labour relations and on developing more harmonious relationships between employers and employees in pursuit of common objectives. In shorthand, this has been defined as 'decentralisation', but it is a more complex process than this mechanical description implies.

Developments in managerial practice since the early 1980s have provided the rationale for changes to legal regulation. In other words, the need for comprehensive legal regulation has been diminished by the growing awareness of shared interests between employees and management. There is now a general understanding of the desirability of management and employees reaching their own agreements without third party intervention. In this process, management, labour and the tribunals have played pivotal roles and the nature of regulation has commenced to change in order to place more emphasis on workplace agreements and productivity growth.

Management has generally initiated change since it has in many cases had no other choice if the enterprise was to survive. Labour has similarly been under great pressure to change work practices and to depart from traditional attitudes in order to maintain job security and to improve remuneration. In some cases, trade unions have facilitated these changes; in others, they have sought to frustrate them.

Statutory tribunals, aided to some extent by changes in the legislative framework, have in general attempted to encourage these changes and to use wage fixation as a spur to workplace change. This has meant some decline in institutional intervention and a greater willingness by management and labour to seek their own solutions to their own problems.

The role of governments has been another matter altogether. Rather than taking a step back from the traditional interventionist approaches adopted in this country, and leaving the direct parties to find solutions, governments have for the most part sought to increase their role. The prime example of this interventionist approach is the Accord negotiated between the federal government and the ACTU at intervals since 1983. This agreement, entered into without employer involvement, sought to determine wage outcomes and general social benefits and thus to become a new form of regulation of the labour market. In so doing, it has had the little-recognised consequence of inhibiting the development of constructive relations between management and labour. A number of other government initiatives at both federal and State level, taken in order to 'reform' the legislative framework, have also encouraged polarisation rather than harmonisation of views. It could be argued that whatever progress has been made has not been due to government effort.

An interesting phenomenon over this period of change has been the continuing decline in the rate of trade-union membership, particularly in the private-sector workforce. The general reasons for this decline are well known and include structural change, the growth of service industries, increased participation of women, and the growth of part-time and casual employment. But there are probably additional reasons connected with the unwillingness of trade unions to reflect in their organisational structures the new emphasis on enterprise level relationships. This is not to depreciate the efforts of many trade unions and the ACTU in encouraging workplace change and fostering better employee–employer relations. Many good things have been done, but much remains to be done.

Employer groups have, however, been at the forefront of change and of management training designed to promote workplace reform. In 1991, Australian Chamber of Commerce and Industry (ACCI) completed the largest supervisor training program ever conducted in Australia, in which 6000 managers and supervisors were trained in the development of constructive workplace change. An independent evaluation of this program found that workplace reform required the development of a new work 'ethos' or spirit, as well as new management approaches and work practices. In part, the report said:

> The kinds of 'workplace culture' changes which are necessary pertain to fostering the development of a collaborative almost communal atmosphere within the enterprise. Promoting the concept of increased individual authority ('ownership' of the job) results in shared objectives, shared values, shared commitment to outcomes (Graffam and Griffin 1992).

ACCI now operates a comprehensive and integrated workplace change program which is designed to bring about better relations between management and labour. As part of this process, ACCI has published a set of guidelines for employers ('Workplace Change and Enterprise Agreements—ACCI Guidelines for Employers', December 1992), which urges management to:

> Communicate directly and fully with employees about the situation of the enterprise and the need to improve efficiency; endeavour to develop a shared vision of the future.

The current situation is:

- there has been a revolution in management thinking and practices in recent years;
- management favours workplace reform and this involves securing the commitment of employees to mutual objectives;
- workplace reform often requires overcoming inappropriate forms of legal regulation;
- ideally workplace reform should proceed faster than at present; and
- workplace reform is an endless continuing process which is necessary to cope with the effects of external change.

If this is the present picture then what does the future hold?

There can be only one outcome of this process of reform and change. This outcome requires a greater degree of voluntarism in labour relations, abolition of the general systems of compulsory arbitration in favour of equitable bargaining systems, and a context in which management and employees will increasingly determine their own solutions to their own problems, employees will have a greater involvement in decision-making processes, and both management and employees will develop greater mutual commitment and understanding.

If this is indeed to be the outcome of present trends and if this will result in more productive and efficient workplaces, the critical question is: how long will these reforms take? The answer to this question depends largely on the removal of a number of barriers. The legislative frameworks for labour relations need to be overhauled so as to encourage a greater degree of voluntarism. We must recognise that neither legislative frameworks nor governments produce outcomes, but that the parties themselves—employers and employees—directly determine the outcomes of their relationship. The institutional mechanisms for legal regulation or state intervention in labour relations must either be dismantled, or the element of general compulsion removed from their operation.

The attitudes of employees must continue to change in order to eradicate the remnants of adversarial labour relations. In addition, trade unions must become to a greater extent facilitators of change and must encourage new forms of workplace-based organisation.

Management must continue the process of transforming its attitudes to employees, including its response to economic challenges. In particular, there must be a greater emphasis on change in small and medium-sized businesses.

Governments must avoid the interventionist approaches of the past and see themselves as encouraging rather than ensuring particular outcomes. The politicisation of labour relations which has been typical of the Australian approach must be sharply reduced.

A solution must be found to the paradox that, while management is attempting to build better relationships with its employees, recessionary economic conditions are leading to widespread redundancies. Since security of employment is a major objective of employees, this insecurity is not conducive to the development of mutual commitments. A resumption of higher levels of economic growth is probably the only solution to this problem. Alternatively, some would look to Japan for solutions to this and other problems of labour–management relations.

Rather than analyse the 'Japanese' approach to labour relations, we might note that:

- there are strong cultural differences between our two countries;
- 'permanency' of employment in Japan is largely confined to larger enterprises (Japan Institute of Labour 1933), and is contracting because of reduced economic growth (*Japan Labour Bulletin* 1993);
- there is a more extensive 'dual' labour market in Japan than there is in Australia;
- the growing expectations of Japanese employees, especially the young, are disturbing traditional patterns of labour relations; and
- reduced rates of growth are also affecting traditional attitudes, and not only in relation to employment security.

In the current (June 1993) issue of the *Japan Labour Bulletin*, it is argued that 'undercurrent moves are progressing towards drastic changes in Japanese employment practices'. The article makes two points in this respect: firstly, a variety of restructurings of management strategies have been taking place continuously since the late 1970s. Also, this trend has been further strengthened as a measure to cope with the recent faltering economy. Introduction of an annual pay system is one such typical measure.

Under the annual pay system, wages vary each year according to an individual's performance and the extent to which he or she attains his or her targets. It is safe to say, therefore, that the annual pay system involves a principle different from that in which pay hikes are determined according to length of service (though there are individual differences by company). What is more important is that introduction of the annual remuneration system is aimed at taking into account the employee's individual performance. This holds the possibility for a vast departure from the traditional management concept which places stress on group-based performance and efficiency.

The second important point to note is that review of Japanese-style employment practices has been made necessary in connection with the argument that the way the Japanese work and the relation between the individual and the company should be re-examined. The pay based on seniority, under which wages and status rise in a stable manner with years of service, and lifetime employment, under which employment is assured unless firms face serious management crises, were ultimately the mechanism by which employees were assured 'stability' by deeply getting involved in the company. This won sympathy from many workers when 'stability' was the first priority. But once economic affluence has to some extent been achieved, workers have shifted their eyes toward private life and away from corporate life. Thus firms, on their part, come to need people who can demonstrate their abilities as individuals as well as in groups or those who can become spiritually independent of firms. These moves from both sides, it may safely be said, are creating a different relationship between the enterprise and the individual in Japan (Kameyama 1993).

The 1993 position paper of *Nikkeiren* (the Japan Federation of Employers' Associations) was entitled 'Choices for Reform and Renewal'. In the section devoted to 'evolving concepts of work and management', Nikkeiren sets out its views on Japanese-style management:

> Employers are beginning to need workers who do not simply work well with others but who also have individuality and creative ability. Types of employment will include not only lifetime employment but flexible working periods and work systems, to make better use of all kinds of employees, among them housewives, older persons, people with international experience, and non-Japanese. This mixed employee structure will require new methods of personnel administration.

Australian worker individualism is clearly undergoing re-alignment towards group objectives, while simultaneously there is a greater individualism emerging in Japan. The Australian workplace is witnessing the development of greater mutual commitment between manager and employee, while in Japan there is some weakening of this traditional link. Nevertheless there are still very large differences in approach and they will probably remain for the foreseeable future.

What are the principal conclusions which can be drawn from this overview?

Firstly, the extensive managerial prerogatives and authoritarian management styles which characterised early labour–management relations in this country have been substantially modified. Secondly, there has been a long tradition of state intervention through direct legal regulation and the establishment of tribunals of compulsory arbitration. Thirdly, employers have in comparatively recent times begun to show an interest in the development of more participative methods of management. The economic pressures to which enterprises have been subjected and the drive for greater efficiency and productivity have encouraged this development. Fourthly, enterprise-focused labour relations are necessitating a reassessment of traditional approaches to labour market regulation, particularly in relation to arbitral tribunals. Finally, the growth of a cooperative model of labour relations requires more emphasis on voluntary arrangements and less emphasis on compulsion.

In the meantime, Australia has an enormous economic challenge to meet. Our ability to meet this challenge will be enhanced by reduced legal regulation of the labour market, and by an increase in enlightened managerial practices which encourage employees to become true participants in the effective operation of enterprises.

11 Management and industrial relations at Toyota and Nissan

Ben Watanabe

I n 1990, scholars at the Massachusetts Institute of Technology published *The Machines that Changed the World*. This book praised Japanese management techniques, and was very well received. Reviewers and critics found special praise for the 'leanness of Japanese management systems', and coined the word 'Toyotism'. They endorsed Japanese management practice as a model for western countries to follow.

What is the Toyota management system? Comparison between General Motors and Toyota gives part of an answer. General Motors in 1990 produced four million cars, and Toyota produced about the same, but the size of the workforce employed by each company is quite different. Fifteen years ago, in 1978, General Motors' total workforce was about 460 000; by 1993, fifteen years later, it had declined to about 200 000 workers. But in that year Toyota employed only 58 000.

How does the Toyota management produce about the same number of cars with a workforce that is so much smaller? When you go to Toyota City, you find twelve Toyota plants there, five assembly plants and seven component plants. But Toyota does not produce electronic harnesses or gear boxes, and its production of engines and transmissions is nowhere near sufficient for its requirements. The manufacture of these components is contracted to outside firms, and in September and October 1992, Toyota attempted to extend this system still further. As a result, its direct employees went on strike.

In Japan, Toyota does not produce engines, electronic harnesses, cushions, mirrors, or steering assemblies. It is difficult to compare out-sourcing with in-sourcing, but roughly speaking, about 20 per cent of

Toyota's components are in-sourced, and about 80 per cent are made by small or medium-sized firms operating from outside Toyota's premises. Whether Toyota decides to out-source or not depends on relative labour costs. The wages of workers in the bottom tier of Toyota's production system are very low—only about 60 per cent of the wages of comparable workers employed directly by the parent company.

Toyota also discriminates sexually and racially in its employment. All workers on the production line are male and Japanese. This contrasts with the employment policy of car manufacturers in the United States, where there is no policy of racial exclusion, where 30 per cent of workers on the production line are female, employed on the same wages and under the same conditions as males.

These features of Toyota's policy have put an end to the myth that private profitability leads to public profitability. So does its use of the just-in-time system.

Toyota's just-in-time management is based on two- or three-hour production phases in body assembly within the parent company's factory. Every two or three hours, trucks from the small out-source companies deliver parts to the parent company in Toyota City. If one of these small companies goes on strike, the assembly line it supplies cannot work, because within the Toyota factory there is no stock. Therefore, Toyota controls all tiers of production to avoid labour disputes.

Absence of stock inside the Toyota plant means that it is neat and clean, but outside the plant there are problems. Early every morning, trucks from Toyota's suppliers begin to line up in the streets outside the parent factory. Members of the local community complain that Toyota have turned the public roads around its plant into a giant warehouse, and this led in 1991 to the Minister of Transportation criticising Toyota's just-in-time management system. Another adverse feature of the system is that Toyota's requirements for parts on Monday morning forces workers in the supplying firms to work on Saturdays and Sundays.

It is difficult to understand why Western countries should try to learn from Japanese management systems. It is all the more difficult if we consider the nature of the industrial relations they produce. On this point, some comparison between Toyota and Nissan is instructive, and so is the story of the rise and fall of Schiogi Ichiro.

Shiogi Ichiro was a leader of the Japanese labour movement and President of the Japanese Automobile Workers' Union from 1962 to 1986. Something about his character and his style of leadership can be inferred from the fact that he owned a 32-foot cruiser, seven foot longer than the one owned by the President of Nissan. He also drove a sports car, a Nissan Parody, specially made for him by that company. He figures prominently in David Halveston's book *Reckoning,* but that book was written in 1985, when he seemed to be at the height of his powers as one of the most powerful leaders of the right-wing of the Japanese labour movement. The next year, he was completely defeated in a battle with the President of Nissan, and forced to quit all of his posts in the labour movement.

The contest between Nissan President Ishihara and Union President Shiogi began not over pressure of labour policy but over Nissan's plans for expansion in the late 1970s, when the trade imbalance between Japan and the United States was getting larger. Well-established Japanese companies were forced to move abroad to stop criticism about surplus exports and to be closer to their selling markets. President Ishihara planned on building a Nissan plant in England. Shiogi, who greatly admired the United States and especially its United Automobile Workers' Union, eagerly proposed building a plant in the United States. President Ishihara hated Shiogi's intrusion into Nissan's management policy on this and every other occasion. At Toyota, the union did not intrude into matters of management policy, but Nissan followed a practice of consulting the union.

Beneath the issue of locating plants overseas was the fundamental issue of control of the production line, and President Ishihara turned the dispute into a holy war to get control back. At Toyota, the union did not have the power to determine whether overtime would be worked, and management had considerable flexibility in the use of labour. But President Ishihara's management could not order even one hour's overtime if a local president of the Nissan union refused it, and the union enforced consultation on all issues.

How was the Nissan union able to exercise such power? The answer begins more than forty years ago. Then, the Nissan local was famous as the most militant union in post-war Japan. In 1953 its President was Mr Masuda; Shiogi began work in April, and was a raw recruit in the Union. The Union went on strike in June, and the strike continued until the company won in late August.

The company's victory depended more than anything else on defection. As the strike intensified, some workers established secret communication with the management and formed a new yellow company union. After they had destroyed the militant Nissan local, Shiogi and Kawamata, Nissan's President, developed a special relationship. Shiogi described it as mutual trust between labour and management.

During the dispute, many workers who had supported the militant union left their jobs, and many middle management officers left the company. As a result, there was a large gap in the company's line of management. The company's recovery depended on filling that gap quickly and efficiently; that became the first task for Shiogi and Kawamata and their new doctrine of mutual trust. Shiogi promised that this union would accept responsibility for keeping the production line moving, and he took over control of the shopfloor himself. He was able to keep his promise, and this allowed him to put strong pressure on the company's executive. He nominated men for removal from or appointment to posts, and in mutual trust, Kawamata always listened to his opinion. The union's role in Nissan's management expanded until the number of stewards was four times that of Toyota's. Correspondingly, the number of staff in Nissan's Department of Human Resources remained small, compared with that of Toyota's. Shiogi further secured peaceful industrial relations by hunting down troublemakers and opponents of his leadership within the union, even to the point of using violence.

The relationship between Shiogi and Kawamata worked smoothly, but real conflict developed after Ishihara succeeded Kawameta as Nissan's President. By that time, Nissan was losing market share to Toyota. Isihara saw the union's control of the production line as the main reason for Nissan's loss of competitiveness. He openly ignored the forms of cooperation with the union, excluded intervention by union officials, and tried to win back control of production for management. As a counter-move, Shiogi refused to support the productivity drive of the management.

The friction between labour and management reached its peak between 1982 and 1984, and the production line frequently stopped. Shiogi claimed the union was eager to support a productivity drive because labour and management trusted one another, but that the productivity drive which management was proposing ignored discussion with the union, neglected safety issues and aimed only at efficiency. This was fundamentally different to the kind of productivity drive the union proposed.

The union's proposal was for a system of labour–management consultation based on a close relationship between the floor managers and blue-collar union officials. These were men who (as in Japan generally) had very limited promotion prospects. They very much distrusted white-collar workers, who often received promotion after only three or four years. Shiogi trusted them, they were loyal to him, and they could make the production line work smoothly.

The basis of their loyalty was the increased opportunities for influencing management that the system at Nissan gave them. This compensated them for having to remain in their dead-end jobs, and it even gave them a sense of superiority. Because Shiogi's productivity drive scheme was based on strengthening their positions of influence, they remained loyal to him and gradually came to support the union's productivity drive. But management thought that what the union proposed was too inflexible, and put too much power in Shiogi's hands. A confrontation between Shiogi and the management became inevitable. It led to his defeat in the spring of 1986, and Shiogi was forced to quit the centre stage of labour history. How did Ishihara manage to defeat him when Shiogi had control of the workplace as a whole?

He was dismissed as president because of the betrayal of blue-collar workers, the very group on which his strength was based. Their loyalty wilted because of a particular tactic the company adopted in its disputes with the union. It ordered its shopfloor managers to refuse absolutely to discuss any issues not specified in the labour contract. There was no written agreement about overtime, or transfer, or mutual trust, or what it meant, so no discussion of these issues was possible. The workers who had supported Shiogi were dismayed and the circumstances of the workplace were completely changed. As an additional blow, Ishihara announced that workers who refused transfers or other orders would be punished according to working rules.

After Shiogi was dismissed, the company signed a new contract with the newly-elected union officials. The new contract differed from that of the Shiogi era in that it was comprehensive, and covered every possibility. Its basic principle was that the union should never oppose the rights and interests of the company. With its former loyal retainer Shiogi gone, the company got all the flexibility in management it wanted.

The new flexibility showed itself in one particularly dramatic way. In September 1986, at the end of the Shiogi era, the number of the union's full-time representatives at Nissan was 222. After the new contract was signed, this number was reduced to 165. Nissan continued to reduce union representation, until only 111 (exactly half of 222) full-time union representatives remained. Flexibility at Nissan meant avoiding union influence on the shopfloor.

What sort of union can co-exist with management systems like this? The union has become a kind of accessory of the company, with no effective rights of consultation. In Australia, the unions are strong and the system of consultation works well. We should ask ourselves what is likely to happen if Australian companies go far in emulating Japanese systems of management.

12 'Good while it lasted': the position and prospects of Australian unions in 1993*

Michael Easson

The title of this chapter, 'Good while it lasted', is meant to imply that the 'good times' for Australian unions have now drawn to a close or are about to. It also suggests significant fluctuations in the fortunes of the Australian labour movement, including a substantial decline in union representation of the workforce, changes in the role of the unions, and transformations in the evolution of the industrial relations system in Australia. It is now appropriate to reflect on some of the labour movement's recent strategies with a view to examining its prospects for the remainder of this decade and beyond. In particular, this chapter will assess the strategies of unions—which, over the last dercade, have included the development of various Accords.

Stuart Macintyre's short monograph *The Labour Experiment* (1989) concludes with this comment:

> The consensus therefore lasted for most of this century and has come under serious assault only over the past decade. The Labor Government led by R.J. Hawke (1983–[1991]) has presided over expansive deregulation of finance and industry, reductions in assistance and protection for domestic producers, and substantial changes to the public sector, including welfare. A conspicuous exception so far to its pattern of economic rationalism and dismantling of public control has been the labour market, though

* I am grateful for the assistance of Labor Council Executive Assistant, Tom Forrest, who undertook much of the research which underpinned this chapter.

it remains to be seen whether the arbitration system can stand alone as a single tree where once there was a forest. If it falls too, the political economy that the Australian labour movement helped to establish will have finally ended.

This passage raises a number of issues: what is meant by the 'Australian labour movement' and the 'political economy' which it helped establish? The problems and prospects of the Australian trade union movement are similar to those of many organisations and individuals struggling to sustain, renew and kindle the range of practices, traditions and activities that constitute a movement. But to speak of a movement suggests that there is something coherent and unified. This is not the case. Australian unions have considerable differences in traditions, styles of activity, industrial relations practices, guiding ideologies (or lack thereof), relations with employers, membership fees, services, structures, membership participation and bargaining experiences.

Ninety-five per cent of union members now belong to unions which are affiliated to the ACTU. Sixty per cent of union members belong to unions affiliated to the ALP in one or more States. The bulk of the remainder belong to unions with key officials in the ALP and which frequently donate funds and resources to the ALP. There is only one national peak council. Australia is not like France. Union membership at the enterprise level is not decided on the basis of politically sectarian preferences. Australian unionism is united in ways that some Europeans and other countries are not. But this 'unity' should not obscure the pluralism between and within different unions. Nor should it obscure the recent history of this 'unity'. After all, it was only after the Commonwealth Association of Government Employees Organisations (CAGEO)—a peak council of federal public-sector unions—merged with the ACTU in 1979, and the Australian Council of Salaried and Professional Associations (ACSPA)—a peak council of white-collar unions—merged with the ACTU in 1981, that a single overwhelmingly representative national peak council has emerged.

Moreover, unionists vary widely. A merchant seaman in a union with a fierce commitment to an isolated occupation will have a very different concept of unionism to that of a stenographer in an office, a nurse in a private hospital, a barman at an hotel, or a foundry worker. Each of those persons and the many other individual types which might be cited, highlight the fact that Australian unions 'cover' nearly every walk of life. Only some of those persons consider themselves part of the trade union movement in any meaningful sense. The sense of belonging to a 'movement' varies from union to union and occupation to occupation, but most unionists are loyal to their own union; for what it delivers and stands for—practical things like bargaining assistance or as employment insurance—rather than because of its encapsulation of metaphysical concepts. Fewer still consider themselves part of political and industrial labour. Amongst the activists—the core of union shop stewards and officials—the number who feel tugs of affinity to the movement are considerably higher, if not overwhelmingly so. Even here precisely what constitutes that affinity remains wide-ranging.

Macintyre and other labour historians clearly have something definite in their minds when they write about 'the political economy' of Australian labour: it includes protection for Australian industry from 'unfair competition', 'sweated labour' from overseas, support for a strong conciliation and arbitration system and for minimum wages and conditions throughout an industry or craft. Those ideals were translated into the politics of 'White Australia', tariff walls and state regulation of industrial relations.

Nonetheless, even here consensus about what it meant in practice was always very loose; there were always some dissident voices within the movement questioning Labor policy, particularly on the formation of so-called 'bosses arbitration courts' and tariff protection for 'petty bourgeois craftsmen'. Although there was subsequent support for a strong conciliation and compulsory arbitration system, this was often espoused with simultaneous support for the unlimited right to take industrial action. Labor views in many areas favoured the paradoxical approach to industrial and political matters over the logically consistent approach.

Macintyre's conclusion, that the labour market might be deregulated under a Labor government, seemed absurd at the time. In 1989, when Macintyre published his monograph, it seemed that the labour movement would never accept significant deregulation of the labour market and that most of the conciliation and arbitration system would remain firmly in place. Further, it seemed that there was no necessary correlation between deregulation of the financial and other markets and the labour market. That optimism now appears partly mistaken and, more importantly, the analysis underlying such optimism appears faulty.

This chapter is unable to explore all these issues exhaustively. To do them justice would require a volume larger than the whole book. Thus some points will be impressionistic and rubric-like. However, in summarising some major themes it is hoped that the argument will remain coherent and intelligible. What factors stand out? Three areas of particular importance arise from the experience of the last decade.

Firstly, anyone examining for the first time the Accord Mark One (as it is now known)—a document adopted in the heat of the 1983 election campaign—would be surprised by the agreement's subsequent evolution. The original Accord brimmed with optimism about the labour movement's capacity to provide full employment, wage indexation and economic growth. It was manifesto politics.

The Accord Mark Seven, adopted in 1993, combined with recent moves by the trade union movement and the federal government to accelerate developments in enterprise bargaining and weaken the powers of the Australian Industrial Relations Commission over compulsory conciliation and arbitration. It is a far cry from the ideas in the original Accord.

Indeed, the original agreement was very rapidly put to the test. There was nothing in Accord Mark One about the discounting of wage movements due to the fall in the consumer price index caused by the introduction of Medicare. Similarly, the Accord Mark Two, which proposed trading a 2-per-cent wage reduction—due to the decline in the Australian dollar and Australia's terms of trade—for support for wage indexation at the April 1986 National Wage Case with tax cuts later in that year, was another proposal not originally contemplated.

There are various ways of assessing these developments. One is to say that the union movement quickly adapted to the economic realities by joining with the federal government to tackle some of the difficult economic and social dilemmas. Or it might be asserted (wrongly in my view) that the Accord was never well suited to the changing economic fortunes of Australia in the 1980s. In any event, whatever view one takes, Accord Seven is radically different from earlier manifestations and in large measure reflects the dilemmas that the union movement faces in 1993. The central dilemma is for the labour movement to be responsible and supportive of its Accord partner, the federal Labor government, while being adaptive to the needs of workers, especially unionists.

The second point is that the confident *élan* of the Australian trade union movement took a battering in the 1980s. The idea of Australian exceptionalism, the proud boast that Australia is the most egalitarian place on earth, went into decline. The trade union movement, despite its propensity to proclaim its difficulties loudly, was largely an optimistic force in the earlier decades. Economic growth and improvements in prosperity all went a long way to dampening the disappointment of twenty-three years of Conservative rule.

Over the course of the 1970s and 1980s, with rising unemployment, significant structural change and a relative decline in the economic fundamentals as measured by GDP growth rates, overseas debt and balance of trade results, the idea of a lucky country—complacency in abundance—gave way to a more sober mood. Although Donald Horne's *The Lucky Country* (1966) captured the mood of the 1960s, Fred Hilmer's *When The Luck Runs Out* (1985), although it sold fewer copies compared with Horne's classic, captured the mood of the late 1980s and predicted that the 1990s would be tough going and more unpredictable than previous periods in the post-war era. This analysis points to the factors that shaped much of the labour movement's outlook in the late 1980s and early 1990s.

Thirdly, over the last decade the trade union movement has been engaged in a number of traumatic battles. The movement has:

- endured the assault of the New Right;
- grappled with the decline in Australia's economic fortunes;
- faced a steady erosion of membership, largely structural; and
- seen the erosion of sustaining ideologies on the far left and the far right of the labour movement; as well as the collapse of the Berlin Wall only a short time after the collapse of the old Movement and Group remnants in the labour movement.

The overall result is a movement lacking confidence in its future directions. Yet it is not a movement standing still, a sandcastle slowly collapsing before an incoming tide. Very substantial structural changes have occurred. New thinking and orientation in trade union activities have developed and found expression in publications like *Australia Reconstructed* (1987), 'The Way Forward' (1989) and 'Future Directions of the Trade Union Movement' (1991).

Those documents and their ideas, debated or unveiled at ACTU Congresses, canvass the need for unions to move away from the old craft orientation towards an industry (or in some cases an occupational) model. Furthermore, they propose that superannuation should be an important social and institutional objective of Australian unionism, nudge the movement towards enterprise negotiations—after an initial period of hostility to the concept—and promote the linkages between education, training, ongoing award restructuring and enterprise negotiation.

The most marked of those challenges has been the creation of twenty large super unions, the result of the various amalgamations that have taken place over the last five years. There is no union unaffected by those changes and the 1993 ACTU Congress was, in some senses, a Congress of the 'children' of its secretary, Bill Kelty— most of the organisations represented at the Congress would not have existed five years earlier. The Communication Workers Union, the

FIMEE, the AMEU and other unions are some of the acronyms of new organisations to make their appearance at the ACTU Congress.

There is, however, considerable irony about some of those developments. The union movement is widely perceived in the community to have never been more responsible. Although the union movement can largely share credit for sustaining the Labor government throughout this period, especially in the 1993 election campaign, there has been a decline in the union movement not only in membership as a percentage of the total workforce, but also in the confidence of its own officials, activists and members.

In another sense, although the union movement has never been better resourced than in this recent period— the sum of membership fees as a percentage of total take home pay is higher than it has ever been—the responsibilities of full-time paid officials must be increased in order for unions to service their members effectively or in order to improve service. A lot of the voluntary activity that used to characterise the union movement has declined during the 1980s and early 1990s. There are many reasons for these trends. Many organisations are experiencing difficulty in maintaining relevance and participation, whether they be Rotary Clubs or Parents and Citizens Associations. But there is also a significant structural and organisational issue that needs to be faced by the union movement.

Four years ago when an assistant secretary of the ACTU decided to quit and move to the private sector, he quipped: 'If you have shares in the union movement, now's the time to sell'. Many people thought at the time that his action was a dramatic indication of disillusionment with the union movement but that his pessimism was unfounded. Some are now wondering what he knew that we didn't. But such an analysis is too pessimistic about the future of the union movement. It is going to be harder for the movement to sustain its position and relevance, particularly given the changes in employment patterns in the Australian workforce—changes that match what is happening around the developed world. Such things as the decline in employment in traditional manufacturing industries, which are highly unionised, will diminish the status of the movement and further reduce its percentage of the total workforce. The iron and steel works in Port Kembla, for example, are at less than one-third of their employment level of fifteen years ago.

As a result the union movement needs to adapt and consider new strategies. Incidentally, there are many comparisons to be drawn between what is happening in Japan and what is happening in Australia. Although it is still common for most unionists and most people to think that there are few similarities between the Japanese and Australian industrial relations systems, it is interesting that there have been common directions and increased convergence in recent years.

At one level, it might be observed that the union movement in Australia, in its representation in the workforce, is very similar to that of Japan. Outside of the large companies and the public service, the union movement is very weakly organised. The peripheral labour force, including part-time and casual employment, is very poorly unionised in both countries. In addition, the peripheral labour force is growing, with the percentage of full-time employees shrinking.

Furthermore, there has been the development of stronger national trade union centres. It is incredible how weak the ACTU was fifteen years ago. Alan Boulton, appointed to the ACTU in early 1978 as its legal officer, was almost not appointed owing to lack of funds. The New South Wales Labor Council offered to pay for the legal officer's position, so poorly resourced was the ACTU. It then only employed a secretary, a president, an assistant secretary, one industrial officer and a librarian, as well as support staff. Now it would employ five or six times as many, and that only tells part of the story. It is obvious from what has already been conveyed that the ACTU's authority has never been greater and the organisation never stronger. Although this growth in centralised union authority parallels that in Japan, a detailed exploration of comparisons between the Australian and Japanese unions is beyond the scope of this chapter.

The Accord discussions from 1979 to 1983 occurred in an atmosphere of scepticism about the viability of what was being proposed. The idea of an Accord fluttered about and fell to obscurity in the 1980 election. The year before had marked the end of the British experiment with a Prices and Incomes policy, the 'winter of discontent' and the defeat of the Callaghan Labour government by Margaret Thatcher's Conservative Party. The possibility that an Australian Accord might keep the lid on wage movements for a time but explode later was one early reservation.

However, the recession of 1981–82 and the industrial problems that occurred, including structural changes and a rise in unemployment, gave impetus to debate about an Australian Accord—discussions that became more intense as the Fraser government in 1982 offered the 'solution' of a six-month wage freeze, voluntary price restraint and a curbing of what it termed 'unlawful union power'. Labor's answer was to create a partnership between the unions and the alternative government—a high-risk political strategy until the election of Bob Hawke as Labor leader while the 1983 election was underway.

One confusing aspect of the evolution of the Accords from 1983 to 1993 is that the demarcation from Mark I onwards to VII was not clear-cut. The president of the ACTU from 1985 to 1990, Simon Crean, liked to refer to the Accord as an evolving Agreement, 'more than a document, it's a state of mind' (a phrase used by the then Treasurer, Paul Keating, in discussions with the ACTU), and resisted media attempts to separate versions of the Accord clearly. Only with the adoption of Accord Mark V did that numbering gain wide currency with subsequent renumbering and conceptualising of earlier 'Accords'.

Union thinking changed over the decade. In 1983 the debate was about 'restoring full indexation'; by 1993 there was no one advocating that course. In 1983, the emphasis and urgency of discussions was about how the trade unions should influence government policy. Today, the emphasis on the various tripartite mechanisms established in the early years of the Accord has considerably diminished. Debate within the movement is more focused on internal changes within the unions, especially on how 'new style unions' might influence bargaining and industrial relations at the company level.

ACTU President Martin Ferguson, in his Presidential Address to the 1993 ACTU Congress, stated hopefully:

> Increasingly, progressive companies are welcoming unions back. They're no longer chanting the old, sterile slogans of the union basher. Because in times of accelerating change, companies have found that a sophisticated union, a truly progressive union, a union with a forward thinking executive, is the best business partner you can have. By no means a sleeping partner, a thinking partner. An active partner, changing companies and structures and approaches and attitudes and services for the better. But the unions we're describing are, of course, new style unions. Unions that have reinvented themselves. Unions that have been as critical of themselves as they have of the companies.

However beautifully appropriate those words describe 'best practice unionism' (another favourite phrase from the early 1990s), the reality remains that the union movement continues to be a mixed bag, consisting of exemplary and mediocre practices.

In many ways, the evolution of the Accord represents a reworking of the Laborist ideal of a partnership between political Labor and industrial labour aimed at:

- providing institutional props supporting each other. An award system and the implicit role of the union movement in updating and policing that system is one example of where regulatory action by government can provide support for the unions;
- ensuring that the social wage issues of interest to the unions,

including Medicare (universal health insurance), child care, child endowment (supplementary payments), and labour market programs (assisting in cushioning the burden of structural adjustment) are given priority in Budget and Cabinet discussions; and

• securing minimum standards of wages and conditions through minimum awards, the regulatory system (including a still-powerful tribunal system), national bodies in the Occupational Health and Safety field, and in the area of equal opportunities.

With respect to industry policy, the union movement is still attracted to the idea without a clear vision of what this means. Unlike the rhetoric at the beginning of the Accord period, it appears that every union document discussing industry policy to come out in the early 1990s is littered with phrases about 'not picking winners'. Furthermore, all agree that the old days of protectionism are over and that tariff walls never did anyone much good. This is policy very much on the defensive.

Recruitment strategies and the development of union services are increasingly debated within the movement. One discussion paper at the 1993 ACTU Congress observed that:

Union recruitment/retention has not kept pace with employment growth. Between 1976 and 1990, unions recruited only seven in every 100 new employees. At a time when the workforce grew by 1 960 400 employees (33.0%) union membership grew by only 146,900 (5.9%). Between 1982 and 1988, union membership *declined* by 31 700. This situation was reversed between 1988 and 1990 when membership increased by almost 5%, with unions recruiting 26 of every 100 new employees.

Between 1990 and 1992, union membership has again fallen by 150 800 or 5.7%, at a time when employment fell by 230 800 or 3.5%. Hence unions suffered heavily in the slower economic conditions losing 65 members for every 100 jobs lost.

Over the period 1976 to 1992, employment rose by 1 804 900 but union membership fell by 3900 and the proportion of employees who were union members fell by 11.4% from 51% to 39.6%. (Emphasis in the original)

It seems likely that there will be a move around the developed world towards the union movement supporting consumer services for its existing and potential members, as well as looking after its traditional producer interests. This orientation can be illustrated by the development by the ACTU and organisations like the Labor Council of New South Wales and the services they provide to attract and retain members. These include salary packaging advice, financial information, banking and insurance products, and discount services. In some senses, this is a return to the cooperative ideal—one of the original motives behind the union movement in Australia and elsewhere. It is a force which diminished with the development of arbitration and state-supported welfare services over this century.

Maybe it is worthwhile noting what is in meant by these developments by referring to Chifley Financial Services in New South Wales. Chifley Financial Services was created by the Labor Council several years ago with a mission not only to provide benefits to members but also to change the orientation of the union movement. It is a move away from asserting that the core business of union movement is industrial relations to saying that the core business is really employee services.

The union movement has, through the 1980s and 1990s, adapted to and, in many cases, heralded major changes: changes in strategy, changes in style, changes in rhetoric, changes in composition and changes in representational power relationships. What good will come from all those changes?

This chapter has noted that in some respects the very economic and circumstantial changes which the union movement has accepted or facilitated have contributed to its own numerical decline. The Accord has placed the industrial wing of the labour movement in an unprecedented position of influence, with considerable benefits for working people. However, the complexity and confusion often associated with the ever-changing wage negotiations have taken many union officials away from their organising function among the rank and file and tied up their time in complex negotiations over 'structural efficiency' improvements and so-called award modernisation.

This, in combination with the dramatic change in the composition of the Australian workforce, has contributed to the recent decline in unionisation. However, it is easy for some within the movement to exaggerate the significance of this point. As Shakespeare's Cassius said to his comrade: 'The fault, dear Brutus, is not in our stars, But in ourselves . . .'

One of the potential disadvantages of the reorganisation of unions into larger conglomerations is the development of cumbersome, more bureaucratic, centralised, and remote institutions. In short, there is potential for the amalgamation process to create large, unresponsive and/or undemocratic unions which appeal less to potential members—a point acknowledged in the ACTU policy document 'The Organisation,

Resources and Services of the Trade Union Movement Strategy' (1991). There is also, in fairness, considerable potential to revitalise union organisation by minimising duplication and freeing up scarce union resources for recruitment in some industries and occupations. The experience is likely to be mixed.

Nonetheless, just as the union movement has adapted to changing circumstances in the past, the recent focus on recruitment and the introduction of innovative financial, legal and other services could, in combination with the enterprise bargaining, demonstrate that unions remain vital and relevant.

The Australian labour movement, through its industrial and political wings and with consultation through the Accord, helped to end the 'political economy' established by the Australian labour movement in the early part of this century. What is significant, however, is not so much the institutional manifestations, but the outcome for the people unions represent. Labor has had a successful recent political history—to the extent that some speak of a Labor hegemony. Many historians fail to recognise that the tremendous pressure of economic change forced on this country during the 1980s was the result of decades of neglect and the maintenance of an inappropriate 'political economy' for the changing post-war circumstances.

During this cathartic period, the union movement has sometimes neglected the tasks of marketing and recruitment. However, the massive changes within its structure have been designed with an eye to the future. Organised labour in this country has not been decimated as in some other Anglo-countries. The vast changes of the 1980s have been accommodated without the massive social dislocation evident under Margaret Thatcher and Ronald Reagan. Political Labor's job is to pursue rational economic changes; industrial labour needs to temper this by understanding its possible impact. The task is to marry economically sensible ideas with a Labor heart—the former and future aim of the Accord processes.

The apparent abandonment of its former ideology, as noted earlier, may prove to be the labour movement's ultimate strength. As political Labor eventually recognised, clinging to outdated ideology will certainly ensure political defeat and numerical decline.

The conclusion about recent Australian experiences is not that the forward march of Labor is halted. The labour movement is not in permanent and unavoidable decline. More than most others, the Australian labour movement is innovatively grappling with new organisational structures and services and exploring the potential of a different kind of labour movement. It is one likely to be less reliant on industrial relations laws and structures, more service-oriented and more like friendly societies. But never just like friendly societies. The union movement is unlikely to lose its important and traditional role of shaping the labour market and organising to maintain industrial fairness.

Bibliography

The following bibliography contains references to works in English dealing with Japanese industrial policy, industrial relations, the labour market, trade unionism, and associated topics including human resource management, general economics and investment relationships between Australia and Japan. Works in Japanese were included if given particular attention by the authors included in this volume.

References to internal, comparative and external studies of Japanese industrial policy and labour markets are included.

A number in square brackets following the reference indicates that the work was felt (by an individual author) to have particular relevance to their own chapter.

The bibliography is divided into three sections as follows:

1 *Australia–Japan*
   Specifically deals with comparative studies of Japan and Australia, or studies carried out by Australian researchers on relevant Japanese topics.

2 *General works: Japan*
   Includes some comparative studies of Japan and countries other than Australia.

3 *General works: Australia*
   This list is limited to studies recommended by the contributors to this book.

Material included in this bibliography substantially post-dates 1983 and is meant to serve as an update of the Australian Department of Industrial Relations' *Japanese Employment and Employee Relations—An Annotated Bibliography* (AGPS, Canberra, 1984). This publication is quite comprehensive, covering material published during the years 1970 to 1983. Journals and serials used in the compilation of that work are listed in the appendix accompanying the current bibliography.

This present bibliography includes not only published works, but also references to unpublished theses and dissertations as taken from the following sources:

* Bishop, E. 1972, *Australian Theses on Asia: A Union List of Higher Degree Theses accepted by Australian Universities to 31 December 1970*, Canberra, [Supplement, 1975].

* *Union List of Higher Degree Theses in Australian University Libraries: Cumulative Edition to 1965*, Hobart 1967. [Supplements 1966–74, Hobart 1971–76].

* *Australian Association of Asian Studies Review* (1977–92). Contains an annual listing of Australian theses and dissertations on Asian subjects. It should be noted that some of the items listed therein (and cited below) are works-in-progress.

It should be noted that in regards to 'Industrial Policy' as applied within this bibliography, the term may refer to (i) government policy towards industry and industrial growth, or (ii) government or private company policy with regards to industrial relations.

The present Australia–Japan section of the bibliography could be further divided into four subject-related sections, as follows:

1   Industrial relations, labour markets, unions, etc. (38%)
2   Management (20%)
3   Economic issues (24%)
4   Non-specific Australia–Japan relationships and comparative studies (18%)

It should be noted that this bibliography also functions as a source of references cited by individual authors in their respective chapters.

Abbreviations

AIRAANZ	Association of Industrial Relations Academics of Australia and New Zealand
AGPS	Australian Government Publications Service
ANU	Australian National University
BIE	Bureau of Industrial Economics
CEDA	Committee for Economic Development of Australia
ILO	International Labour Organisation
JACE	Japan Association of Corporate Executives
JIL	Japan Institute of Labor
MITI	Ministry of International Trade and Industry
OECD	Organisation for Economic Cooperation and Development
UNSW	University of New South Wales

1 Australia–Japan

Access Economics 1991, *Japanese Investment in Australia: a report prepared for the Australia–Japan Foundation*, Barton.

Akaneya, T. 1987, *The Development of Post-war Japan-Australia Relations and the Impact of Declining American Hegemony*, Pacific Economic Papers, No. 153, Australia–Japan Research Centre, ANU, Canberra.

Atkinson, J.M. 1978, Aspects of the Development of Anglo-Japanese Commercial Relations 1856–1899, MA thesis, Department of History, University of New England.

Australia–Japan Economic Institute, *Newsletter*, 1981- , Sydney.

Australia-Japan Research Centre 1989, *The Australia–Japan Relationship: Towards the Year 2000*, ANU, Canberra.

Bamber, G., Howell, F. & Shadur, M.A. 1990, 'To what extent are Japanese management styles transferable to Australia?', in *Current Research in Industrial Relations*, 5th AIRAANZ Conference Proceedings, ed. G. Griffin, University of New South Wales, Kensington, pp. 169–91.

Barker, S. 1982, Tsukiai and the Japanese white collar employee, BA(Hons) thesis, Japanese Department, Monash University.

Batliwalla, S.B. 1979, An examination of manpower planning in Japanese multinational firms in Australia, MBA thesis, University of Queensland.

Best, O.A. 1989, Japanese Management in the Telecommunications Industry, MBA thesis, Department of Management, University of Queensland.

BIE 1987, *North–East Asia and Australia: Economic Relations*, Bureau of Industry Economics, Department of Industry, Technology and Commerce, AGPS, Canberra.

Boyles, C. 1981, *Issues in the Study of Japanese and Australian Labour Markets: A Seminar Report*, Research Paper no. 76, Australia–Japan Research Centre, ANU, Canberra.

Broadbent, K.J. 1990, A comparative case study between an Industrial Federation in Australia and Japan, PhD thesis, Commerce and Administration, Griffith University.

Buxey, G. & Petzall, S. 1991, 'Australian Automobile Industry: JIT [Just in time] Production and Labour Relations', *Industrial Magazine and Data Systems*, vol. 91, no. 1, pp. 8–16.

Butlin, N.G. 1984, *Select Comparative Economic Statistics 1900–1940: Australia, Britain, Canada, Japan, New Zealand and USA*, Source Paper no. 4, ANU, Canberra, December.

CEDA & JACE 1989, *Labour-Management Relations, Australia and Japan: A Comparative Study*, Committee for Economic Development of Australia and the Japan Association of Corporate Executives, Research Study P33, Sydney.

Chalmers, N.J. 1981, *Japanese Perspectives on Australian Industrial Relations*, Research Paper No 16, Centre for the Study of Australian–Asian Relations, Griffith University.

Crawford, J.G. & Okita, S. 1976, *Australia, Japan and Western Pacific Economic Relations: A Report to the Governments of Australia and Japan*, AGPS, Canberra.

Das, A. 1991, The managerial practices of Japanese firms in their domestic and international environment, BA(Hons) thesis, Division of Asian and International Studies, Griffith University.

Dedoussis, E. 1990, Japanese-style management: Adaptation to a foreign environment, PhD thesis, Commerce and Administration, Griffith University.

Drysdale, P. & Tsukuda, C. 1989, *Long-Run Adjustment of the Japanese Iron and Steel Industry and its Implications for Australia: An Overview*, Pacific Economic Papers no. 176, Australia-Japan Research Centre, ANU, Canberra, October.

Easson, M. 1992, 'Matching the Wattle with the Chrysanthemum: Comparisons between Australian and Japanese Unions', in *What Should Unions Do?*, eds M. Crosby and M. Easson, Pluto Press, Sydney, pp. 97–149.

Edgington, D.W. 1990, *Japanese Business Downunder: Patterns of Japanese Investment in Australia*, Routledge, London.

Ford, W.G. 1986, 'Learning from Japan: the concept of skill formation', *Australian Bulletin of Labour*, vol. 12, no. 2, March, pp. 119–27.

—— 1986, 'Cross-cultural differences in enterprise skill formation: can Australia learn from Japan?', *Economic and Industrial Democracy*, vol. 7, no. 2, May, pp. 205–13.

—— 1986, 'The concept of skill formation: perspective', *Engineers Australia*, vol. 58, no. 13, July, pp. 40–3.

—— 1988, 'Reconstruction and skill formation: developing discussions on concurrent and integrated changes', *Unicorn*, vol. 14, no. 4, November, pp. 208–18.

Forster, C. 1981, 'Australian and Japanese economic development', in *Japan & Australia: Two societies and their interaction,* eds P. Drysdale & Hironobu Kitaôji , Australian National University Press, Canberra, pp. 49–75. [2]

Garnaut, R. 1989, *Australia and the Northeast Asian Ascendancy*, AGPS, Canberra.

Goddard, I. 1992, An analysis of Japanese and Australian Management, MBA thesis, Graduate School of Management, University of Queensland.

Graves, A. 1978, Women's wage differentials: Australia, Japan, Taiwan—a comparative study, BA(Hons) thesis, Modern Asian Studies, Griffith University.

Gregory, R.G. & Foster, W.F. 1982, *A preliminary look at some labour market dynamics in Australia, Japan and North America*, Discussion Paper no. 52, Centre for Economic Policy Research, ANU, Canberra.

Griffiths, A. 1990, Fordism and Flexibility: Australia, Italy and Japan, BA(Hons) thesis, Humanities, Griffith University.

Grimm, R.J. 1980, A comparison of Japanese and Australian companies with respect to the duties and powers of their offices and members, LLM thesis, Monash University.

Hanami, T. & Blanpain, R. (eds) 1989, *Industrial Conflict Resolution in Market Economies—A Study of Australia, the Federal Republic of Germany, Italy, Japan and the USA*, 2nd edn, Kluwer, Deventer.

Hancock, K., Sano, Y., Chapman, B. & Fayle, P. (eds) 1983, *Japanese and Australian Labour Markets: A Comparative Study*, Pacific Economic Papers no. 99, Australia–Japan Research Centre, ANU, Canberra.

Hawke, B. 1982, Economic and trade relations, industrial relations and Australia's trade with Japan, Australia-Japan Relations Symposium: Stocktaking and the Future, AJRS, Melbourne.

Henderson, A.G. 1985, *Japanese and Australian Labour Markets: A Comparison of their Institutions, Structure and Performance*, Pacific Economic Papers no. 119, Australia–Japan Research Centre, ANU, Canberra, February.

—— 1985, 'A Comparison of Japanese and Australian Labour Markets', *Australian Bulletin of Labour*, vol. 12, no. 1, December, pp. 22–45.

—— 1985, 'A Comparison of Japanese and Australian Labour Markets: Flexibility versus Rigidity', *Institute of Public Affairs Review*, vol. 39, no. 2, Spring, pp. 14–16.

Hildebrand, D. 1987, *A Comparative Reappraisal of Japanese and Australian Industrial Disputes*, Working Paper no. 9, Japanese Studies Centre, Monash University, Clayton.

Howell, F.M.E. 1990, Japanese and Australian management practice: a case study of the Daikyo Group in Australia, MBA thesis, Management, University of Queensland.

Iida, T. 1983, 'Transferability of Japanese management systems and practices into Australian companies', *Human Resource Management Australia*, vol. 21, no. 3, pp. 23–27.

—— 1985, The relationship between management systems and organisational problems in Australia-based Japanese subsidiaries, PhD thesis, La Trobe University.

Ishida, H. 1983, 'Industrial Relations in Japan', in *Japanese and Australian Labour Markets: A Comparative Study*, eds K. Hancock, Y. Sano, B. Chapman & P. Fayle, Australia–Japan Research Centre, ANU, Canberra.

Jamieson, G.J. 1979, Management and culture: a study of the quality of work life in a subsidiary of a Japanese company operating in Australia, BA(Hons) thesis, Economics, University of Melbourne.

Japanese Studies Association of Australia, *Newsletter*, 1981– .

Kawaguchi, A. 1990, Australian and Japanese Labour Markets: A Comparative Study, PhD thesis, AJRC, Research School of Pacific Studies and Research School of Social Sciences, ANU.

Kelso, A. 1992, The Japanisation of Australia, MIntS thesis, GPA, University of Sydney.

Kojima, K. 1982, *A Perspective of the Australian Economy: A Japanese View*, Research Paper no. 91, Australia–Japan Research Centre, ANU, Canberra.

Kriegler, R. 1984, *Japanese Personnel Practices in Australia: The Case of Mitsubishi Motors*, National Institute of Labour Studies, Working Papers Series.

Kriegler, R. & Wooden, M. 1985, 'Japanese management practices in Australia: The case of Mitsubishi', *Work and People*, vol. 11, no. 1, pp. 3–8.

Kuwahara, Y. 1987, 'Japanese Industrial Relations', in International and Comparative Industrial Relations, eds G. Bamber & R. Lansbury, Allen & Unwin, Sydney, pp. 211–31.

Lockwood, R. 1987, *War on the Waterfront: Menzies, Japan and the Pig-iron Dispute*, Hale & Iremonger, Sydney.

McCormack, G. (ed) 1991, *Bonsai Australia Bonsai: Multi-function polis and the making of a special relationship with Japan*, Pluto Press, Leichhardt.

McMahon, P.L. 1986, 'An Internal Comparison of Labour Force Participation 1977–1984', *Monthly Labour Review*, vol. 109, no. 5, May, pp. 3–12.

Middleton, J. 1987, A case study of the operations of an Australian corporation in Japan, BA(Hons) thesis, Japanese, Monash University.

Mortenson, W. 1988, Japanese Work Practices and Four Australian Companies—A Case Study of Learning from Abroad, unpublished, CEDA (Centre for Economic Development of Australia).

Namai, K. 1983, The Australian–Japan Commerce Agreement 1957 and its Australian background, MEc thesis, Government, University of Sydney.

Ohtomo, H. 1979, Early Australian–Japanese Relations to Federation, MA thesis, History, University of Queensland.

Pethiyagoda, C. 1991, Japanese manufacturing management techniques and the possibility of applying these technologies in Australian manufacturing industry, MBA thesis, Graduate School of Management, Monash University.

Purcell, W.R. 1978, *The nature and extent of Japanese commercial interests in Australia 1932–41*, Research Paper no. 53, Australia–Japan Economic Relations Unit, ANU, Canberra.

—— 1981, 'The Development of Japan's Trading Company Network in Australia 1890–1941', *Australian Economic History Review*, vol. 21, no. 2.

—— 1982, Japanese–Australian economic and commercial relations 1932-41, PhD thesis, Economic History, UNSW.

Rix, A. 1984, *Australia and Most-favoured Nation Treatment for Japan, 1947–55*, Pacific Economic Papers no. 115, Australia–Japan Research Centre, ANU, Canberra, November.

—— 1983, *Coming to Terms: The Politics of Australia's Trade with Japan 1945–1957*, Allen & Unwin, Sydney.

Sasaki, M. 1977, Recognition and enforcement of foreign awards in Japan and Australia, LLM thesis, Monash University.

Schultze, C.L. 1984, 'Industrial Policy: A Dissent', *Australian Bulletin of Labour*, vol. 10, no. 3, June, pp. 134–43.

Sekine, M. 1992, 'Labor Problems in Australia', in *The Australian Economy in the Japanese Mirror*, ed. K. Sheridan, University of Queensland Press, St Lucia, pp. 65–91.

Sheridan, K. (ed.) 1992, *The Australian Economy in the Japanese Mirror*, University of Queensland Press, St Lucia.

Shore, W.J. 1992, The debate on foreign labourers in Japan and its relationship to the structure of Japanese Studies, BA(Hons) thesis, Asian Studies, University of Adelaide.

Smith, G. 1991, 'Contending interests in the supply of Australian coal to the world market', *Australian Quarterly*, vol. 63, no. 2, Winter, pp. 143–50.

Squires, J. 1978, Development of Japanese attitudes to the Australian region 1918–45, PhD thesis, History, University of Queensland.

Stening, B.W. 1979, Interpersonal perceptions of expatriate and local managers in Australian subsidiaries of Japanese corporations, PhD thesis, Department of Organisational Behaviour, UNSW.

Stockwin, J.A.A.1972, *Japan and Australia in the Seventies*, Angus & Robertson, Sydney.

Sugimoto, Y. 1977, 'Comparative Analysis of Industrial Conflict in Australia and Japan', in *Sharpening the Focus*, ed. R.D. Walton, School of Modern Asian Studies, Griffith University.

Townsend, L.C. 1984, 'Japanese labour relations and Australian [vehicle manufacturing] industry', *Human Resource Management Australia*, vol. 22, no. 3, August, pp. 26–28.

—— 1984, Japanese labour relations and Australian [vehicle manufacturing] industry, *SAE Australia*, vol. 44, no. 5, Sept– Oct, pp. 218–20.

Tsokhas, K. 1988, *The Wool Industry and the 1936 Trade Diversion Dispute Between Australia and Japan*, Working Papers in Economic History no. 109, ANU, Canberra.

Ungerer, C. 1992, The effect of Japanese MCN activity in Australia on the manufacturing industry, MA(CW) thesis, Division of Asian and International Studies, Griffith University.

Utick, S.E. 1988, *Japan: how to make collaboration work: a study with special reference to pre-competitive research and development*, Department of Industry, Technology and Commerce, AGPS, Canberra.

Wheelwright, T. 1991, 'Labour and Globilisation Down Under', *Pacific Basin Studies Review*, vol. 2, no. 1, pp. 2–4.

Williams, L. 1989, Australian-Japan relations: the case of Belmont-Adachi, BA(Hons) thesis, University of Western Australia.

Williams-Wynn, M. 1989, *Japanese Management Practices and their Relevance to Australia*, Committee for Economic Development of Australia (CEDA), Public Information Pamphlet no. 22, May.

Withers, G. 1986, 'Australian wages and labour market adjustment: a comparative international assessment', in *Wage Fixation in Australia*, ed. J. Niland, Allen & Unwin, Sydney, pp. 243–55.

Yamaguchi, J.T. 1986, 'Acculturation and alienation of the expatriate managers of Japanese firms in Australia', in *The Enterprise and*

Management in East Asia, eds S.R. Clegg, D.C. Dunphy & S.G. Redding, Centre of Asian Studies, University of Hong Kong, pp. 413–41.

Yano, Y. 1982, Japanese labour in Australia 1880–1914, BA(Hons) thesis, Economic History, UNSW.

—— 1984, Japan–Australia relations and Japanese labour in Australia circa 1870–1914, MA thesis, Economic History, UNSW.

—— 1986, Japanese labour immigration to Australia during the 1890s, MComm(Hons) thesis, Economic History, UNSW.

Yasuba, Y. 1985, *The Japanese Economy and Economic Policy in the 1930s*, Working Papers in Economic History no. 52, ANU, Canberra.

Yoshimitsu, K. 1982, Communication patterns adopted by a Japanese trading company in Melbourne, MA thesis, Japanese, Monash University.

2 General: Japan

Abe, K. 1979, Comparisons of the productivity of manufacturing industries in the United Kingdom, Japan and the United States for the period 1964–75, PhD thesis, University of Liverpool.

Abegglen, J.C. 1958, *The Japanese Factory: Aspects of Its Social Organisation*, Free Press, Illinois. [4]

Abegglen, J.C. & Stalk, G. Jr. 1985, *Kaisha: Japanese Corporation*, Basic Books, New York. [6]

Ackroyd, S., Burrell, G., Hughes, M. & Whitaker, A. 1988, 'The Japanisation of British Industry', *Industrial Relations Journal*, vol. 19, no. 1, pp. 11–23.

Adams, F.G. & Ichimura, S. 1983, 'Industrial Policy in Japan', in *Industrial Policies for Growth and Competitiveness*, eds F.G. Adams, & L.R. Klein, Lexington Books, Lexington, pp. 307–23.

Aganon, M.E. 1982, *Transfer of Japanese Industrial Relations Practices: The Case of Japanese Joint Venture Enterprises in the Philippines. A Socio-economic Exploration*, Institute of Social Studies, The Hague.

Akio, M. 1992, 'A critical moment for Japanese management', *Japan Echo*, vol. 19, no. 2, Summer, pp. 8–14. [Written by the chairman of Sony]

Allen, G. 1981, 'Japan', in *Trade Unions in the Developed Economies*, ed. E. Owen-Smith, Croom Helm, London.

Allen, M. 1991, Stories from the Coal Mouth: An Ethnographic Account of a Japanese Coalmining Community's Past and Present, PhD thesis, Anthropology, University of Sydney.

Alston, J.P. 1985, *The American Samurai: Blending American and Japanese Managerial Practices*, Walter de Gruyter, Berlin.

Amante, M.S.V., Aganon, M.E. & Ofreneo, R.E. 1992, *Japanese Industrial Relations Interface in the Philippines*, School of Labor and Industrial Relations, University of the Philippines, Quezon City.

Amaya, T. 1990, *Recent Trends in Human Resource Management*, Japanese Industrial Relations Series no. 17, Japan Institute of Labour, Tokyo.

Ando, Yoshio 1975, *Kindai Nippon Keizai-shi Yôran* [Selected Materials of Modern Japanese Economics], (2nd edition), Tokyo University Press, Tokyo (in Japanese). [2]

Ayusawa, Iwao 1966, *A History of Labor in Modern Japan*, East-West Centre, Honolulu.

Ballon, R. 1969, *The Japanese Employee*, Charles E. Tuttle, Rutland.

Bamber, G.J. 1988, 'Japanisation, excellence and new technology: some cautionary comments based on comparative studies of industrial relations and organisational behaviour', *Management Research News*, vol. 11, no. 1&2, pp. 57–59.

Beck, J.C. 1989, The change of a lifetime: individuals, organisations and environment in Japan's employment system, PhD thesis, Organisational Behaviour, Harvard University.

Bergmann, J. & Shigeyoshi, T. 1987, *Economic and Social Aspects of Industrial Relations: a comparison of the German and Japanese systems*, Campus Press, Frankfurt. [6]

Bethlehem Steel, 1983, *Japanese Government Promotion of the Steel Industry: Three Decades of Industrial Policy*, Bethlehem Steel Co. Washington.

Boswell, D. 1991, Converting judgements to settlements: dispute resolution in post-war Japan, BA(Hons) thesis, East Asian Studies, University of Sydney.

Bosworth, D. & Westaway, T. 1987, 'Labour hoarding, discouraged workers and recorded unemployment: an international comparison', *Australian Bulletin of Labour*, vol. 13, no. 3, June, pp. 143–61.

Bowen, D. 1986, The role of technology in modern [Japanese] industrial policy, MA thesis, Modern Asian Studies, Griffith University.

Bradshaw, N. 1989, Current trends in the sub-contracting system of Japan's automobile industry, BA(Hons) thesis, Asian Studies, University of Adelaide.

Bray, M. 1992, *Literature Review of Decentralised Bargaining in the USA, Canada and Japan, Workplace Bargaining in the International Perspective*, ACIRRT and Commonwealth Department of Industrial Relations, AGPS, Canberra.

Briggs, P. 1988, 'The Japanese at Work: Illusions of the Ideal', *Industrial Relations Journal*, vol. 19, no. 1, pp. 24–30.

Broadbent, K. 1987, The development of Zenmin Rokyo and the effect on the labour movement and political parties [in Japan], BA(Hons) thesis, Modern Asian Studies, Griffith University.

—— 1992, Flexibility and work in the [Japanese] retail industry, PhD thesis, Division of Asian and International Studies, Griffith University.

Broadbridge, S. 1966, *Industrial Dualism in Japan*, Frank Cass & Co. London.

Brunello, G. & Wadhwani, S. 1989, *The Determinants of Wage Determination in Japan: Some Lessons from a Comparison with the United Kingdom using Micro-data*, Working Paper no. 1116, Centre for Labour Economics, London School of Economics and Political Science.

Castelvetere, T. 1990, Labour in occupied Japan, PhD thesis, Department of History, Latrobe University.

Caves, R.E. & Uekusa, M. 1976, *Industrial Organization in Japan*, Brookings Institution, Washington.

Chalmers, N.J. 1989, *Industrial Relations in Japan—The Peripheral Workforce*, Nissan Institute/Routledge Japanese Studies Series, Routledge, London.

Chalmers, S. 1991, *Perceptions of Women in the Japanese Workforce: Gender and Work*, PhD, Division of Asian and International Studies, Griffith University.

Chamswasdi, R. 1991, Japanese Manufacturing Techniques, MBA thesis, Graduate School of Management, University of Queensland.

Chick, M. (ed) 1990, *Government, Industries, and Markets: Aspects of Government–Industry Relations in the United Kingdom, Japan, West Germany and the USA since 1945*, Aldershot, Hants.

Clark, R. 1979, *The Japanese Company*, Yale University Press, New Haven.

Clegg, S.R., Dunphy, D.C. & Redding, S.G. (eds) 1986, *The Enterprise and Management in East Asia*, Centre of Asian Studies, University of Hong Kong, Hong Kong.

Clegg, S.R., Higgins, W. & Spybey, T. 1990, '"Post-Confucianism", Social Democracy and Economic Culture', in *Capitalism in Contrasting Cultures*, eds S.R. Clegg, S.G. Redding, S.G. & M. Cartner, Walter de Gruyter, Berlin, pp. 31–78.

Cole, Robert E. 1971, *Japanese Blue Collar—The Changing Tradition*, University of California Press, Berkeley.

—— 1984, 'Diffusion of participatory work structures in Japan, Sweden and the United States', in *Change in Organizations: New Perspectives* on *Theory, Research and Practice*, ed. P.S. Goodman, Jossey-Bass, San Francisco.

—— 1971, 'The Theory of Institutionalization: Permanent Employment and Tradition in Japan', *Economic Development and Cultural Change*, no. 20 (October), pp. 47–70. [2]

Committee for the Study of Labor Issues 1993, *Choices for Reform and Renewal—Nikkeiren Position Paper 1993*, Committee for the Study of Labor Issues—Japan Federation of Employers' Associations (Nikkeiren), Tokyo. [10]

Cook, A. H. 1966, Japanese Trade Unionism, Cornell University Press, Ithaca.

Cook, A.H., Levine, S.B. & Mitsufuji, T. 1971, *Public Employee Labor Relations in Japan: Three Aspects*, Institute of Labor and Industrial Relations, University of Michigan, Ann Arbor. [Includes three separate articles 1. Industrial Relations in the Public Sector in Japan; 2. Labor Relations and Local Government in Japan; 3. Teacher Unionism in Japan.]

Crawcour, S. 1978, 'The Japanese Employment System', *Journal of Japanese Studies*, vol. 4, no. 2. [4]

Deutschmann, C. 1987, 'Economic restructuring and company unionism: the Japanese model', *Economic and Industrial Democracy*, vol. 8, no. 4, November, pp. 463–88.

Dore, R.P. 1973, *British Factory, Japanese Factory: the Origins of National Diversity in Industrial Relations*, Allen & Unwin, London. [2] [4] [6]

—— 1986, *Flexible Rigidities: Industrial Policy and Structural Adjustment in the Japanese Economy 1970–80*, Athlone Press, London.

Dore, R.P., Bounine-Cabale, J. & Tapiola, K. 1989, *Japan at Work: Markets, Management and Flexibility*, OECD, Paris.

Dore, R.P. & Sako, M. 1990, *How the Japanese Learn to Work*, Routledge, London.

Dunkley, G. 1988, *The Japanese Social Contract, 1974–1980*, Research Paper no. 3, John Reid Faculty of Business, Footscray Institute of Technology.

Dunphy, D.C. 1986, 'An historical review of the literature on the Japanese enterprise and its management', in *The Enterprise and Management in East Asia*, eds S.R. Clegg, D.C. Dunphy & S. Gordon Redding, Centre for Asian Studies, University of Hong Kong, pp. 343–68.

Dunphy, D.C. & Stenning, B. 1984, *Japanese Organisation Behaviour and Management: An Annotated Bibliography*, Asian Research Press, Hong Kong.

Dunning, J. 1986, *Japanese Participation in British Industry*, Croom Helm, London.

Eisenstadt, S.N. & Eyal, B. 1990, *Japanese Models of Conflict Resolution*, K. Paul International, London.

Ferber, M.A. 1987, *Women and Work: Paid and Unpaid. A Select Annotated Bibliography*, Garland, New York.

Ford, W.G., Easther, M. & Brewer, A. 1984, *Japanese Employment and Employee Relations—An Annotated Bibliography*, Department of Employment and Industrial Relations, AGPS, Canberra.

Freeman, R.B. & Weitzman, M.L. 1986, *Bonuses and Employment in Japan*, Working Paper no. 1878, National Bureau of Economic Research, Cambridge, Massachussets.

Friedman, D. 1988, *The Misunderstood Miracle: Industrial Development and Political Change in Japan*, Cornell University Press, Ithaca US.

Fucini, J.J. & Fucini, S. 1990, *Working for the Japanese*, Free Press, New York [6]

Fujita, Y. 1984, *Employee Benefits and Industrial Relations*, Japanese Industrial Relations Series no. 12, Japan Institute of Labor, Tokyo.

Fuke, H. 1977, Japanese and British telecommunications system: a comparative industrial relations analysis, MLitt thesis, University of Glasgow.

Fukuzawa, Yukichi 1931, *Bunmei-ron no gairyaku [Essence of Study on Civilization]*, Iwanamishoten (Bunko), Tokyo. [2]

Furstenberg, F. 1984, 'Japanese industrial relations from a Western European perspective', *Work and People*, vol. 12, no. 2, pp. 11–14.

Garon, S. 1987, *The State and Labor in Modern Japan*, University of California Press, Berkeley.

Garrahan, P. 1986, 'Nissan in the North East of England', *Capital and Class*, no. 27.

George, A. 1980. Farmers and politics: the political role of the Japanese agricultural co-operative unions, PhD thesis, Political Science, ANU, Canberra.

Giesecke, T. 1985, 'Industrial relations and management in Japan: other views', *Work and People*, vol. 11, no. 3, pp. 21–26.

Gordon, A.D. 1981, Workers, managers and bureaucrats in Japan: labor relations in heavy industry 1853–1945, PhD thesis, Harvard University [University Microfilms International, Ann Arbor, 1981].

—— 1985, *The Evolution of Labor Relations in Japan: Heavy Industry, 1853–1955*, Council on East Asian Studies, Harvard University, Cambridge (Mass.). [2] [4] [6]

Gordon, A.D., Ellington, L. & Rice, R. 1990, 'Japan Labor Relations During the Twentieth Century', *Journal of Labor Research*, vol. 11, no. 3, pp. 239–52.

Gordon, D.D. 1988, *Japanese Management in America and Britain: Revelation or Requiem for Western Industrial Democracy*, Gower, Aldershot.

Gordon, R.J. 1982, 'Why US wage and employment behaviour differs from that in Britain and Japan', *Economic Journal*, no. 92, March, pp. 13–44.

Gould, W.B. 1984, *Japan's Reshaping of American Labor Law*, MIT Press, Cambridge.

Graham, I. 1988, 'Japanisation as Mythology', *Industrial Relations Journal*, vol. 19, no. 1, pp. 69–75.

Hamada, K. & Kurosaka, Y. 1983, *The Relationship between Production and Unemployment in Japan*, International Seminar on Macroeconomics, Maison des sciences de l'homme, Paris.

Hanami, T. 1979, *Labor Relations in Japan*, Kodansha International, Tokyo. [6]

—— 1985, *Labor Law and Industrial Relations in Japan*, Kluwer Law and Taxation, Deventer.

—— 1989, 'Japan—Conflict Resolution in Industrial Relations', in *Industrial Conflict Resolution in Market Economies—A Study of Australia, the Federal Republic of Germany, Italy, Japan and the USA*, 2nd edn, eds T. Hanami & R. Blanpain, Kluwer, Deventer, pp. 203–15.

—— 1991, *American Enterprise in Japan*, State University of New York Press, Albany.

Hanley, S.B. & Yamamura, Kozo 1977, *Economic and Demographic Change in Preindustrial Japan 1600–1868*, Princeton University Press, Princeton (New Jersey). [2]

Harada, S. 1928, *Labor Conditions in Japan*, Columbia University Press, New York.

Hayashi, K. 1989, 'Cross-cultural interface management: the case of Japanese firms abroad', *Japanese Economic Studies*, no. 15, p. 341.

Hirschmeier, J. & Yui, Tsunehiko 1981, *The Development of Japanese Business 1600–1980*, 2nd edn, Allen & Unwin, London. [2]

Horie, Yasuzô 1968, *Nippon Keizaishi Dokuhon [Reading of Japanese economic history]*, Tôyôkeizai-shinpôsha, Tokyo. [2]

Hosomi, T. & Okumura, A. 1982, 'Japanese Industrial Policy', in *National Industrial Strategies and the World Economy*, ed. J. Pinder, Allanhead, Osmun & Co. New Jersey.

IIRA 1983, *Viability of the Japanese Model of Industrial Relations*, paper no. 5, International Industrial Relations Association, 6th World Conference, Kyoto.

ILO 1982, *Labor Relations and Development: Country Studies on Japan, the Phillipines, Singapore and Sri Lanka*, International Labour Office, Geneva.

Imai, M. 1986, *Kaizen—the Key to Japan's Competitive Success*, McGraw-Hill, New York.

Imaoka, H. 1989, 'Japanese corporate employment and personnel systems and their transfer for Japanese affiliates in Asia', *The Developing Economies*, no. 27, December, pp. 407–25.

Inagami, T. 1988, *Japanese Workplace Industrial Relations*, Japan Institute of Labour, Tokyo.

Inoue, Kiyoshi 1963, *Nippon no Rekishi [History of Japan]*, vol. 1, Iwanami-shoten (Shinsho), Tokyo. [2]

——, 1965, *Nippon no Rekishi [History of Japan]*, vol. 2, Iwanami-shoten (Shinsho), Tokyo. [2]

Ishida, H. 1981, 'Human Resources Management in Overseas Japanese Firms', *Japanese Economic Studies*, no. 10, pp. 53–79.

—— 1986, 'Transferability of Japanese Human Resource Management Abroad', *Human Resource Management*, vol. 25, no. 1, pp. 103–20.

Iwata, R. 1982, *Japanese-style Management: Its Foundations and Prospects*, Asian Productivity Organisation, Tokyo.

Iyori, H. 1986, 'Antitrust and Industrial Policy in Japan: Competition and Cooperation', in *Law and Trade Issues of the Japanese Economy: American and Japanese Perspectives*, eds G.R. Saxonhouse & K. Yamamura, University of Washington Press, Washington.

Japan Foreign Press Centre 1978, *Labour Problems and Industrial Relations*, Foreign Press Centre, Tokyo.

Japan Institute of Labour 1993, 'Employment Practices at Crossroads— Managers Asked to Retire Early', *Japan Labour Bulletin*, March. [10]

Japan Institute of Labour 1991 [1933], *Labour–Management Relations in Japan [Nihon no roshi kankei]*, Japan Institute of Labour, Tokyo. [10]

Japan Productivity Centre 1985, *In search of a new industrial relations model: summary of 1984 white paper on labour movement relations*, Asian Productivity Organisation, Monograph Series no. 6, Tokyo.

Japanese Economic Studies, [journal], 1971– .

JIL 1967, *Labor Relations in the Asian Countries: Proceedings of the 2nd International Conference on Industrial Relations*, Japan Institute of Labor, Tokyo.

——, *Japan Labor Bulletin*, Japan Institute of Labor, Tokyo.

——, *Japanese Industrial Relations Series*, Japan Institute of Labor, Tokyo, 1979-1990.

    1   Employment and Employment Policy, 1979 (1983)

    2   Labor Unions and Labor-Management Relations, 1979 (1983)

    3   Wages and Hours of Work, 1979

    4   Labor and the Economy Illustrated, 1980

    5   Social Security, 1980

6   The Japanese Employment System, 1980
7   Vocational Training, 1981
8   Problems of Working Women, 1981
9   Industrial Safety and Health, 1982
10   Human Resource Development in Industry, 1983
11   Labor-Management Communication at the Workshop Level, 1983
12   Employee Benefits and Industrial Relations, 1984
13   Technological Innovation and Industrial Relations, 1985
14   Japanese Workplace Industrial Relations, 1988
15   Shunto Wage Offensive: Historical Overview and perspective, 1989
16   Industrial Relations System in Japan: A New Interpretation, 1989
17   Recent Trends in Human Resource Management, 1990.

—— 1983–88, *Highlights in Japanese Industrial Relations: a selection of articles from the Japan Labor Bulletin*, Japan Institute of Labor, Tokyo, 1983-88.

——1984– , *Japanese Working Life Profile*, Japan Institute of Labor, Tokyo.

—— 1989, *Searching for a New System in Industrial Relations*, Japan Institute of Labour, Tokyo.

—— 1991, *Labor–Management Relations in Japan*, Japan Institute of Labor, Tokyo.

Johnson, C. 1982, *MITI and the Japanese Miracle: The Growth of Japanese Industrial Policy, 1925 to 1975*, Stanford University Press, Stanford.

—— 1988, 'Japanese–Style Management in America', *California Management Review*, Reprint Series, vol. 30, no. 4.

Kamata, S. 1983, *Japan in the Passing Lane: An Insider's Account of Life in a Japanese Auto Factory*, Allen & Unwin, London.

Kameyama, N. 1993, 'Japanese-style Employment Practices at a Turning Point?', in *Japan Labour Bulletin*, June. [10]

Kassalow, E.M. 1983, 'Japan as an industrial relations model', *Journal of Industrial Relations*, vol. 25, no. 2, pp. 201–19.

Katayama, S. 1976, *The Labor Movement in Japan*, Slienger, London.

Kawada, H. 'Industrial Relations in Japan', *Indian Journal of Industrial Relations*, vol. 1, no. 2, October, pp. 195–207.

Kawanishi, H.J. 1992, *Enterprise Unionism in Japan*, Kegan Paul International, London, New York. [6]

Kendrick, D.M. 1988, *The Success of Competitive-Communism in Japan*, Macmillan, Basingstoke.

Kenny, M. & Florida, R. 1988, 'Beyond Mass Production: Production and the Labor Process in Japan', *Politics and Society*, vol. 16, no. 1, March.

Kim, Y. 1986, 'Social Factors of Japanese Industrial Policy', *Asian Profile*, vol. 14, no. 2, April, pp. 129–32.

Kiyokawa, Yukihiko 1986, 'Seiô seishi gijutu no dônyû-teichaku [The introduction of western silk reeling technology and the permeation and establishment of factory system]', *Economic Review* (Japan), vol. 37, no. 3, pp. 234–47. [2]

Koike, K. 1977, Sho*kuba no rôdôkumiai to sanka: rôshikankei no nichibei hikaku* [Trade unions and participation: A comparative study of the industrial relations between Japan and the USA], Tôyôkeizai-shinpôsha, Tokyo. [2]

—— 1988, *Understanding Industrial Relations in Modern Japan*, Macmillan, London. [6]

Kojima, Yasuhisa 1987, *Nippon no Rôdô Undô [Trade union movement of Japan]*, Kawadeshobô-shinsha, Tokyo. [2]

Komai, H. 1989, *Japanese Management Overseas: Experiences in the United States and Thailand*, Asian Productivity Organisation, Tokyo.

Komiya, R., Okuno, M. & Suzumura, K. (eds) 1988, *Industrial Policy of Japan*, Academic Press, Tokyo.

Kono, S. 1958, The Japanese Work Force: A Demographic Analysis, PhD thesis, Sociology, Brown University.

Koshiro, K. 1986, *Labour Market Flexibility in Japan—With Special Reference to Wage Flexibility*, Discussion Paper Series 86-2, Centre for International Trade Studies, Yokohama national University.

—— 1986, *Small Business and the Labour Market in Japan—The Inter-relationship between Large and Small Enterprises since 1970*, Discussion Paper Series 86-4, Centre for International Trade Studies, Yokohama national University.

—— 1989, 'Labour Dispute Settlement in the Japanese Postal Service', in *Industrial Conflict Resolution in Market Economies—A Study of Australia, the Federal Republic of Germany, Italy, Japan and the USA*, 2nd edn, eds T. Hanami & R. Blanpain, Kluwer, Deventer, pp. 217–35.

Kotkin, J. & Kishimoto, Y. 1986, 'Theory F—The One Ingredient that Makes Japanese Management Work: Fear', *Good Weekend (Sydney Morning Herald* magazine), 10 May, pp. 14–21.

Kowalewski, D. 1986, 'Asian Strikes against Transnationals: Characteristics and Consequences', *Asian Profile*, vol. 14, no. 3, June, pp. 287–99.

Kumara, U.A. 1990, 'Work-related Values and Attitudes: A Study of Japanese Manufacturing Workers', *Asian Profile*, vol. 18, no. 5, October, pp. 415–25.

Kume, I. 1988, 'Changing Relations among Government, Labor and Business in Japan after the Oil Crisis', *International Organization*, vol. 42, no. 2, Autumn, pp. 659–87.

Kuwahara, Y. 1985, *Decision-making Structures and Processes in Multinationals in Japan, Multinational Enterprises Programme*, Working Paper no. 36, International Labour Office, Geneva.

—— 1989, *Industrial Relations System in Japan: A New Interpretation*, Japan Institute of Labor, Tokyo.

Large, S.S. 1970, 'The Japanese Labor Movement, 1912–1919: Bunji and the Yuaikai', *Journal of Asian Studies*, vol. 29, no. 3, May, pp. 559–79.

—— 1981, *Organized Workers and Socialist Politics in Interwar Japan*, Cambridge University Press, Cambridge. [4]

—— 1972, *The Yuaikai: The Rise of Labor in Japan, 1912-19*, Sophia University Press, Tokyo. [4]

Lee, S.M. & Schwendiman, G. (eds) 1982, *Japanese Management: Cultural and Environmental Considerations*, Praeger, New York.

Lee, K.H. 1988, The history of the early Japanese Labour Movement, MA thesis, Oriental Studies, University of Sydney.

Lesbirel, S.H. 1988, The Political Economy of Industrial Adjustment in Japan: The Case of Coal, unpublished manuscript, Australia-Japan Centre, ANU, Canberra.

Levine, Soloman B. 1958, *Industrial Relations in Post-War Japan*, University of Illinois Press, Urbana.

—— 1982, 'Japanese Industrial Relations: An External View', in *Industrial Relations in Japan*, eds Y. Sugimoto, H. Shimada & S.B. Levine Japanese Studies Centre, Monash University, Melbourne, pp. 39–57.

—— 1983, 'Careers and Modility in Japan's Labor Market', in *Work and Lifecourse in Japan*, ed. D.W. Plaith, State University of New York Press, Albany, pp. 66–108.

—— 1984, 'Employers Associations in Japan', in *Employer Associations and Industrial Relations*, eds A. Gladstone & J. Windmuller, Clarendon Press, Oxford.

Lincoln, J.R. & Kalleberg, A.L. 1985, 'Work Organisation and Workforce Commitment: A Study of Plants and Employees in the US and Japan', *American Sociological Review*, no. 50, December, pp. 738–60.

Littler, C.R. 1992, 'Employment relations and trade unionism in East Asia', Labour Management and Industrialisation Conference, 4-5 September 1992, Australian Graduate School of Management, UNSW, Sydney.

Long, J. 1986, Female labour force in Japan, BA(Hons) thesis, Japanese, Monash.

Mackie, V.C. 1988, 'Division of Labour', in *The Japanese Trajectory: Modernisation and Beyond*, eds G. McCormack & Y. Sugimoto, Cambridge University Press, pp. 218–32.

—— 1989, 'Equal opportunity in an inequal labour market: the Japanese situation', *Australian Feminist Studies*, no. 9, Autumn, pp. 97–109.

Maehara, Y. 1981, The duration of jobs in the United States and Japan, PhD thesis, London School of Economics.

Magaziner, I.C. & Hout, T.M. 1982, *Japanese Industrial Policy*, Institute of International Studies, University of California, Berkeley.

Marchington, M. 1988, 'Japanisation: a lack of chemical reaction', *Industrial Relations Journal*, vol. 19, no. 4, pp. 272–86.

Marsland, S.E. & Beer, M. 1985, 'Japanese Management and Employment Systems', in *Readings in Human Resource Management*, eds S.E. Marsland. & M. Beer, Free Press, New York, 1985.

Matsuzaki, Hajime 1993, *Historical Development of Japanese Construction Unionism,* Industrial Relations Research Centre, University of New South Wales, Sydney (forthcoming). [2]

—— 1992, *Japanese Business Unionism: The Historical Development of a Unique Labour Movement*, Monograph no. 1, Studies in Human Resource Management and Industrial Relations in Asia, UNSW, Kensington.

Masuda, Shirô 1992, 'Chûsei toshi [Medieval cities]', in *Keizaigaku-jiten [Dictionary of Economics],* ed. Institute of Economics, Osaka Municipal University, Iwanami-shoten, Tokyo, pp. 894–95. [2]

McGown, V.J. 1978, Paternalism and labour relations in small-medium scale industry in Japan, MA thesis, Japanese, Monash University.

McMillan, C.J. 1989, *The Japanese Industrial System*, 2nd edn, Walter de Gruyter, Berlin.

Minami, Ryôshin 1986, *The Economic Development of Japan: A Quantitative Study,* Macmillan, London. [2]

Ministry of Labour 1989, *White Paper on Labour*, Tokyo.

Mitsufuji, T. 1971, 'Industrial Relations in the Public Sector in Japan', in *Public Employee Labor Relations in Japan: Three Aspects*, eds A.H. Cook, S.B. Levine & Tadasshi Mitsufuji, Institute of Labor and Industrial relations, University of Michigan–Wayne State University, Ann Arbor, pp. 3–28.

Mizuno, A. 1985, *An Empirical Analysis of Wage Flexibility and Employment Fluctuations in Japan*, Pacific Economic Papers no. 124, Australia–Japan Research Centre, Research School of Pacific Studies, ANU, Canberra.

Mogi, S. 1933, Letter from S. Mogi, Japanese Federation of Labour, Tokyo, to Edo Fimmen, International Transport Workers Federation, Amsterdam, 31 March 1933, in *ITWF Papers*, Modern Records Centre, University of Warwick. [4]

Monden, Y., Shibakawa, S., Takayanagi, S. & Nagao, T. 1985, *Innovations in Management: The Japanese Corporation*, Industrial Engineering and Management Press, Atlanta.

Moore, J.B. 1983, *Japanese Workers and the Struggle for Power, 1945–1947*, University of Wisconsin Press, Madison. [6]

—— 1987, 'Japanese Industrial Relations', *Labour and Industry*, vol. 1, no. 1, October, pp. 140–55.

—— 1990, 'Nikkeiren (Japan Federation of Employers' Associations) and restoration of the right to manage in post-war Japan', *Labour and Industry*, vol. 3, nos. 2&3, June/October, pp. 281–301.

Mori, H. 1983, *Labor Administration in Japan: a Historical Perspective*, Japan Institute of Labour, Tokyo.

Morris, J. 1988, 'The who, why, and where of Japanese manufacturing investment in the United Kingdom', *Industrial Relations Journal*, vol. 19, no. 1, pp. 31–40.

Nagagawa, K. (ed) 1979, *Labor and Management: Proceedings of the 4th Fuji International Conference on Business History*, no. 4, University of Tokyo Press, Tokyo.

Nakagi, Yasuo 1992, 'Nôson kôgyô [Country industry]', in *Keizaigaku-jiten [Dictionary of Economics]*, ed. Institute of Economics, Osaka Municipal University, Iwanami-shoten, Tokyo, pp. 1075–76. [2]

Nakamura, K. 1991, 'Types and functions of industry-wide labor organisations in Japan', *Japan Labor Bulletin*, no. 1, pp. 5–8.

Nakane, C. 1970, *Japanese Society*, Weidenfeld & Nicolson, London. [4]

Nakanishi, T. 1983, 'Equality or Protection? Protective Legislation for Women in Japan', *International Labour Review*, vol. 122, no. 5, Sept–Oct, pp. 609–21.

Nester, W. 1989, 'Japan's Corporate "Miracle": Ideals and Realities at Home and Abroad', *Asian Profile*, vol. 17, no. 6, December, pp. 497–511.

Ng, J. 1988, Japan's recruiting system—case studies, BA(Hons) thesis, Japanese, Monash University.

Nikkeiren Committee 1985, *Towards a more vital society: Report of the Committee for the Study of Labor Questions*, Japan Federation of Employers' Associations (Nikkeiren), Tokyo.

Nimura, K. 1990, 'Japan', in *The Formation of Labour Movements 1870-1914: An International Perspective*, vol. 2, eds M. van der Linden & J. Rojahn, Brill, Leiden, pp. 673–97. [2]

—— 1984, 'Kigyobetsu-kumiai no rekishiteki haikei [Historical background of enterprise unionism]', *Journal of the Ohara Institute for Social Research*, no. 305 (March), pp. 2–21. [2]

—— 1987, 'Nihon rôshikankei no rekisiteki tokushitu [Historical feature of Japanese labour-management relations]', in *Nihon no rôshikankei no rekisiteki tokushitu [Historical feature of Japanese labour-management relations]*, Annual of the Institute of Social Policy, no. 31, pp. 77–95. [2]

—— 1975, 'Rôdôsha-kaikyû no jôtai to rôdôundô [State of working class and labour movement]', *Nihon rekishi [Japanese history]*, vol. 18 (modern vol. 5), Iwanami-shoten, Tokyo, pp. 91–140. [2]

—— 1969, 'The Steady Development and the Defeat of Labour Movements in the Pre-war Period', in *Rôdôundôshi Kenkyû (Labour History Review)* no. 50. [4]

Nishikawa, S. (ed.) 1980, *The Labor Market in Japan: Selected Readings*, University of Tokyo Press, Tokyo.

Nishinarita, Y. 1988, *Kindai Nihon Roshikankeishi no Kenkyû*, Tokyo Daigaku Shuppankai, Tokyo. [4]

Nitta, M. 1989, 'Conflict Resolution the [Japanese] Steel Industry— Collective Bargaining and Workers' Consultation in a Steel Plant', in *Industrial Conflict Resolution in Market Economies—A Study of Australia, the Federal Republic of Germany, Italy, Japan and the USA*, 2nd edn, eds T. Hanami & R. Blanpain, Kluwer, Deventer, pp. 238–51.

Noble, G. 1989, 'The Japanese Industrial Policy Debate', in *Pacific Dynamics*, eds S. Haggard & C. Moon, Westview Press, Boulder.

Notar, E.J. 1979, Labor Unions and the Sangyo Hokuku Movement, 1930–1945: a Japanese model for industrial relations, PhD thesis, University of California, Berkeley.

Odaka, K. 1992, *Towards Industrial Democracy: Management and Workers in Modern Japan*, Harvard University Press, Cambridge.

OECD 1972, *The Industrial Policy of Japan*, Paris.

—— 1977, *The Development of Industrial Relations Systems: Some Implications of Japanese Experience*, Paris.

—— 1989, *Japan at Work: Markets, Management and Flexibility*, Paris.

Ohta, T. 1988, 'Work Rules in Japan', *International Labour Review*, vol. 127, no. 5.

Okochi, K., Karsh, B. & Levine, S.B. (ed.) 1974, *Workers and Employers in Japan*, University of Tokyo Press, Tokyo. [6]

Okimoto, D.I. 1989, *Between MITI and the Market: Japanese Industrial Policy for High Technology*, Stanford University Press, California.

O'Neill, M. 1982, 'Japanese Labour Relations', *Dyason House Papers*, no. 8, March, pp. 7–15.

Ono, T. & Mouer, R. 1986, *Labour Policy in Japan: a Survey of Issues in the Eighties*, Japanese Studies Centre Papers no. 14, Melbourne University, Clayton.

Osaki, R.S. 1991, *Human Capitalism: the Japanese Enterprise System as World Model*, Kodansha International, Tokyo.

Osawa, M. 1986, *The Wage Gap in Japan: Changing Patterns of Labour Force Participation, Schooling and Tenure*, Discussion Paper Series 86-1, Economic Research Centre & National Opinion Research Centre, Chicago.

—— 1989, 'The service economy and industrial relations in small and medium-size firms in Japan', *Japan Labor Bulletin*, 1 July 1989, pp. 4–8.

Otsuka, Hisao 1992, 'Kyokuchîteki shijôken [Local market area]', in *Keizaijaku-jiten [Dictionary of Economics]*, ed. Institute of Economics, Osaka Municipal University, Iwanami-shoten, Tokyo, pp. 240. [2]

Owen, B. 1990, 'Organisation and industrial change at Nissan New Zealand', in *Perspectives on Contemporary Human Resource Management: Function in Search of a Future*, ed. P. Boxhall, Longman Paul, Auckland.

Owen Smith, E. (ed.) 1981, *Trade Unions in the Developed Economies*, Croom Helm, London. [6]

Ozawa, T. 1982, *People and Productivity in Japan*, Pergammon Press, New York.

Paltern, S. 1988, Japan's equal opportunity law and the future of professional women, BA(Hons) thesis, Japanese, Monash University.

Patrick, H. 1983, *Japanese Industrial Policy and its Relevance for United States Industrial Policy*, Research Paper no. 105, Australia–Japan Research Centre, ANU, Canberra.

Plaith, D.W. (ed.) 1983, *Work and Lifecourse in Japan*, State University of New York Press, Albany.

Price, J. 1989, *From Quality Circle to Team Concept: a Critical Review of the Japanese Labour Relations Model*, Working Paper no. 31, Institute of Asian Research, Vancouver.

Pugal, T.A. 1984, 'Japan's industrial policy: instruments, trends and effects', *Journal of Comparative Economics*, no. 8, pp. 420–35.

Rapp, W.V. 1975, 'Japan's Industrial Policy', in *The Japanese Economy in International Perspective*, ed. I. Frank, John Hopkins University Press, Baltimore, pp. 37–66.

Reitsperger, W.D. 1986, 'Japanese management coping with British industrial relations', *Journal of Management Studies*, vol. 23, no. 1.

Roberts, B.C. (ed.) 1979, *Towards Industrial Democracy: Europe, Japan and the United States*, Allanheld, Osmun, Montclair. [6]

Rostow, W.W. 1978, *The World Economy: History & Prospect*, Macmillan, London. [2]

Sakura, Y. 1992, A study of cross cultural management in Japan and Korea, MA(CW) thesis, Division of Asian and International Studies, Griffith University.

Sandkull, B. 1986, 'Industrial management, production technology and working conditions in Japan and Sweden—a cross-cultural comparison', in *The Enterprise and Management in East Asia*, eds S.R.Clegg, D.C. Dunphy & S.G. Redding, Centre for Asian Studies, University of Hong Kong, pp. 169–85.

Sasaki, N. 1990, *Management and Industrial Structure in Japan*, 2nd edn, Pergamon Press, Oxford.

Sato, K. 1980, *Industry and Business in Japan*, Croom Helm, London.

Saxonhouse, G.R. 1986, *Industrial Policy and Factor Markets: Biotechnology in Japan and the United States*, Research Paper no. 136, Australia–Japan Research Centre, ANU, Canberra.

Schonberger, R.J. 1982, 'The transfer of Japanese manufacturing management approaches to US industry', *Academy of Management Review*, vol. 7, no. 3, pp. 479–87.

Schnitzer, M. 1974, *Income Distribution: A Comparative Study of the United States, Sweden, West Germany, East Germany, the United Kingdom and Japan*, Praeger, New York.

Schwendiman, G. 1982, *Japanese Management: Cultural and Environmental Considerations*, Praeger, New York.

Sekine, M. 1990, *Guest Workers in Japan*, Occasional Paper no. 21, Centre for Multicultural Studies, University of Wollongong.

Sethi, S.P., Namiki, N. & Swanson, C.L. 1984, *The False Promise of the Japanese Miracle: Illusions and Realities of the Japanese Management System*, Pitman, Boston.

Sheard, P. 1982, The Japanese industrial system: a case study of linkages in the auto industry, PhD thesis, Geography, Monash University.

—— 1983, 'Auto production systems in Japan: organisational and locational features', *Australian Geographical Studies*, no. 21, April, pp. 49–68.

—— 1987, *How Japanese firms handle industrial adjustment: a case study of aluminium*, Pacific Economic Papers no. 151, Australia–Japan Research Centre, ANU, Canberra.

Shenk, V.T. 1982, Redundancy and redeployment in the Japanese synthetic fibre industry 1973-79, MA thesis, University of Sheffield.

Shiba, Ryôtarô 1991, *Meiji' to iu kokka [A state called 'Meiji']*, Nippon Hôsô-kyôkai Shuppankai, Tokyo. [2]

Shibagaki, K., Trevor, M. & Abo, T. 1989, *Japanese and European Management: Their International Adaptability*, University of Tokyo Press, Tokyo.

Shigeyoshi, T. & Bergmann, J. (eds) 1984, *Industrial Relations in Transition: The Cases of Japan and the Federal Republic of Germany*, University of Tokyo Press, Tokyo.

Shimada, Haruo 1982, 'Japanese Perceptions of Industrial Relations', in *Industrial Relations in Japan*, eds Y. Sugimoto, H. Shimada & S.B. Levine, Japanese Studies Centre, Monash University, Melbourne, pp. 21–38.

—— 1984, 'Japanese Industrial Relations—A New General Model?: A Survey of the English Language Literature', in *Contemporary Industrial Relations in Japan*, ed. T. Shirai, University of Wisconsin Press, Madison.

—— 1988, 'Japanese Trade Unionism: Post-war Evolution and Future Prospects', *Labour and Society*, vol. 13, no. 2, April.

—— 1988, 'Contemporary Challenges for Japanese Trade Unionism', *Japan Labour Bulletin*, 1 January, pp. 4–8.

Shimada, Haruo & Higuchi, Y. 1985, 'An Analysis of Trends in Female Labor Force Participation in Japan', *Journal of Labour Economics*, vol. 3, no. 1, January (Supplement), pp. 355–74.

Shiozawa, M. & Hiroki, M. 1988, *Discrimination Against Women Workers in Japan*, Asian Women Workers' Centre, Tokyo.

Shirai, T. (ed) 1984, *Contemporary Industrial Relations in Japan*, University of Wisconsin Press, Madison. [6]

Shirai, T. & Shimada, H. 1978, 'Japan', in *Labor in the Twentieth Century*, eds J.T. Dunlop & W. Galenson, Academic Press, New York, pp. 241–322. [2]

Shoven, J.B. 1988, *Government Policy Towards Industry in the United States and Japan*, Cambridge University Press, Cambridge.

Smith, D. 1988, 'The Japanese example in South West Birmingham', *Industrial Relations Journal*, vol. 19, no. 1, pp. 41–50.

Smith, P.B. & Misumi, J. n.d. 'Japanese Management—A Sun Rising in the West?', *International Review of Industrial and Organisational Psychology*, John Wiley, Chichester, pp. 329–69.

Smith, T.C. 1971, 'Pre-modern Economic Growth: Japan and the West', *Past and Present*, no. 60 (August), pp. 127–60. [2]

Sorrentino, C. 1984, 'Japan's low unemployment: an in-depth analysis', *Monthly Labor Review*, March.

Storry, R. 1960, *A History of Modern Japan*, Penguin Books, London. [2]

Sugawara, A. 1992, Japanese Management Practices: Past, Present and Future, MBA thesis, Graduate School of Management, University of Queensland.

Sugayama, S. 1989, 'Interwar Employment System in Japan: A Comparative Study of the Employment Conditions of White Collar Staff and Workers', *Shakai Keizai Shigaku (Socio-Economic History)*, vol. 56, no. 4. [4]

Sugeno, K. 1992, *The Role of the State in Industrial Relations in Japan: The State's Guiding Role in Socio-economic Developments*, Proceedings of the IIRA 9th World Congress, Sydney, 30 August– 3 September 1992, International Industrial Relations Association, no. 1, pp. 62 & 150–63.

Sugimoto, Y. 1977, 'Labor Reform and Industrial Turbulance: The Case of the American Occupation of Japan', *Pacific Sociological Review*, no. 20, October, pp. 492–513.

—— 1982, 'Japanese Society and Industrial Relations', in *Industrial Relations in Japan*, eds Y. Sugimoto, H. Shimada & S.B. Levine, Japanese Studies Centre, Monash University, Melbourne, November, pp. 1–20.

Sugimoto, Y., Shimada, H. & Levine, S.B. 1982, *Industrial Relations in Japan*, Japanese Studies Centre Papers no. 4, Monash University, Melbourne.

Sumiya, M. 1973, 'The Emergence of Modern Japan', in *Workers and Employers in Japan*, eds K. Okochi, B. Karsh & S.B. Levine, University of Tokyo Press, Tokyo, pp. 15–48. [2]

—— 1990, *Japanese Industrial Relations Reconsidered*, Japanese Institute of Labor, Tokyo.

Suzumura, K. & Okuno-Fujiwara, M. 1987, *Industrial Policy in Japan*, Pacific Economic Papers no. 146, Australia–Japan Research Centre, ANU, Canberra.

Tabata, H. 1988, *Changes in Plant-level Trade Union Organisations: A Case Study of the Automobile Industry*, Occasional Papers in Labor Problems and Social Policy no. 3, Institute of Social Science, University of Tokyo.

Taira, K. 1983, 'Japan's low unemployment: economic miracle or statistical artefact?', *Monthly Labor Review*, Bureau of Labor Statistics, US Department of Labor, July, pp. 3–10.

—— 1961, The Dynamics of Japanese Wage Differentials 1881–1959, PhD thesis, Economics, Stanford University.

—— 1970, *Economic Development and the Labor Market in Japan*, Columbia University Press, New York. [4] [6]

Takagi, H. 1985, *The Flaw in Japanese Management*, Research for Business Decisions no. 83, UMI Research Press, Ann Arbor.

Takezawa, S. 1976, *The Quality of Working Life: Trends in Japan*, Research Series no. 11, International Institute for Labor Studies, Geneva.

Takezawa, S. et al. 1982, *Improvements in the quality of working life in three Japanese industries*, International Labour Office, Geneva.

Tanaka, H. 1988, *Personality in Industry—The Human Side of a Japanese Enterprise*, Pinter, London.

Tasker, P. 1989, *Inside Japan: Wealth, Work and Power in the New Japanese Empire*, Penguin, Harmondsworth.

Thompson, A.G. 1986, 'Work incentives and the efficiency of international labour markets', *Journal of Industrial Relations*, vol. 28, no. 1, March, pp. 40–56.

Thurley, K. 1986 (July), Japanese Industrial Relations and Industrial Relations in Japanese Companies Overseas, BUIRA Annual Conference, University of Bath.

Tokyo Civil and Building Workers' Union (TCBWU) 1989, *Tokyo doken 40nen shi [40-year history of TCBWU]* TCBWU, Tokyo. [2]

Totten, G.O. 1967, 'Collective Bargaining and Works Councils as Innovations in Industrial Relations in Japan during the 1920s', *Aspects of Social Changes in Modern Japan*, ed. R.P. Dore, Princeton. [4]

Tresize, P.H. 'Industrial Policy in Japan', in *Industrial Vitalization*, ed. M.E. Dewar, Pergammon, New York, pp. 177–95.

Tsurumi, E.P. 1988, 'Serving in Japan's Industrial Army: Female Textile Workers, 1868–1930', *Canadian Journal of History*, no. 22, August.

—— 1990, *Factory Girls: Women in the Thread Mills of Meiji Japan*, Princeton University Press, Princeton.

—— 1991, 'Old Wine in New Bottles: Management Practices in Contemporary Japan', *Journal of Contemporary Asia*, vol. 21, no. 3.

Tsurumi, Y. 1978, *Japanese Business: a Research Guide with Annotated Bibliography*, Praeger, New York.

Turnbull, P. 1986, 'The Japanisation of British Industrial Relations at Lucas', *Industrial Relations Journal*, vol. 17, no. 3, pp. 203–4.

Tussing, A.R. 1966, Employment and Wages in Japanese Industrialization: A Quantitative Study of Yamanashi Prefecture in the Meiji Era, PhD thesis, School of Economics, Washington University, Seattle.

Uekusa, M. & Ide, H. 1986, 'Industrial Policy in Japan', *Pacific Economic Papers* no. 135, Australia–Japan Research Centre, ANU, Canberra.

Ueno, H. 1980, 'The conception and evaluation of Japanese industrial policy', in *Industry and Business in Japan*, ed. K. Sato, Croom Helm, London, pp. 375–434.

Walker, M.H. 1940, Manufacturers Guilds (Kyogo Kumiai) in Japanese small scale industries, PhD thesis, School of Economics, University of California, Berkeley.

Watanabe, B. n.d. 'The Japanese Labour Movement—Toward Total Dissolution?', *AMPO Japan–Asia Quarterly Review*, vol. 20, no. 4, pp. 62–3; vol. 21, no. 1, pp. 69–70.

Werveke, H. van and Miller, E. (ed.) n.d., *The Cambridge Economic History of Europe, Vol. III, Economic Organisation and Politics in the Middle Ages*, Cambridge University Press, London, pp. 3–41. [2]

White, M. & Trevor, M. 1983, *Under Japanese Management: The Experience of Japanese Workers*, Heinemann, London. [6]

Wickens, P. 1985, 'Nissan (UK): the thinking behind the union agreement', *Personnel Management*, August.

Wilkinson, B. 1990, *Japanisation: the emerging agenda for research*, Key Centre in Strategic Management, Working Paper Series no. 12, University of Queensland.

Whittaker, D.H. 1989, *The End of Japanese-style Employment*, Occasional Paper no. 89-17, US–Japan Program, Harvard University.

Yamaguchi, J.T. 1971, Postwar demographic transition and labour development in Japan, PhD thesis, ANU, Canberra.

Yamamoto, Kiyoshi, 1990, *Japanese-style Industrial Relations and an Informal Employee Organisation: A Case Study of the Ohgi-kai at T Electric*, Occasional Papers in Labor Problems and Social Policy no. 8, Institute of Social Science, University of Tokyo.

Yamashita, S. 1991, *Transfer of Japanese Technology and Management to the ASEAN Countries*, University of Tokyo Press, Tokyo.

Yamazaki, R. 1992, 'Nihon shihonshugi ronsô [Issue on Japanese capitalism]' and 'Manyufakuchâ ronsô [Issue on manufacture]' in *Keizaigaku-jiten [Dictionary of Economics]*, ed. Institute of Economics, Osaka Municipal University, Iwanami-shoten, Tokyo, pp. 1036–37 & 1237. [2]

Young, M. 1986, 'Structurally Depressed and Declining Industries in Japan: A Case Study in Minimally Intrusive Industrial Policy', in *Japan's Economy and Trade with the United States*, ed. D. Nanto, Joint Economic Committee, Washington.

Zenkensôren 1985, *50-man eno michi [the road to five hundred thousand]*, Zenkensôren, Tokyo. [2]

3 General: Australia

Australian Bureau of Statistics 1990, *Incidence of Industrial Awards, Determinations and Collective Agreements*, May 1990, cat 6315.0. AGPS, Canberra. [9]

—— 1992, *Industrial Disputes, 1970–1991*, cat 6322.0, AGPS, Canberra. [9]

Australian Council of Trade Unions 1987, Future Strategies of the Trade Union Movement, mimeo Australian Council of Trade Unions Congress document. [12]

—— 1989, The Way Forward, mimeo, Australian Council of Trade Unions. [12]

—— 1991, 'The Organisation , Resources and Services of the Trade Union Movement Strategy', policy statement, Australian Council of Trade Unions Congress, September, in 1991 ACTU Congress book, Australian Council of Trade Unions. [12]

—— 1991, Future Directions of the Trade Union Movement, mimeo, Australian Council of Trade Unions. [12]

—— 1993, Union Services and Membership Growth, paper prepared for the 1993 ACTU Congress, mimeo, Australian Council of Trade Unions. [12]

Australian Council of Trade Unions/Trade Development Council 1987, *Australia Reconstructed,* AGPS, Canberra. [12]

Bowden, B. 1993, *Driving Force: The History of the Transport Workers' Union 1883–1992,* Allen & Unwin, Sydney. [5]

Boyne Smelters Case 1993: Re Boyne Smelters; ex p FIMEE (1993) 112 ALR 359. [9]

Bray, M. & Taylor, V. 1986, *Managing Labour? Essays in the political economy of Australian industrial relations,* McGraw-Hill, Sydney 1986. [7]

Butlin, N.G. (1964) 1972, *Investment in Australian Economic Development, 1861–1900,* ANU, Canberra. [3]

—— 1993, *Economics and the Dreamtime: A Hypothetical History,* Cambridge University Press, Melbourne. [5]

Callus, R. et al. 1991, *Industrial Relations at Work,* Department of Industrial Relations, AGPS, Canberra.[7]

Cameron, C. 1992, *Unions in Crisis,* Hill of Content, Melbourne. [7]

Carney, S. 1988, *Australia in Accord. Politics and Industrial Relations Under the Hawke Government,* Sun Books, Crows Nest. [12]

Commonwealth of Australia 1985, *Australian Industrial Relations Law and Systems: Report of the Committee of Review,* AGPS, Canberra. [7]

—— 1988, Industrial Relations Act, No. 86 of 1988 (Cth) as amended to 22 December 1993, AGPS, Canberra. [9]

Confederation of Australian Industry & Australian Council of Trade Unions 1988, *Joint Statement on Participative Practices: a co-operative approach to improving efficiency and productivity in Australian industry,* Confederation of Australian Industry and Australian Council of Trade Unions, Melbourne. [10]

Confederation of Australian Industry, Business Council of Australia & Australian Council of Trade Unions 1986, 'Issues Related to Productivity Improvement—Joint Statement', 24 September. [10]

Confederation of Australian Industry, Industrial Council 1987, *Employee Participation: A Guide to Realising Employee Potential and Commitment*, Confederation of Australian Industry, Industrial Council, Melbourne. [10]

Confederation of Australian Industry, National Employers' Industrial Council 1978, *Involving Employees in the Enterprise (Workers' Participation)—a Guide to Employers*, Confederation of Australian Industry, Hawthorn, Vic. [10]

Cooksey, R.(ed.) 1970, *The Great Depression in Australia*, Australian Society for the Study of Labour History, Canberra. [5]

Costa, M. & Easson, M. (eds.) 1991, *Australian Industry. What Policy?* Pluto Press/Lloyd Ross Forum, Leichardt, pp 187–206. [12]

Cupper, L. 1976, 'Legalism in the Australian Conciliation and Arbitration Commission: The Gradual Transition', *Journal of Industrial Relations*, vol. 18. [9]

Dabscheck, B. 1989, *Australian Industrial Relations in the 1980s,* Oxford University Press, Melbourne. [7] [9]

Davidson, A. 1969, *The Communist Party of Australia*, Hoover Institution Press, Stanford. [5]

Deakin, A. 1903, *Commonwealth Parliamentary Debates*, vol. 15, 30 July 1903, AGPS, Canberra. [9]

Deery, S.J. & Plowman, D.H. 1991, Australian Industrial Relations, 3rd edn, McGraw-Hill, Sydney. [7]

Drago, R. et al. 1988, *The BCA/NILS Industrial Relations Study: An Overview of the Employee Survey*, National Institute of Labour Studies Working Paper no. 100. [9]

Dufty, N.F. 1972, *Industrial Relations in the Australian Metal Industries,* West Publishing, Sydney. [7]

Dyster, B. and Meredith, D. 1990, *Australia in the International Economy in the Twentieth Century*, Cambridge University Press, Melbourne. [5]

Easson, M. 1992, 'Matching the Wattle With The Chrysanthemum: Australian and Japanese Union Comparisons', in *What Should Unions Do?* eds M. Crosby & M. Easson, Pluto Press/Lloyd Ross Forum, Leichardt, pp. 97–149. [12]

Ewer, P, Higgins W. & Stevens, A. 1987,*Unions and the Future of Australian Manufacturing,* Allen & Unwin, Sydney. [7]

Ferguson, M. 1993. Presidential Address to the 1993 ACTU Congress, mimeo, Australian Council of Trade Unions. [12]

Fitzpatrick, B. 1941, *The British Empire in Australia: An Economic History 1834–1939*, Melbourne University Press, Melbourne. [5]

—— 1946, *The Australian People 1788–1945*, Melbourne University Press, Melbourne. [5]

Foenander, O. de R. 1947, *Industrial Regulation in Australia*, Melbourne University Press, Melbourne. [5]

Ford, B. & Plowman, D.H, (eds) 1989, *Australian Unions: An Industrial Relations Perspective*, Macmillan, Melbourne. [7]

Forster, C. (ed.) 1970, *Australian Economic Development in the Twentieth Century*, Allen & Unwin, London. [5]

Francis, R. 1993, *The Politics of Work: Gender and Labour in Victoria, 1880–1939*, Cambridge University Press, Melbourne. [5]

Gardner, M. & Palmer, G. 1992, *Employment Relations*, Macmillan, Melbourne 1992. [7]

Gollan, R. 1963, *The Coalminers of New South Wales. A History of the Union, 1860–1960*, Melbourne University Press, Melbourne. [3] [5]

Gramsci, A. 1971, *Selections From the Prison Notebooks of Antonio Gramsci*, Lawrence and Wishart, London. [5]

Great Britain. Committee of Inquiry into Industrial Democracy in the United Kingdom 1977, *Report of the Committee of Inquiry into Industrial Democracy in the United Kingdom*, HMSO, London. [10]

Great Britain. Royal Commission on Trade Unions and Employers' Associations 1968, *Report of the Royal Commission on Trade Unions and Employers' Associations*, HMSO, London. [10]

Gregory, R., Ho, V. and McDermott, L. 1985, *Sharing the Burden: The Australian Labour Market During the 1930s*, Working Papers in Economic History, no. 47, August, The Australian National University, Canberra. [5]

Griffin, G. & de Rozairo, S. 1993, 'Trade Union Finances in the 1970s and 1980s', *Journal of Industrial Relations*, vol. 35, no.3, September, pp. 424–35. [12]

Hagan, J. & Wells, A. (eds) 1992, *The Maritime Strike: A Centennial Retrospective. Essays in Honour of E.C. Fry*, Five Islands Press, Wollongong. [3]

Hagan, J. 1966, *Printers and Politics: A History of the Australian Printing Unions 1850–1950*, ANU Press, Canberra. [5]

—— 1981, *The History of the ACTU*, Longman Cheshire, Melbourne. [3] [5][7]

Head, B. (ed) 1983, *State and Economy in Australia*, Oxford University Press, Melbourne. [7]

Hilmer, F. 1985, When The *Luck Runs Out. The Future For Australians At Work*, Harper & Row, Sydney. [12]

Horne, D. 1966, *The Lucky Country*, Angus & Robertson, Sydney. [12]

HR Nicholls Society 1986, *Arbitration in Contempt*, HR Nicholls Society, Melbourne. [7]

Hutson, J. 1971, *Six Wage Concepts*, Amalgamated Engineering Union, Sydney. [7]

Inaba, Kouichi 1991 [started], Industrial relations in the Australian Engineering Industry Between the Wars, PhD thesis, Department of History and Politics, University of Wollongong (in progress).

Iremonger, J., Merritt, J. and Osborne, G. (eds) 1973, *Strikes: Studies in Twentieth Century Australian Social History*, Angus &Robertson, Sydney. [5]

Larmour, C. 1985, *Labour Judge: the Life and Times of Judge Alfred William Foster*, Hale & Iremonger, Sydney. [9]

Lever-Tracy, C. & Quinlan, M. 1988, *A Divided Working Class*, Routledge & Kegan Paul, London. [7]

Lincoln Mills Case 1957: Textile Workers Union of America v Lincoln Mills of Alabama 353 US 448. [9]

Macarthy, P. 1967, The Harvester Judgment: An Historical Assessment, PhD Thesis, ANU. [3]

—— 1976, 'Justice Higgins and the Harvester Judgment', in *Social Policy in Australia. Some Perspectives, 1901–75*, ed. J. Roe, Cassell, Stanmore, pp. 41–59. [3]

Macintyre, S. 1983, 'Labour, Capital and Arbitration, 1890–1920', in *State and Economy in Australia*, ed. B. Head, Oxford University Press, Melbourne. [3]

—— 1984, *Militant: The Life and Timnes of Paddy Troy*, Allen & Unwin, Sydney. [7]

—— 1986, *The Oxford History of Australia: Volume Four 1901–1942; The Succeeding Age*, Oxford University Press, Melbourne. [5]

—— 1989, 'Neither Capital nor Labour: The Politics of the Establishment of Arbitration', in *Foundations of Arbitration. The Origins and Effects of State Compulsory Arbitration, 1890–1914*, eds S. Macintyre & R. Mitchell, Oxford University Press, Melbourne, pp. 178–202. [3]

—— 1989, *The Labour Experiment*, McPhee Gribble, Melbourne. [12]

Markey, R. 1982, 'The ALP and the Emergence of a National Social Policy, 1880–1900', in *Australian Welfare History. Critical Essays*, ed. R. Kennedy, Macmillan, Melbourne, pp. 103–37. [3]

—— 1985, 'New Unionism in Australia, 1880–1900', *Labour History*, no. 48, May, pp. 15–28. [3]

—— 1987, 'Populism and the Formation of a Labor Party in New South Wales, 1890–1900', *Journal of Australian Studies*, no. 20, May, pp. 38–48. [3]

—— 1988, 'The Aristocracy of Labour and Productive Re-organisation in New South Wales, c. 1880–1900', *Australian Economic History Review*, XXVIII/1, March, pp. 43–59. [3]

—— 1988, *The Making of the Labor Party in New South Wales, 1880–1900*, NSW University Press, Kensington. [3]

—— 1990, 'A Century of Labour and Labor, New South Wales, 1890–1990', in *The Foundation of Labor*, ed. M. Easson, Pluto Press, Sydney, pp. 47–8. [3]

—— 1990, 'Australia', in *The Formation of Labour Movements, 1870–1914. An International Perspective*, vol. 2, ed. M. van der Linden & J. Rojahn, Brill, Leiden, pp. 579–608. [3]

—— 1990, 'Trade Unions, the Labor Party and the Introduction of Arbitration in New South Wales and the Commonwealth', in *Foundations of Arbitration. The Origins and Effects of State Compulsory Arbitration, 1890–1914*, eds S. Macintyre & R. Mitchell, Oxford University Press, Melbourne, pp. 156–77. [3]

McCallum, R. 1994, 'The Internationalisation of Australian Industrial Law: The Industrial Relations Reform Act 1993', *Sydney Law Review*, vol. 15. [9]

Merritt, A. 1982, 'The Historical Role of Law in the Regulation of Employment—Abstentionist or Interventionist', *Australian Journal of Law and Society*, no. 1, pp. 56–86.

Merritt, J. 1973, 'W.G. Spence and the 1890 Maritime Strike', *Historical Studies*, vol. 15, no. 60, April, pp. 594–609. [3]

—— 1986, *The Making of the AWU*, Oxford University Press, Melbourne. [3]

Nairn, N.B. 1967, 'The Role of the Trades and Labour Council in New South Wales, 1871–1891', *Historical Studies Australia and New Zealand. Selected Articles*, Second Series, Melbourne University Press, Melbourne, pp. 151–78. [3]

National Employee Participation Steering Committee 1979, *Employee Participation: A Broad View*, AGPS, Canberra. [10]

—— 1980, *Employee Participation—Ways and Means*, AGPS, Canberra. [10]

National Labour Consultative Council 1984, *Guidelines on Information Sharing*, AGPS, Canberra. [10]

New South Wales Government, *Report of the Royal Commission on Strikes*, NSW, 1891, Appendix to Evidence. [3]

O'Lincoln, T. 1993, *Years of Rage: Social Conflicts in the Fraser Era*, Bookmarks Australia, Melbourne. [7]

Oxnam, D.W. 1968, 'The Changing Pattern of Strike Settlements in Australia, 1913–1963', *Journal of Industrial Relations*, vol. 10, pp. 11–24. [9]

Plowman, D. 'Forced March—the Employers and Arbitration' in *Foundations of Arbitration. The Origins and Effects of State Compulsory Arbitration 1890–1914*, eds S. Macintyre & R. Mitchell, Oxford University Press, Melbourne. [10]

—— 1988, 'Employer Associations and Bargaining Structures: An Australian Perspective', *British Journal of Industrial Relations*, vol. 26. [9]

—— 1989, 'Forced March: The Employers and Arbitration', in *Foundations of Arbitration. The Origins and Effects of State Compulsory Arbitration, 1890–1914*, eds S. Macintyre & R. Mitchell, Oxford University Press, Melbourne, pp. 135–55. [3] [9] [10]

—— 1989, *Holding the Line: Compulsory arbitration and national employer co-ordination in Australia*, Cambridge University Press, Melbourne. [7]

Quinlan, M. 1989, "Pre-Arbitral' Labour Legislation in Australia and its Implications for the Introduction of Compulsory Arbitration' in *Foundations of Arbitration. The Origins and Effects of State Compulsory Arbitration 1890–1914*, eds S. Macintyre & R. Mitchell, Oxford University Press, Melbourne. [10]

Ranger Uranium Case 1987: Re Ranger Uranium Mines Pty Ltd; ex p Federated Miscellaneous Workers' Union (1987) 163 CLR 656. [9]

Rawson, D.W. 1978, *Unions and Unionists in Australia*, Allen & Unwin, Sydney. [7]

Ryan, E. 1984, *Two Thirds of a Man: Women and Arbitration in New South Wales, 1902–08*, Hale and Iremonger, Sydney. [3]

Schedvin, C.B. 1970, *Australia and the Great Depression*, Sydney University Press, Sydney. [5]

Sheridan, T. 1976, *Mindful Militants: the Amalgamated Engineering Union in Australia 1920–1972*, Cambridge University Press, Cambridge. [7]

—— 1989, *Division of Labour: Industrial Relations in the Chifley Years, 1945–1949*, Oxford University Press, Melbourne. [7] [9]

Singleton, G. 1990, *The Accord and the Australian Labour Movement*, Melbourne University Press, Carlton, Vic. [7] [12]

Social Welfare Case 1983: R v Coldham; ex p Australian Social Welfare Union (1983) 153 CLR 297. [9]

Special Report of the Conference Between the Steamship Owners' Association of Australasia and the Federated Seamen's Union of Australasia and the Stewards' and Cooks' Union of Australia (Federated) on the Subject of the Proposed Reduction of Wages, Sydney, September 1886. [3]

Stilwell, F. 1986, *The Accord .... And Beyond: The Political Economy of the Labor Government*, Pluto Press, Leichardt. [12]

Thomas, M. 1985, *Manufacturing and Economic Recovery in Australia, 1932–1937*, Working Papers in Economic History no. 46, August, The Australian National University, Canberra. [5]

Thompson, E.P. 1968, *The Making of the English Working Class*, Penguin, Harmondsworth. [5]

Troubleshooters Case 1991: Building Workers' Industrial Union of Australia v Odco Pty Ltd (1991) 29 FCR 104. [9]

Turner, I. 1983, *In Union is Strength. A History of Trade Unions in Australia, 1788–1983*, 3rd edn., Nelson, Melbourne. [3]

Walker, K.F. 1970, *Australian Industrial Relations Systems*, Harvard University Press, Cambridge. [7]

Wells, A. 1990, *Constructing Capitalism: An Economic History of Eastern Australia, 1788–1901*, Allen & Unwin, Sydney. [5]

Willis, W.C. 1965, *Industrial Labour and Politics*, ANU Press, Canberra. [3]

Wise, B.R. 1900, *New South Wales Parliamentary Debates*, vol. 103, 4 Jul 1900, Government Printer, Sydney. [9]

Wooden, M. & Creigh, S. 1983, *Strikes in Post-War Australia: a review of research and statistics*, National Institute of Labour Studies Working Paper no. 60, Bedford Park, SA. [9]

Alphabetic Listing of Journals Cited

The following is a listing of journals and periodicals cited in Ford et al. 1984, *Japanese Employment and Employee Relations—An Annotated Bibliography*, AGPS, Canberra, and within the current bibliography.

Academy of Management Review
Across the Board
Administrative Science Quarterly
Aging and Work
American Journal of Sociology
American Sociological Review
AMPO Japan-Asia Quarterly Review
Asia Pacific Community
Asian Survey
Atlanta Economic Review
Australian Bulletin of Labour
Australian Economic History Review
Australian Feminist Studies
Australian Geographical Studies
Australian Quarterly
British Journal of Industrial Relations
Bulletin of Comparative Industrial Relations
Bulletin of Concerned Asian Scholars
Business Horizons

Business Week
Canadian Journal of History
Capital and Class
Columbia Journal of World Business
Developing Economies
Economia
Economic Analysis and Workers' Management
Economic and Labour Relations Review
Economic Development and Cultural Change
Economic Studies Quarterly
Economist
Economic and Industrial Democracy
Engineers Australia
European Industrial Relations Review
Evaluation Review
Far Eastern Economic Review
Harvard Business Review
Hitotsubashi Journal of Social Studies
Human Organization
Human Relations
Human Resource Management
Human Resource Management Australia
Indian Journal of Industrial Relations
Industrial and Commercial Training
Industrial and Labour Relations Review
Industrial Relations Journal
International Economic Review
International Institute for Labour Studies Bulletin
International Labour Review
International Organization
Japan Echo
Japan Interpreter
Japan Labor Bulletin
Japan Quarterly
Japanese Economic Studies
Journal of Asian and African Studies
Journal of Comparative Economics
Journal of Contemporary Asia
Journal of Industrial Relations
Journal of Labor Research
Journal of Japanese Studies
Journal of Management Studies
Journal of Political Economy

Keio Economic Studies
Kyoto University Economic Review
Labour and Industry
Labour and Society
Long Range Planning
Management Research News
Monthly Labor Review
Monumenta Nipponica
MSU Business Topics
New Scientist
Now in Japan
Organization Studies
Pacific Affairs
Pacific Basin Studies Review
Peace, Happiness and Prosperity for All
Personnel Journal
Personnel Management
Population Research and Political Review
R & D Management
Research Management
Sociological Quarterly
Sohyo Review
Studies in Comparative Economic Development
Sumitomo Quarterly
The Wheel Extended: A Toyota Quarterly Review
Unicorn
Work and People

Index

References are to Australian organisations and topics unless otherwise indicated, excepting specific Japanese terms.